Our Global Neighborhood

THE COMMISSION ON GLOBAL GOVERNANCE

Our Global Neighborhood

THE REPORT OF THE COMMISSION ON GLOBAL GOVERNANCE

OXFORD UNIVERSITY PRESS

Oxford University Press, Great Clarendon Street, Oxford OX2 6DP

Oxford New York

Athens Auckland Bangkok Bogota Buenos Aires Calcutta
Cape Town Chennai Dar es Salaam Delhi Florence Hong Kong Istanbul
Karachi Kuala Lumpur Madrid Melbourne Mexico City Mumbai
Nairobi Paris São Paolo Singapore Taipei Tokyo Toronto Warsaw

and associated companies in
Berlin Ibadan

Oxford is a registered trade mark of Oxford University Press

Published in the United States by
Oxford University Press Inc., New York

First published 1995
Reprinted 1995, 1996, 1998

British Library Cataloguing in Publication Data

Data available

Library of Congress Cataloging in Publication Data

Data available

ISBN 0-19-827998-1
ISBN 0-19-827997-3 (Pbk.)

Printed in Great Britain
on recycled paper by
Biddles Ltd, Guildford and King's Lynn

TABLE OF CONTENTS

CHAPTER FIVE

REFORMING
THE
UNITED
NATIONS
225

Acronyms

BIS	Bank for International Settlements
CSCE	Conference on Security and Co-operation in Europe
CSD	UN Commission on Sustainable Development
DA	Development Alternatives (of India)
ECA	Economic Commission for Africa
ECE	Economic Commission for Europe
ECLAC	Economic Commission for Latin America and the Caribbean
ECOSOC	UN Economic and Social Council
ECWA	Economic Commission for West Asia
ESAF	Enhanced Structural Adjustment Facility
ESC	Economic Security Council
ESCAP	Economic and Social Commission for Asia and the Pacific
EU	European Union
FAO	UN Food and Agriculture Organization
GATT	General Agreement on Tariffs and Trade
GDP	gross domestic product
GEF	Global Environment Facility
IDA	International Development Association (of the World Bank)
ILC	International Law Commission
ILO	International Labour Organisation
IMF	International Monetary Fund
INBio	Instituto Nacional de Biodiversidad
IOM	International Organisation for Migration
ITU	International Telecommunications Union
NAFTA	North American Free Trade Agreement

NATO	North Atlantic Treaty Organization
NGO	non-governmental organization
NPT	Nuclear Non-Proliferation Treaty
OAS	Organization of American States
ODA	official development assistance
OECD	Organisation for Economic Co-operation and Development
PPP	purchasing power parity
SDR	Special Drawing Rights
TNC	transnational corporation
UNCED	UN Conference on Environment and Development
UNCTAD	UN Conference on Trade and Development
UNDP	UN Development Programme
UNESCO	UN Educational, Scientific, and Cultural Organization
UNHCR	UN High Commissioner for Refugees
UNICEF	UN Children's Fund
UNIDO	UN Industrial Development Organization
UPU	Universal Postal Union
WEU	Western European Union
WFP	World Food Programme
WHO	World Health Organization
WTO	World Trade Organization

Co-Chairmen's Foreword

AND FOR THESE ENDS...
to practice tolerance and live
together in peace with one
another as good neighbours...

—Charter of the United Nations

The Charter of the United Nations was written while
the world was still engulfed in war. Face to face with
untold sorrow, world leaders were determined never to
let it happen again. Affirming their faith in the dignity
and worth of the human person, they set their minds on
the advancement of all peoples. Their vision produced
the world's most important political document.

Half a century has passed since the Charter was
signed in San Francisco. There has been no world war
in that time, but humanity has seen much violence,
suffering, and injustice. There remain dangers that
could threaten civilization and, indeed, the future of
humankind.

But our dominant feeling is of hope. We believe
the most notable feature of the past fifty years has been
the emancipation and empowerment of people. People
today have more power to shape their future than ever
before, and that could make all the difference.

At the same time, nation-states find themselves
less able to deal with the array of issues—some old,
some new—that face them. States and their people,
wishing to control their destinies, find they can do so
only by working together with others. They must

xiii

secure their future through commitment to common responsibility and shared effort.

The need to work together also guided the visionary men and women who drew up the Charter of the United Nations. What is new today is that the interdependence of nations is wider and deeper. What is also new is the role of people and the shift of focus from states to people. An aspect of this change is the growth of international civil society.

These changes call for reforms in the modes of international co-operation—the institutions and processes of global governance.

The international system that the UN Charter put in place needs to be renewed. The flaws and inadequacies of existing institutions have to be overcome. There is a need to weave a tighter fabric of international norms, expanding the rule of law world-wide and enabling citizens to exert their democratic influence on global processes.

We also believe the world's arrangements for the conduct of its affairs must be underpinned by certain common values. Ultimately, no organization will work and no law upheld unless they rest on a foundation made strong by shared values. These values must be informed by a sense of common responsibility for both present and future generations.

■ ■ ■

It was Willy Brandt who brought the two of us together as co-chairmen of the Commission on Global Governance.

Both of us had worked with him in the past, in various roles. And we knew him as a man who personified political courage allied to political vision, perhaps better than anyone else.

Twice, Willy Brandt made important personal contributions that changed the course of events. His 'ostpolitik' paved the way for the peaceful resolution of the cold war. His attention to global interdependence, and his initiatives to change the dynamics of North-South relations, gave the world a vision of greater peace and justice.

In 1989, when the Berlin Wall had fallen and events in Moscow signalled the end of the cold war, Willy Brandt clearly sensed that we were on the edge of a new time. He invited to a meeting in Königswinter in Germany the members of his own Commission, on international development issues, together with some who had served on other Commissions—Olof Palme's on disarmament and security, Gro Harlem Brundtland's on environment and development, Julius Nyerere's South Commission.

That meeting in Königswinter started a process of looking at the future of the world in a more integral way, in which the two of us participated, together with Jan Pronk. This work led, in 1991, to a meeting in Sweden and the presentation there of a document entitled 'Common Responsibility in the 1990s: The Stockholm Initiative on Global Security and Governance'. That document and its proposals were endorsed by many world leaders (their names are listed in the annex to this report). As a sequel to the Stockholm Initiative, Willy Brandt consulted Gro Harlem Brundtland and Julius Nyerere, and then invited the two of us to co-chair a Commission on Global Governance.

One of those who supported the Stockholm Initiative in 1991 was Dr. Boutros Boutros-Ghali. Soon after he had been appointed Secretary-General of the United Nations in early 1992, we met him in Geneva and explained the idea for a Commission. He gave it his full endorsement.

After that, we began to approach the twenty-six men and women whom we wanted to join us as members of the Commission. They needed no persuasion; the service we invited them to share with us was of a kind they wished to give.

The members of the Commission have all served in their personal capacities, and they are from many backgrounds and orientations. Yet, over the last two years together, we have been united by one single desire: to develop a common vision of the way forward for the world in making the transition from the cold war and in managing humanity's journey into the twenty-first century. We believe this report offers such a vision.

Each member of the Commission would have chosen different words if he or she were writing this report alone. Everyone might not have fully embraced each and every proposal; but we all agreed on the overall substance and direction of the report. The strongest message we can convey is that humanity can agree on a better way to manage its affairs and give hope to present and future generations.

■ ■ ■

The development of global governance is part of the evolution of human efforts to organize life on the planet, and that process will always be going on. Our work is no more than a transit stop on that journey. We do not presume to offer a blueprint for all time. But we are convinced that it is time for the world to move on from the designs evolved over the centuries and given new form in the establishment of the United Nations nearly fifty years ago. We are in a time that demands freshness and innovation in global governance.

As this report makes clear, global governance is not global government. No misunderstanding should arise from the similarity of the terms. We are not proposing movement towards world government, for were we to travel in that direction we could find ourselves in an even less democratic world than we have—one more accommodating to power, more hospitable to hegemonic ambition, and more reinforcing of the roles of states and governments rather than the rights of people.

This is not to say that the goal should be a world without systems or rules. Far from it. A chaotic world would pose equal or even greater danger. The challenge is to strike the balance in such a way that the management of global affairs is responsive to the interests of all people in a sustainable future, that it is guided by basic human values, and that it makes global organization conform to the reality of global diversity.

This report deals with how the world has been transformed since 1945, making changes necessary in our governance arrangements. We make many recommendations, some quite radical, for promoting security in its widest sense, including the security of people and of the planet. We make recommendations for managing economic interdependence, and for reforming the United Nations in ways that also offer a larger role to people through the organizations of international civil society. And we address the need for extending on the global stage the rule of law that has been so great a civilizing influence in national societies.

We conclude by urging the international community to mark the fiftieth anniversary of the United Nations by beginning a determined process of rethinking and reform. That process could draw on a wide range of ideas that the commemoration itself will prompt, including those advanced in this report. This is a time for the international community to be bold, to explore new ideas, to develop new visions, and to demonstrate commitment to values in devising new governance arrangements.

In the final chapter of this report, we draw attention to what has been a pre-eminent strand in the thinking of the Commission: the world's need for enlightened leadership that can inspire people to acknowledge their responsibilities to each other, and to future generations. It has to be leadership that upholds the values we need to live together as neighbours, and to preserve the neighbourhood for those who follow us.

Many pressures bear on political leaders, as they seek both to be effective and to retain support at the national level. Notwithstanding the drawbacks of nationalism, however, the history of even this century encourages us to believe that from the very best of national leaders can come the very best of internationalism. Today, a sense of internationalism has become a necessary ingredient of sound national policies. No nation can make progress heedless of insecurity and deprivation elsewhere. We have to share a global neighbourhood and strengthen it, so that it offers the promise of a good life to all our neighbours.

■ ■ ■

The Commission is grateful to those governments and foundations that have given financial and other support for its work, and to the many organizations and individuals who assisted it in innumerable ways. They are listed in the annex on the work of the Commission. The members of the Commission were greatly encouraged that so many groups and individuals attached importance to its work and were willing to identify with it and contribute to it in practical ways.

The responsibility for the report is, of course, the Commission's alone. We are mindful that it is not all-encompassing; we did not set out to make it so. It is neither a work of academic research nor a handbook on world affairs. It is primarily a call to action, based on the Commission's assessment of where the world stands and of what needs to be done to improve the way our human community manages its affairs.

As the Commission's Co-chairmen, we want to express our special gratitude to our colleagues for their help and support, and at times their forbearance, as the Commission worked its way through a formidable agenda. We are similarly grateful to Hans Dahlgren, the Secretary-General of the Commission, to the members of his small Secretariat team, and to the staff of our offices for their support throughout our work.

■ ■ ■

Time is not on the side of indecision. Important choices must be made now, because we are at the threshold of a new era. That newness is self-evident; people everywhere know it, as do governments, though not all admit to it. We can, for example, go forward to a new era of security that responds to law and collective will and common responsibility by placing the security of people and of the planet at the centre. Or we can go backwards to the spirit and methods of what one of our members described as the 'sheriff's posse'—dressed up to masquerade as global action.

There should be no question of which way we go. But the right way requires the assertion of the values of internationalism, the primacy of the rule of law world-wide, and institutional reforms that secure and sustain them. This report offers some suggestions for such responses.

Fifty years ago, another generation, recoiling from the horror of war and the unleashed potential for human self-destruction, sought to secure a future free from fear and free from want. The result of that effort was the United Nations system, established in the name of the peoples of the world. Today, with the need as great and urgent, and with a heightened sense among people of an endangered future, humanity must renew that effort. That is why this report is a call for action.

It is a call for action on many fronts, but essentially for better global governance—better management of survival, better ways of sharing diversity, better ways of living together in the global neighbourhood that is our human homeland. There is no question of capacity to take the action for which the Commission calls. There is only a question of the will to take that action.

Removed from the sway of empires and a world of victors and vanquished, released from the constraints of the cold war that so cramped the potential of an evolving global system throughout the post-war era, seized of the risk of unsustainable human impacts on nature, mindful of the global implications of human deprivation—the world has no real option but to rise to the challenge of change, in an enlightened and constructive fashion. We call on our global neighbours, in all their diversity, to act together to ensure this—and to act now.

Ingvar Carlsson
Stockholm

Shridath Ramphal
London

November 1994

Our Global Neighborhood

CHAPTER ONE

A NEW WORLD

The collective power of people to shape the future is greater now than ever before, and the need to exercise it is more compelling. Mobilizing that power to make life in the twenty-first century more democratic, more secure, and more sustainable is the foremost challenge of this generation. The world needs a new vision that can galvanize people everywhere to achieve higher levels of co-operation in areas of common concern and shared destiny.

Fifty years ago, international co-operation, collective security, and international law were powerful concepts. In 1945, world leaders met in San Francisco to sign the United Nations Charter, a document expressing the universal hope that a new era in international behaviour and governance was about to begin. The onset of the cold war did not entirely smother that hope, but it greatly diminished its fulfilment.

As the cold war ended in 1989, revolution in Central and Eastern Europe extended the movement towards democratization and economic transformation, raising the prospect of a strengthened commitment to the pursuit of common objectives through multilateralism. The world community seemed to be uniting around the idea that it should assume greater collective responsibility in a wide range of areas, including security—not only in a military sense but in economic and social terms as well—sustainable development, the promotion of democracy, equity and human rights, and humanitarian action.

In the three years since the idea for the Commission on Global Governance was advanced by the Stockholm Initiative and endorsed by leaders around the world, the mood has changed significantly. Today, given such experiences as the Gulf War, the enormities of ethnic cleansing in the Balkans, brutal violence in Somalia, and genocide in Rwanda, there is far less assurance. And there is deepening disquiet over the actions—and in some cases the inaction—of governments and of the United Nations. Instead of coming together around a common vision of the way forward, the world seems in danger of losing its way.

THE CONCEPT OF GLOBAL GOVERNANCE

There is no alternative to working together and using collective power to create a better world.

Governance is the sum of the many ways individuals and institutions, public and private, manage their common affairs. It is a continuing process through which conflicting or diverse interests may be accommodated and co-operative action may be taken. It includes formal institutions and regimes empowered to enforce compliance, as well as informal arrangements that people and institutions either have agreed to or perceive to be in their interest.

Examples of governance at the local level include a neighbourhood co-operative formed to install and maintain a standing water pipe, a town council operating a waste recycling scheme, a multi-urban body developing an integrated transport plan together with user groups, a stock exchange regulating itself with national government oversight, and a regional initiative of state agencies, industrial groups, and residents to control deforestation. At the global level, governance has been viewed primarily as intergovernmental relationships, but it must now be understood as also involving non-governmental organizations (NGOs), citizens' movements, multinational corporations, and the global capital market. Interacting with these are global mass media of dramatically enlarged influence.

When the United Nations system was created, nation-states, some of them imperial powers, were dominant. Faith in the ability of governments to protect citizens and improve their lives was strong. The world was focused on preventing a third world war and avoiding another global depression. Thus the establishment of a set of international, intergovernmental institutions to ensure peace and prosperity was a logical, welcome development.

Moreover, the state had few rivals. The world economy was not as closely integrated as it is today. The vast array of global firms and corporate alliances that has emerged was just beginning to develop. The huge global capital market, which today dwarfs even the largest national capital markets, was not foreseen. The enormous growth in people's concern for human rights, equity, democracy, meeting basic material needs, environmental protection, and demilitarization has today produced a multitude of new actors who can contribute to governance.

Many Actors in Global Governance

A wide range of actors may be involved in any one area of governance. To cite just one example, those with a role in bringing order to international trade in sugar and sweeteners include transnational firms, national and international authorities in charge of competition policy, a global group (the International Sugar Council) with specific responsibility for trade, and a host of smaller private associations, including plantation workers, beet farmers, and dietitians. An international organization may easily develop an interest in a local issue, as when the World Bank finances an agricultural project in a country. A local voluntary association may just as easily become a participant in an international regime.

All these emerging voices and institutions are increasingly active in advancing various political, economic, social, cultural, and environmental objectives that have considerable global impact. Some of their agendas are mutually compatible; others are not. Many are driven by positive concerns for humanity and the space it inhabits, but some are negative, self-serving, or destructive. Nation-states must adjust to the appearance of all these forces and take advantage of their capabilities.

Contemporary practice acknowledges that governments do not bear the whole burden of global governance. Yet states and governments remain primary public institutions for constructive responses to issues affecting peoples and the global community as a whole. Any adequate system of governance must have the capacity to control and deploy the resources necessary to realize its fundamental objectives. It must encompass actors who have the power to achieve results, must incorporate necessary controls and safeguards, and must avoid overreaching. This does not imply, however, world government or world federalism.

There is no single model or form of global governance, nor is there a single structure or set of structures. It is a broad, dynamic, complex process of interactive decision-making that is constantly evolving and responding to changing circumstances. Although bound to respond to the specific requirements of different issue areas, governance must take an integrated approach to questions of human survival and prosperity. Recognizing the systemic nature of these issues, it must promote systemic approaches in dealing with them.

Effective global decision-making thus needs to build upon and influence decisions taken locally, nationally, and regionally, and to draw on the skills and resources of a diversity of people and institutions at many levels. It must build partnerships—networks of institutions and processes—that enable global actors to pool information, knowledge, and capacities and to develop joint policies and practices on issues of common concern.

In some cases, governance will rely primarily on markets and market instruments, perhaps with some institutional oversight. It may depend heavily on the co-ordinated energies of civil organizations and state agencies. The relevance and roles of regulation, legal enforcement, and centralized decision-making will vary. In appropriate cases, there will be scope for principles such as subsidiarity, in which decisions are taken as close as possible to the level at which they can be effectively implemented.

The creation of adequate governance mechanisms will be complicated because these must be more inclusive and participatory—that is, more democratic—than in the past. They must be flexible enough to respond to new problems and new understanding of old ones. There must be an agreed global framework for actions and policies to be carried out at appropriate levels. A multifaceted strategy for global governance is required.

This will involve reforming and strengthening the existing system of intergovernmental institutions, and improving its means of collaboration with private and independent groups. It will require the articulation of a collaborative ethos based on the principles of consultation, transparency, and accountability. It will foster global citizenship and work to include poorer, marginalized, and alienated segments of national and international society. It will seek peace and progress for all people, working to anticipate conflicts and improve the capacity for the peaceful resolution of disputes. Finally, it will strive to subject the rule of arbitrary power—economic, political, or military—to the rule of law within global society.

Effective global governance along these lines will not be achieved quickly: it requires an enormously improved understanding of what it means to live in a more crowded, interdependent world with finite resources. But it does provide the beginning of a new vision for humanity, challenging people as well as governments to see that there is no alternative to working together and using collective power to create a better world. This vision of global governance can only flourish, however, if it is based on a strong commitment to principles of equity and democracy grounded in civil society.

It is our firm conclusion that the United Nations must continue to play a central role in global governance. With its universality, it is the only forum where the governments of the world come together on an equal footing and on a regular basis to try to resolve the world's most pressing problems. Every effort must be made to give it the credibility and resources it requires to fulfil its responsibilities.

Vital and central though its role is, the UN cannot do all the work of global governance. But it may serve as the principal mechanism through which governments collaboratively engage each other and other sectors of society in the multilateral management of global affairs. Over the years, the UN and its constituent bodies have made vital contributions to international communication and co-operation in a variety of areas. They continue to provide a framework for collaboration that is indispensable for global progress. But both the United Nations itself and the broader UN system need to be reformed and revitalized, and this report addresses these needs in the context of the new world that has emerged.

The first challenge for us as a Commission is to demonstrate how changes in the global situation have made improved arrangements for the governance of international affairs imperative, and to point to the concepts and values that should underpin these arrangements so they may produce a world order that is better able to promote peace and progress for all the world's people. That is what we attempt to do in the first two chapters of this report. It is against this background that we offer the substantive recommendations set out in the subsequent chapters.

The Phenomenon of Change

Never before has change come so rapidly, on such a global scale, and with such global visibility.

Nelson Mandela's inauguration as President of the Republic of South Africa in May 1994 marked the virtual completion of a major transformation of modern times. The enfranchisement of South Africa's black population may be seen as part of the final phase in the liberation from colonialism and its legacy. This process has nearly quadrupled the world's sovereign states and fundamentally altered the nature of world politics.

One effect of World War II was to weaken the traditional great powers of Europe—the United Kingdom and France—and so trigger a fundamental shift in the relative standing of world powers and the structure of world politics. Just as important was the role of the war in the collapse of the old colonial order. The most important development of the last five decades may be the emergence of new economic and political powers out of the developing world. In a relatively short time, countries such as India and Indonesia have become significant regional powers. For countries such as Brazil and China the path has been different, but the result the same. To comprehend the immensity of these changes, just imagine the difference between the delegates present in San Francisco and those who would be present—and the influence they would exercise—if such a conference were convened in 1995, or

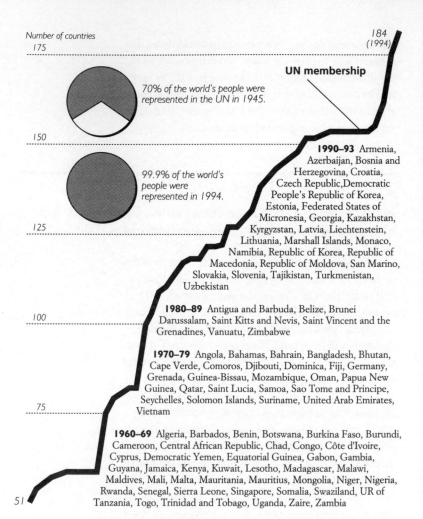

Number of countries

175

70% of the world's people were represented in the UN in 1945.

99.9% of the world's people were represented in 1994.

184 (1994)

UN membership

150

1990–93 Armenia, Azerbaijan, Bosnia and Herzegovina, Croatia, Czech Republic, Democratic People's Republic of Korea, Estonia, Federated States of Micronesia, Georgia, Kazakhstan, Kyrgyzstan, Latvia, Liechtenstein, Lithuania, Marshall Islands, Monaco, Namibia, Republic of Korea, Republic of Macedonia, Republic of Moldova, San Marino, Slovakia, Slovenia, Tajikistan, Turkmenistan, Uzbekistan

125

1980–89 Antigua and Barbuda, Belize, Brunei Darussalam, Saint Kitts and Nevis, Saint Vincent and the Grenadines, Vanuatu, Zimbabwe

100

1970–79 Angola, Bahamas, Bahrain, Bangladesh, Bhutan, Cape Verde, Comoros, Djibouti, Dominica, Fiji, Germany, Grenada, Guinea-Bissau, Mozambique, Oman, Papua New Guinea, Qatar, Saint Lucia, Samoa, Sao Tome and Principe, Seychelles, Solomon Islands, Suriname, United Arab Emirates, Vietnam

75

1960–69 Algeria, Barbados, Benin, Botswana, Burkina Faso, Burundi, Cameroon, Central African Republic, Chad, Congo, Côte d'Ivoire, Cyprus, Democratic Yemen, Equatorial Guinea, Gabon, Gambia, Guyana, Jamaica, Kenya, Kuwait, Lesotho, Madagascar, Malawi, Maldives, Mali, Malta, Mauritania, Mauritius, Mongolia, Niger, Nigeria, Rwanda, Senegal, Sierra Leone, Singapore, Somalia, Swaziland, UR of Tanzania, Togo, Trinidad and Tobago, Uganda, Zaire, Zambia

51

1946–59 Afghanistan, Albania, Austria, Bulgaria, Cambodia, Finland, Ghana, Guinea, Hungary, Iceland, Indonesia, Ireland, Israel, Italy, Japan, Jordan, Lao PDR, Libyan Arab Jamahiriya, Malaysia, Morocco, Myanmar, Nepal, Pakistan, Portugal, Romania, Spain, Sri Lanka, Sudan, Sweden, Thailand, Tunisia, Yemen

Original 51 members Argentina, Australia, Belgium, Bolivia, Brazil, Byelorussian SSR, Canada, Chile, China, Colombia, Costa Rica, Cuba, Czechoslovakia, Denmark, Dominican Republic, Ecuador, Egypt, El Salvador, Ethiopia, France, Greece, Guatemala, Haiti, Honduras, India, Iran, Iraq, Lebanon, Liberia, Luxembourg, Mexico, Netherlands, New Zealand, Nicaragua, Norway, Panama, Paraguay, Peru, Philippines, Poland, Saudi Arabia, South Africa, Soviet Union, Syrian Arab Republic, Turkey, Ukrainian SSR, United Kingdom, United States, Uruguay, Venezuela, Yugoslavia

| 1945 | 50 | 55 | 60 | 65 | 70 | 75 | 80 | 85 | 90 |

how different the Security Council would be if it were created from scratch today.

The transformation from colonialism was accompanied—indeed, it was fuelled—by a revolution in communication. Thirty years before Mandela made the transition from liberation leader to head of government before a global audience, no satellites carried images of the trial at which he was sentenced to life imprisonment. Over the years of struggle, the communications media revealed, and to some degree reinforced, progress towards liberation. In 1945, as the delegates of fifty countries assembled to form the United Nations, television itself was in its infancy. Many people probably had no idea what had happened in San Francisco. In the fifty years since then, the revolution in communications has quickened the pace of interaction and strengthened the imperative of response.

The last few decades have also witnessed extraordinary growth in global industrial and agricultural productivity, with profound social consequences. Among these have been migration and urbanization that in turn have upset traditional household structures and gender roles. The same forces have depleted non-renewable natural resources and produced environmental pollution. They also first subdued and subsequently reinforced ethnicity, nationality, and religion as sources of identity and the focus of political commitment.

The very tendencies that now require and even facilitate the development of global governance have also generated obstacles to it. For example, the perceived need for co-operation between developing states— whether through regional organizations or such broader groups as the Non-Aligned Movement or the Group of 77—had to contend with the strong nationalism and regard for sovereignty borne out of independence struggles. The Commission believes that such contradictions can be resolved, and that this may best be achieved through a system of global governance that includes the whole range of associations and interests—both local and global, formal and informal—that exist today.

Deregulation, interacting with accelerating changes in communications and computer technology, has reinforced the movement towards an integrated global market. The changing patterns of economic growth of the last few decades have produced new poles of dynamism. Germany and Japan, vanquished in World War II, have dislodged the United Kingdom and France in economic league tables. The European Union matches the United States as an economic power. New areas of economic vibrancy are appearing in Latin America. The striking performance of the four Asian 'tigers' and of China, with countries such as India and Indonesia not far behind, is shifting the world centre of economic gravity.

Developments such as these are even shifting the meaning of traditional terms and rendering many of them less useful. There is no longer an East to be juxtaposed against the West. With the abandonment of communism, capitalism has become even more of an omnibus term that hides important distinctions between different ways of organizing market economies. Similarly, the North-South dichotomy is becoming less sharp. And the problems of Africa are now strikingly different from those of South-east Asia or South America. More and more, it is disparities within nations and regions, both North and South, no less than the disparities among nations and blocs that reveal injustice and cause insecurity.

The term globalization has been used primarily to describe some key aspects of the recent transformation of world economic activity. But several other, less benign, activities, including the drug trade, terrorism, and traffic in nuclear materials, have also been globalized. The financial liberalization that seems to have created a borderless world is also helping international criminals and creating numerous problems for poorer countries. Global co-operation has eradicated smallpox. And it has eliminated tuberculosis and cholera from most places, but the world is now struggling to prevent the resurgence of these traditional diseases and to control the global spread of AIDS.

Technological advances have made national frontiers more porous. States retain sovereignty, but governments have suffered an erosion in their authority. They are less able, for example, to control the transborder movement of money or information. They face the pressures of globalization at one level and of grassroots movements and, in some cases, demands for devolution if not secession at another. In the extreme case, public order may disintegrate and civil institutions collapse in the face of rampant violence, as in Liberia and Somalia.

Mounting evidence indicates that human activities have adverse—and sometimes irreversible—environmental impacts, and that the world needs to manage its activities to keep the adverse outcomes within prudent bounds and to redress current imbalances. The links among poverty, population, consumption, and environment and the systemic nature of their interactions have become clearer. So has the need for integrated, global approaches to their management and world-wide embrace of the discipline of sustainable development counselled by the World Commission on Environment and Development and endorsed at the June 1992 Earth Summit. The call is for fundamental changes in the traditional pattern of development in all countries.

The last fifty years have radically and rapidly transformed the world and the agenda of world concern. But this is not the first generation to live on the cusp of a great transformation. The turbulence of the last decade is not unlike those that accompanied the rise of Islam in the century following the death of the Prophet, the European colonization of the Americas after 1492, the

THE NEED FOR VISION

onset of the Industrial Revolution in the eighteenth century, and the creation of the contemporary international system in this century. Yet there is a distinction between the contemporary experience of change and that of earlier generations: never before has change come so rapidly—in some ways, all at once—on such a global scale, and with such global visibility.

A time of change when future patterns cannot be clearly discerned is inevitably a time of uncertainty. There is need for balance and caution—and also for vision. Our common future will depend on the extent to which people and leaders around the world develop the vision of a better world and the strategies, the institutions, and the will to achieve it. Our task as a Commission is to enlarge the probability of their doing so by suggesting approaches to the governance of the global, increasingly interdependent human society.

MILITARY TRANSFORMATIONS

The strategic terrain is now sharply different from what it was even five years ago.

On 6 August 1945, the United States dropped the first atomic bomb on Hiroshima. The death toll, some 140,000 by the end of 1945, was to rise to around 227,000 by 1950—all from a single explosion that was small and primitive by current standards of nuclear weaponry. From then onward, the destructive power of nuclear weapons increased exponentially, and the world lived with the possibility that life on earth could end in one apocalyptic blast.

During the past fifty years, trillions of dollars have been spent on weapons that have never been used, chiefly by the United States and the Soviet Union. It has been argued that nuclear weapons prevented the bitter rivalry between these two countries from erupting in a full-scale war between them. It cannot, however, be denied that the development of nuclear arms brought enormous risks for humanity while absorbing money that could have supported worthier, life-enhancing purposes.

Nuclear weapons came to be seen as a badge of great-power status and a potential shield against a hostile world. All the permanent members of the Security Council felt it necessary to acquire their own nuclear capabilities. Several other countries also invested heavily in developing the ability to produce these weapons: Argentina, Brazil, India, Iraq, Israel, North Korea, Pakistan, and South Africa. Others are widely believed to have started on the same road. And there has been a further dispersion of nuclear weapons material and technology following the breakup of the Soviet Union.

At the same time, there were large-scale sales of conventional weapons, particularly to developing countries. The Third World became increasingly militarized, drawing funds away from vitally needed economic and social development.

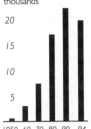

Nuclear warheads deployed
thousands

The first steps have been taken toward nuclear disarmament, but the goal remains distant

---

The lessening of tensions in the 1980s between the United States and the Soviet Union started a process that led to dramatic reductions in the nuclear stockpiles of these countries. But the end of the East-West confrontation does not stop the spread of nuclear weapons: as long as these weapons exist, the risk of their use remains.

The world may, in fact, be on the verge of a new race to acquire weapons of mass destruction. These include biological and chemical weapons in addition to nuclear ones. The new arms race could also involve more countries. Even non-state entities—drug syndicates, political movements, terrorist groups—could join it. A much wider range of interests and motives will have to be taken into account in efforts to discourage proliferation, and the factors to be considered in plans to deter the use of weapons of mass destruction will be vastly more complicated. There will also be higher

A NEW ARMS RACE

risks of accidental war as the number of countries with these weapons rises.

In all these respects, the strategic terrain is now sharply different from what it was even five years ago. But weapons of mass destruction are only one factor in the global military equation. And for most people, they are still an abstract and distant threat compared with the threat that conventional arms pose.

| THE ARMS TRADE | The period since 1945 may be regarded as a long peace only in the restricted sense that there has been no war between major powers. In other respects, and for much of the world, it has been a period of frequent wars. In a few of these, the United States and the Soviet Union were directly involved; in many others, their support was a key factor. |

By one estimate, between 1945 and 1989 there were 138 wars, resulting in some 23 million deaths. But military force was also used elsewhere, without an actual war breaking out, as in Hungary in 1956, Czechoslovakia in 1968, and Grenada in 1983. The Korean War, which caused 3 million deaths, and the Vietnam War, which killed 2 million people, were the most deadly conflicts. All 138 wars were fought in the Third World, and many were fuelled by weapons provided by the two major powers or their allies.

Between 1970 and the end of the cold war in 1989, weapons worth $168 billion were transferred to the Middle East, $65 billion worth went to Africa, $61 billion to the Far East, $50 billion to South Asia, and $44 billion to Latin America (all in 1985 dollars). The Soviet Union and the United States accounted for 69 per cent of the $388 billion total. The surfeit of weapons, especially small arms, left over from this era is a key enabling factor in many conflicts now scarring the world.

Yet the arms trade continues. Although the demand for arms has declined as many countries face economic difficulties or feel less threatened since the end of the cold war, those that are buying find many countries eager to sell. The five permanent members of the Security Council provide 86 per cent of the arms exported to developing countries. In 1992, the United States alone accounted for 46 percent of the deliveries of weapons to these states. For arms exporters—the United States, Russia, United Kingdom, France, and Germany are the top five—strategic considerations now matter less than protecting jobs and industrial bases. And the huge research and development costs of major weapons often mean that even the largest domestic market cannot guarantee a profit.

In each of the last few years, at least thirty major armed conflicts—defined as those causing more than 1,000 deaths annually—have been in progress. Many have gone on for several years. Each has its own historic origins and proximate causes. Structural factors at the regional or global level are significant in many conflicts. The wars of Afghanistan and Angola are direct legacies of cold war power politics. Other conflicts, including those in Azerbaijan, Bosnia, Georgia, and Somalia, were in different ways precipitated by the end of the cold war and the collapse of old regimes. In many cases, structural factors have combined with tension across social cleavages, whether ethnic, religious, economic, or political, to fuel antagonisms. Personal ambitions and missed opportunities have played some part.

THE RISE IN CIVIL CONFLICT

The risks of war between states have not been eliminated, and several sources of discord that could spark interstate war remain. Flashpoints have existed in many regions; the dissolution of the Soviet Union, leaving troublesome sources of contention between some of its successor republics, may have added to these. Meanwhile, it is conflicts originating within national polities—in Yemen, Rwanda, and the former Yugoslavia, for example—that have posed a formidable new challenge to the world community.

Until recently, the United Nations has had very little to do with these conflicts. The peace and security provisions of the UN Charter were designed to deal with wars between states, and it was not envisaged that the UN would intervene in the domestic affairs of sovereign states. But the United Nations is under public pressure to take action when violent strife within countries leads to extensive human suffering or threatens the security of neighbouring countries.

WIDESPREAD VIOLENCE	A disturbing feature of the contemporary world is the spread of a culture of violence. Civil wars brutalize thousands of young people who are drawn into them. The systematic use of rape as a weapon of war has been an especially pernicious feature of some conflicts. Civil wars leave countless weapons and a legacy of continuing violence. Several political movements ostensibly dedicated to the liberation of people have taken to terrorism, showing scant regard for the lives of innocent civilians, including those in whose name they are fighting. Violence is sometimes perceived as an end in itself.

The ascendance of the military in many countries has contributed to an ethos inimical to human rights and democratic values. In some societies, the trade in narcotics has been responsible for raising the general incidence of violence. Russia and some parts of Eastern Europe have seen a surge of violence as criminal syndicates seek to exploit the new freedoms. Widespread criminalization can threaten the very functioning of a state. In the United States, the easy availability of weapons goes with a startling level of daily killings. Ethnic violence in several parts of the world has shown extreme savagery.

Conflict and violence also leave deep marks on the lives of children, innocent victims who are rarely able to rid themselves of the legacy of war. The culture of violence is perpetuated in everyday life. Violence in the home, particularly against women, has long been an underestimated phenomenon, both widespread and tolerated, and part of both the roots and the consequences of violence within and between societies. The world over, people are caught in vicious circles of disrespect for the life and integrity of others.

A hopeful scenario portrays the present level of violence as a transitional phenomenon. In this view, the world is likely to become much more peaceful and secure for most of its inhabitants once it recovers from the disruptions caused by the sudden end of the cold war. Another scenario envisages a world divided into two: a prosperous and secure part that would include most of Western and Central Europe, East Asia, and North America, and a larger part of impoverished and violently conflicted territories without stable governments, which would include large areas of Africa, the Middle East, and South Asia and possibly bits of Central and South America.

In a third scenario, the entire world would be engulfed in spreading violence, and large areas would become ungovernable. Crime, drug abuse, high unemployment, urban stress, economic mismanagement, and ethnic tensions would lead to low-level violence or graver conflict in regions and cities throughout the world. In this view, the Chiapas rebellion in Mexico, the Los Angeles riots, the murders of journalists and academics in Algeria, and the appearance of neo-fascist movements in Europe—different though they are in character and scale—bode ill for their respective societies and the world as a whole.

Unless the optimism of the first scenario is borne out—even if the world does not move fully towards the forbidding situations projected in the other two scenarios—global governance faces a grave test.

ECONOMIC TRENDS

The dazzling performance of several developing countries has tended to blur the relentless growth in the number of the very poor.

At the end of World War II, the United States, as the world's only thriving industrial economy, was thrust into an unparalleled position of economic leadership. From the early days of the war, U.S. and British officials set about designing a set of international institutions to promote economic recovery, full employment, free trade, and economic stability. The United Nations Relief and Rehabilitation Administration, the Bretton Woods institutions, and the General Agreement on Tariffs and Trade, together with the Marshall Plan launched by the United States to revive Europe, helped lay the foundation for the most rapid and sustained expansion of the international economy in history.

The driving force of the long post-war boom was the private sector. Major extractive, service, and manufacturing firms in Europe and North America had already developed a substantial international presence during the first half of the century. After 1945, the weight of these transnational corporations (TNCs) in the world economy grew as the pioneers matured and were joined by Japanese and subsequently by other Asian and Latin American enterprises. Complementing these were a number of massive state-owned firms, mostly in the energy and service sectors. Together and often through joint ventures, these transnational firms extended and intensified industrialization and brought about a globalization of production, trade, and investment that dramatically increased world economic interdependence. At the same time, however, it increased the vulnerability of the weak through uneven distribution of gains and pressures on natural resources.

From the early 1950s, the world's output grew at a historically unprecedented rate. During the four decades up to 1990, real output increased fivefold. The benefits of economic expansion were especially obvious in Western industrial countries. In one generation after 1950, per capita income increased in most of Europe as much as it had during the previous century and a half. A tide of new consumer goods flooded U.S. and European markets, transforming societies that only recently had suffered the hardships of the Great Depression and the ravages of World War II. The quality of life improved dramatically. Particularly in Europe, extensive social security systems were constructed. The welfare state, with widely accessible, high-quality health care and enlarged educational opportunities, appeared. In many countries, unemployment was kept at very low levels.

Many developing countries also achieved higher growth rates than those in the already industrialized world. Great strides were made in combating hunger and disease, improving sanitary conditions, and providing education. The gains, however, were not equally shared. Some groups began to enjoy vastly increased prosperity while others languished in poverty.

Since the 1970s, a succession of challenges has shaken confidence in the post-war order and slowed growth in many countries. A series of shocks—including the US government's 1971 decision to sever the dollar-gold link and the dramatic rise in oil prices starting in 1973—signalled the end of the easy growth years. At the end of the decade, recession in the industrial countries and anti-inflationary policies precipitated a sharp rise in real interest rates. Mexico's declared inability to service its debt in 1982 marked the onset of a debt crisis that engulfed much of Latin America and also Africa, where it aggravated already deep economic problems.

Literacy rates are improving and people are living longer

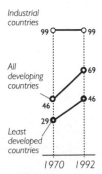

Adult literacy rate
percentage

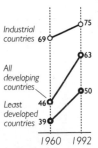

Life expectancy in years

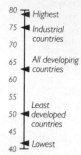

Life expectancy in
years (1992)

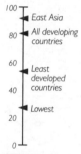

Percentage of the
population with
access to health
services (1985-91)

Many countries were caught in a debt trap, unable to maintain interest payments, let alone repay debt, public or private. Investment and imports were curtailed, exacerbating the difficulties of growing out of debt. Growth rates fell sharply, with average income per head actually falling on the two continents. Africa is today poorer than at the start of the 1970s. Everywhere, the poor suffered greatly from falling real incomes and rising unemployment.

The 'lost decade' of development—for some, actually a 'lost generation'—had roots both in domestic conditions and the international economic environment. Economic policies that were too inward-looking left countries unable to respond to external shocks, and proved unsustainable. Inadequate global economic governance both contributed to the crisis and, perhaps worse, postponed its resolution. Most countries have faced up to the crisis by introducing difficult and often painful structural adjustment programmes. Some, but not all, have as a result reversed economic decline. With policies for macro-economic stability and a market-driven recovery, a number of middle-income countries are experiencing a revival in economic strength. The crisis, especially in terms of human development, is still far from over, but most countries have a better sense of what could lead to sustainable economic development.

At the same time, some developing countries had a radically different, much more positive experience during the 1980s. Particularly in Asia, a number of countries weathered adverse trends and in fact benefited from strong demand in the industrial world, achieving high levels of export-led growth. In the wake of the spectacular economic success of Hong Kong, Singapore, South Korea, and Taiwan, many other developing countries, including some of the world's most populous—China, Indonesia, Malaysia, and Thailand in Asia; Brazil, Chile, and Mexico in Latin America—

achieved several years of high, sometimes double-digit, growth. The Indian subcontinent, home to more than a billion people, has also shown greater economic vigour. These developments are not uniformly benefiting all people. Sustained growth, however, is providing greater opportunities for many millions, and is fundamentally transforming global economic relations.

The dazzling performance of several developing countries in Asia has tended to blur a less admirable aspect of the economic changes of the post-war world: the relentless growth in the number of the very poor. Though the global economy has expanded fivefold in the last four decades, it has not rooted out dire poverty or even reduced its prevalence. Even some otherwise successful countries have not managed to eliminate poverty.

PERSISTENT POVERTY

The entrenchment of poverty is borne out by the fact that the number of people falling in the World Bank's category 'the absolute poor' had climbed to 1.3 billion in 1993. This level of poverty spells acute destitution; it is life at the edge of existence. For the absolute poor, for example, a nearby source of safe drinking water is a luxury; in several countries— Bhutan, Ethiopia, Laos, Mali, Nigeria—less than half the population has even this.

Geographical, gender, and age distributions of poverty also deserve attention. By the late 1980s, the chronically undernourished in Asia had fallen to 19 per cent of the population, half the level of two decades earlier. But the same twenty years saw little change in Africa, where undernourishment continued to afflict about a third of a rapidly growing population. Sub-Saharan Africa and South Asia stand out as the poorest regions in the world today. In all, about 800 million people do not have sufficient and regular supplies of food.

Such levels of poverty and malnutrition are shocking. Equally shocking is the 'feminization' of poverty and the ways in which these evils and their associated deprivations blight the lives of children throughout the world. Women who enter the labour market continue to receive less reward than men for equivalent work and to be confined to stereotypical and low-status tasks. At the same time, their unpaid work in the home and the field goes unrecognized, even though no national economy could survive without it. Their low incomes are reinforced by cultural patterns that place women behind men in the queues for food and education in countries where these are scarce. A third of adults in the developing world are illiterate; of these, two thirds are women.

Deprivation is passed on to the next generation. In low-income developing countries, seventy-three out of every 1,000 babies do not live until their first birthday. The rate of infant mortality is ten times that in rich countries. Of the children that survive, many do not receive an education. Just over 40 per cent of eligible children attend secondary school.

Absolute poverty provides scant basis either for the maintenance of traditional society or for any further development of participation in civic life and governance. Yet poverty is not only absolute but relative. The destitution of perhaps a fifth of humanity has to be set alongside the affluence of the world's rich. Even using income data based on purchasing power parity (PPP) to correct for different price levels in different countries, the poorest fifth earn less than one twentieth as much as the richest fifth. Per capita incomes in the United States and India, for instance, were $22,130 and $1,150 respectively in 1991 on a PPP basis.

Unfair in themselves, poverty and extreme disparities of income fuel both guilt and envy when made more visible by global television. They demand, and in recent decades have begun to receive, a new standard of global governance.

The collapse of the Soviet bloc has opened up new opportunities for the people of Central and Eastern Europe. Except in the already industrialized parts of Central Europe, the early years of the Communist economic system did bring some improvement in economic and social conditions. But politically motivated isolation from the world community and world economy, combined with an emphasis on militarization and heavy industry, eventually led to stagnation and decline. Efforts to secure progress through command economies proved impossible to sustain and environmentally disastrous. These people are now engaged in fundamental transformations of their economies and integration into the European and world economies.

Transformation into successful market economies is an extremely difficult process. The breakdown of old structures has everywhere precipitated a severe decline in output. For many people, the quality of life has deteriorated. The situation in Russia and Ukraine, as evidenced by a dramatic rise in mortality and criminality, gives special cause for concern. It is not clear yet that these countries will be able to achieve the right combination of national liberation, shared responsibility, and mutual respect and tolerance, or to strike the right balance between radical transformation and stability or between market reform and political, social, environmental, and other objectives.

Nevertheless, signs of new economic creativity are to be found everywhere in the region. Its countries, home to more than 300 million people, possess both human and natural resources that should enable them to develop relatively quickly once functioning market institutions have been created. Their integration into the international economy will increase competition on the world market. That may well cause economic

EASTERN EUROPE'S EXPERIENCE

dislocation, for example in European agriculture. But there is also much scope for mutually beneficial trade, not least with the dynamic Asian economies and other parts of the developing world. If the transformation finds sustainable forms, global economic relations could acquire a fundamentally positive new dimension.

REGIONAL GROUPS

The emergence of regional economic groups enlarges the prospect for a new geo-economic landscape. The uniting of Europe has created a single regional economy that accounts for about 40 per cent of the world's imports and exports. As this integration proceeds, the European Union will take on more and more of the global economic roles and responsibilities traditionally shouldered by its member-states. The North American Free Trade Agreement has brought into being another regional body that could play an increasingly important role in the global economy.

In Asia, the Association of South-East Asian Nations now has a significant regional economic role, and there is some prospect of an eventual emergence of a larger Asian economic community. Asian and Pacific leaders recently formed the Asia-Pacific Economic Co-operation forum, which will allow them to discuss common problems and develop co-ordinated policies. There have also been moves to set up an East-Asian Economic Caucus.

Progress towards closer regional co-operation has also been evident in recent years in Central America, the Caribbean, and South America, where democratization and new initiatives have revived established forums and fostered new ones such as MERCOSUR and the Association of Caribbean States. Elsewhere—in South Asia and Africa—regional arrangements have fared less well or failed to emerge. In Europe, there is debate about the speed and scope of integration, including its extension to Central and Eastern Europe and Mediterranean countries.

It is also unclear whether regional organizations will become building blocks of a more balanced global economic order or degenerate into instruments of a new protectionism that divides the world. It is therefore important that they become an integral part of a more democratic system of global governance.

Another phenomenon of recent years that holds immense but as yet unclear consequences for the evolution of global governance is the burgeoning of private enterprise. The demands created during two world wars and the general economic dislocation brought about by war and depression resulted in massive state intervention during the first half of the twentieth century even in countries most strongly committed to free enterprise. Twice in a generation, world business leaders became civil servants entrusted with the management of military and civilian supplies by warring states.

This experience left its mark on the attitudes of policy makers towards the private sector in industrial and developing countries alike after 1945. Economic

THE PRIVATE SECTOR

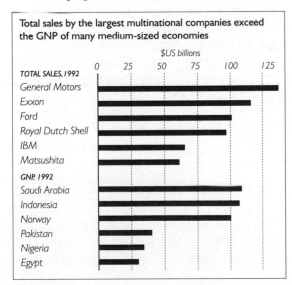

Total sales by the largest multinational companies exceed the GNP of many medium-sized economies

policy makers were confident of their ability to guide and regulate market forces for the public good. This was reflected in the economic policies adopted by most industrial countries to stimulate growth and improve living and working conditions. It was also revealed in the institutions created by the architects of the post-war order to govern the international economy; in ambitious strategies of import substitution adopted by India, Mexico, and Brazil; and in the restrictive systems of regulation imposed on foreign-owned firms in these and many other developing economies.

But the extensive movement in favour of market-driven approaches since the end of the 1970s has recast transnational corporations into mobilizers of capital, generators of technology, and legitimate international actors with a part to play in an emerging system of global governance. Many TNCs now manufacture on several continents, buying and selling world-wide. Numerous consumer products and brand names have become ubiquitous. The change in the economic policy environment has also helped many vigorous small entrepreneurs emerge, particularly in developing countries. This is another facet of the trend towards greater empowerment world-wide.

SOCIAL AND ENVIRONMENTAL CHANGE

People are beginning to assert their right to participate in their own governance.

Along with political and economic transformations, the past five decades have seen far-reaching social and environmental change. Rapid population growth has been accompanied by many changes in the way people live as increasing economic activity has helped raise living standards and spread literacy. The media, aided by new technology to become pervasive in its reach, reflects some of these changes and influences others.

Increasing population and economic growth have placed additional pressure on natural resources and the environment, and the management of both demographic and economic change to safeguard the interests of future generations has become an issue of paramount importance.

As significant as these changes is the increasing capacity of people to shape their lives and to assert their rights. The empowerment of people is reflected in the vigour of civil society and democratic processes. These point to the potential of human creativity and co-operation, both vital to meet the many challenges—security, economic, environmental, social—that the world faces and that governance must address.

POPULATION

More than twice as many people inhabit the earth today as when the post-war era began. Indeed, more people have been added to the world's population in the past five decades than in all the previous millennia of human existence. Although the rate at which population is growing has been slowing for some time, annual additions remain high, reaching a near-peak level of 87 million in 1993. In 1950, by comparison, only 37 million people were added to the global total.

The fertility of the earth and farm technology—new seeds, fertilizer, pesticides, machines, irrigation—have so far prevented a Malthusian crisis in which numbers completely outstrip the ability of humankind to feed itself. As highlighted at the 1994 International Conference on Population and Development, the prospect of continuing demographic growth raises disturbing questions. These are not just about food supplies, though in some parts of the world rising population is contributing to growing food insecurity. They are also about the capacity of the earth to withstand the impact of human consumption as numbers multiply if present trends of rising economic activity and rising consumption continue unchanged. The distribution of future expansion is also worrying: the fastest population growth will be in Africa, both the poorest and ecologically the most fragile of regions.

UN demographers now believe world population growth will slow much more gradually than they had expected. In 1982, they thought global population would reach a peak of 10.2 billion at the end of the next century. Now they say that it could go on climbing for another century and more, until it hits 11.6 billion. Developing countries already have 78 per cent of the people in the world; as much as 94 per cent of the current increase is also taking place in these countries. Their cities will face severe strains as more and more people leave rural areas that cannot support them. These countries are urbanizing much faster than today's industrial ones did at a comparable stage in their development.

They are also urbanizing faster than they are industrializing. Cities are attracting people ahead of their economic capacity to provide jobs, homes, water, sanitation, and other basic services. This is the road to urban squalor, with social tensions, crime, and other problems to follow. Large cities have long ceased to be exclusive to industrially advanced countries. By 1960, three of the ten largest cities in the world were in developing countries. By the end of the 1990s, these states will have as many as eighteen of the twenty-four cities with more than 10 million people. The problems are much more acute in the rapidly growing cities of the developing world. The city is a vital subject of all levels of governance. Global governance has an important contribution to make in tackling causes of excessively rapid population growth and urbanization, and in strengthening regional, state, and local capacities to cope with their consequences.

Rapid growth in population is closely linked to the issue of environmental security through the impact that people have on the earth's life-supporting resources. Evidence has accumulated of widespread ecological degradation resulting from human activity: soils losing fertility or being eroded, overgrazed grasslands, desertification, dwindling fisheries, disappearing species, shrinking forests, polluted air and water. These have been joined by the newer problems of climate change and ozone depletion. Together they threaten to make the earth less habitable and life more hazardous.

Both the rate at which and the way key resources are used are critical factors in determining environmental impact. Industrial countries account for a disproportionate use of non-renewable resources and energy. Despite a substantial rise in energy use in developing countries in recent decades, per capita consumption of fossil fuels in industrial countries is still nine times as high. With less than a fourth of the world's people, industrial countries (including Eastern Europe and the former Soviet Union) accounted for 72 per cent of the world's use of fossil fuels in 1986–90. The pattern for key metals shows even larger disparities. Developing countries use only 18 per cent of the copper consumed each year, for example, and per capita use in industrial countries is seventeen times as high as in developing ones.

In developing countries, the main environmental pressure is linked to poverty. Poor people press on the land and forests, over-exploiting them to survive and undermining the resource base on which their well-being and survival depend. These countries must be helped to climb out of poverty and so ease pressure on their habitat. But as they become less poor, their living standards and therefore consumption levels will rise. The world must find ways to ensure they can do so without endangering environmental safety. They must have access to technologies that use fewer resources, such as energy-saving technologies. To keep global resource use within prudent limits while the poor raise their living standards, affluent societies need to consume less.

Population, consumption, technology, development, and the environment are linked in complex relationships that bear closely on human welfare in the global neighbourhood. Their effective and equitable management calls for a systemic, long-term, global approach guided by the principle of sustainable development, which has been the central lesson from the mounting ecological dangers of recent times. Its universal application is a priority among the tasks of global governance.

GLOBAL MEDIA

Innovations in communications technology, in addition to driving economic globalization, have also transformed the media world and the spread of information, with important consequences for national as well as global governance. This began with radio broadcasting in the 1940s and has since been extended through television and satellite transmission to give even those in remote places immediate access to sound and images from a wider world. In some countries, new communications systems have even brought people news of domestic events that is not available locally. Direct-dial international telephone and fax services have swelled the transborder flow of news and other messages. Another important development has been the sharing of information through links between computers around the world.

Exposure through the media to foreign cultures and life-styles can be both stimulating and destabilizing; it can inspire both appreciation and envy. Concern that the dominance of transnational media could result in cultural homogenization and could damage indigenous cultures is not limited to non-Western countries. Many people are worried that media images will strengthen the consumerist ethos in societies in the early stages of development. There are questions about distortion and imbalance as the world's news is filtered predominantly through Western prisms, and dissatisfaction that information flows from and within the developing world are inadequate. Apprehension about concentration in media ownership is linked to worries that this sector's power to shape the agenda of political action may not be matched by a sense of responsibility. These varied concerns have given rise to the suggestion that civil society itself should try to provide a measure of global public service broadcasting not linked to commercial interests.

The wider access to information has been healthy for democracy, which gains from a better-informed citizenry, as well as beneficial for development, scientific and professional collaboration, and many other activities. The wide linkages now facilitated can also help pull the world's people closer together. Media images of human suffering have motivated people to express their concern and their solidarity with those in distant places by contributing to relief efforts and by demanding explanations and action from governments. The media's influence on the shaping of foreign policy is considerable in many countries.

Although there has been a spectacular expansion in the reach of some communications media, serious imbalances remain in access to information and in the distribution of even the most basic technology. Two billion people—more than one in three individuals in the world—still lack electricity. In 1990, Bangladesh, China, Egypt, India, Indonesia, and Nigeria together had fewer telephone connections than Canada, which has only 27 million people. These disparities are repeated in the ownership of communications satellites, the key to media globalization.

AGENTS OF CHANGE IN CIVIL SOCIETY

Among the important changes of the past half-century has been the emergence of a vigorous global civil society, assisted by the communications advances just described, which have facilitated interaction around the world. This term covers a multitude of institutions, voluntary associations, and networks—women's groups, trade unions, chambers of commerce, farming or housing co-operatives, neighbourhood watch associations, religion-based organizations, and so on. Such groups channel the interests and energies of many communities outside government, from business and the professions to individuals working for the welfare of children or a healthier planet.

Important non-governmental organizations and movements have existed for as long as the modern state. But the size, diversity, and international influence of civil society organizations have grown dramatically during the past five decades. The spectacular flourishing of such organizations at first centred mainly on industrial countries with high living standards and democratic systems. More recently, such organizations have begun to blossom in developing countries and in former Communist countries in Europe.

The NGO community has changed with shifts in economic and social patterns. Trade unions, which were among the largest and most powerful NGOs nationally and internationally, have declined somewhat with changes in industrial employment and trends towards free market ideologies in labour relations, although their influence and membership remains considerable in many countries. Conversely, issue-oriented mass membership and specialist organizations have become much more numerous.

All in all, citizens' movements and NGOs now make important contributions in many fields, both

International NGOs*

28,900

176

1909   1964 1993

The growth of non-governmental organizations reflects their increasing role

*Operating in at least three countries

OUR GLOBAL NEIGHBOURHOOD

nationally and internationally. They can offer knowledge, skills, enthusiasm, a non-bureaucratic approach, and grassroots perspectives, attributes that complement the resources of official agencies. Many NGOs also raise significant sums for development and humanitarian work, in which their dedication, administrative efficiency, and flexibility are valuable additional assets. NGOs have been prominent in advancing respect for human rights and are increasingly active in promoting dispute settlement and other security-related work.

Growing awareness of the need for popular participation in governance, combined with disenchantment with the performance of governments and recognition of their limited capabilities, has contributed to the growth of NGOs. The proliferation of these groups broadens effective representation, and can enhance pluralism and the functioning of democracy. Civil society organizations have attained impressive legitimacy in many countries. Yet, some governments and powerful interests remain suspicious of independent organizations, and issues of legitimacy and accountability will continue to arise everywhere as assessments of the NGO sector become more careful and nuanced. The sector includes a huge range of bodies, not all of which are democratic in structure or broadly representative in participation.

Some NGOs serve narrow interests, and this pattern may intensify as the sector is seen to take on greater political importance. NGOs increasingly span the entire range of interests and political positions on particular issues. Civil society organizations make tremendous contributions in mobilizing the energies and commitment of people, but the focus on single issues that gives some of them strength and expertise may also block out perspectives on wider concerns. As such organizations become more institutionalized, they become more dependent on tactics to raise membership or obtain funding.

Share of country memberships in international NGOs

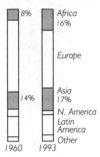

Countries' participation in international NGOs has grown fastest in Africa and in Asia

In developing countries, civil society organizations often face particularly difficult dilemmas of securing funding and access to current information while retaining independence and avoiding being portrayed as foreign-influenced. Overall, however, civil society organizations and the NGO sector in general are vital and flourishing contributors to the possibilities of effective governance. They must occupy a more central place in the structures of global governance than has been the case.

As at the national level, civil servants in intergovernmental organizations have been cautious in acknowledging that NGOs can be useful partners. UN-NGO relationships are, however, improving. Collaboration is now an established feature of international life, though much remains to be done. It reached a high point in Rio with the UN Conference on Environment and Development in 1992: more than 1,400 NGOs were accredited to the official conference and thousands more participated in the parallel Global Forum—the largest number to attend a UN event and perhaps the closest collaboration ever between the official and independent sectors.

Strong NGO participation has also marked the UN conferences held after Rio: on human rights in Vienna in 1993, on small island states in Barbados in 1994, and on population and development in Cairo, also in 1994. It is likely to be repeated at the World Summit on Social Development in Copenhagen in March 1995, the World Conference on Women in Beijing in September 1995, and the Conference on Human Settlements in Istanbul in June 1996.

The growing range of actors involved makes the challenge of governance more complex. Policy makers have to serve, engage, and mobilize a much wider variety of institutions—and hence to cope with a broader range of interests, values, and operating styles. Although institutional diversity may complicate the process, it could also greatly increase the capacity of the governance system to meet the complex demands placed on it. Problems that may go unobserved by one set of institutions may be detected by another; those beyond the capacity of certain organizations may be easily addressed by others.

This is especially true in the area of sustainable development: many development mistakes have occurred because bureaucrats, national and international, failed to foresee or ignored the likely effects of new projects. Civil society organizations play important roles in identifying genuine development needs, initiating projects, and in some cases implementing projects as funding or co-funding agencies. In projects funded by governments and intergovernmental agencies, involving NGOs in the preparation and evaluation of projects may increase the likelihood of success.

Finding ways for so many different organizations to participate constructively in international activities is a challenging task, but the progress made in Rio and since then provides a good foundation. Official bodies need, of course, to relate to the independent sector on a regular basis, not simply at or in preparation for a major conference. They must reach out to civil society in a positive spirit and seek its contributions at all stages, including the shaping of policy. The agents of change within civil society can help this process through arrangements to ensure balanced representation of their own varying interests and positions and through manageable modes of participation.

THE EMPOWERMENT OF PEOPLE

The new vigour of civil society reflects a large increase in the capacity and will of people to take control of their own lives and to improve or transform them. This has been helped by wider educational facilities, improved opportunities for women, and greater access to information as well as political progress. A number of governments, political movements, and other institutions have also made conscious efforts to empower people.

Empowerment depends on people's ability to provide for themselves, for poverty translates into a lack of options for the individual. Economic security is essential if people are to have the autonomy and means to exercise power. While the number of productive jobs world-wide has multiplied, particularly through the growth of the small-scale private sector, practically all societies are affected by debilitating unemployment. And the situation seems to be worsening, with marginalization eating away at communities. No empowerment will be sustained if people lack a stable income.

The most egregious failure in the process of empowerment is in respect of women; despite wide campaigning for their emancipation and many advances, a large share of the world's women remains voiceless and powerless. The struggle to achieve equal opportunity and remuneration for women in the economic sphere continues, and it should be joined by a comparable struggle to achieve equal access and voice for women in the political sphere.

The number and proportion of people who can make their voices heard is nevertheless vastly greater in all parts of the world today than in 1945. This is principally the product of decolonization, economic improvement, and the spread of democracy. Beyond elections, however, people are beginning to assert their right to participate in their own governance. They include indigenous peoples long deprived by settlers of control over traditional lands, ethnic minorities seeking a role in government, and regional and local groups who feel their interests have been neglected by national leaders. These groups have become more effective in asserting their rights.

More generally, attitudes towards governments are changing. Tensions between the government of the day and opposition groups are a vital part of any democracy. But there is now greater disenchantment with the political process itself; both government and opposition parties and politicians of all hues have been losing credibility. This may partly derive from the increasing demands of electors and the growing inability of politicians to deliver results, as in an increasingly interdependent world, individual states are constrained in what they can achieve. There are also deeper causes, such as corruption and criminalization of politics.

Many people expect more from democracy. Two minutes in a voting booth every few years does not satisfy their desire for participation. Many resent politicians who, having won elections in democratic systems, neglect large sectors of the community—sometimes even a majority of the electorate—who have voted for the 'losers'. The widening signs of alienation from the political process call for the reform of governance within societies, for decentralization, for new forms of participation, and for the wider involvement of people than traditional democratic systems have allowed.

Enlightened Leadership

Leadership is urgently needed that represents all the world's countries and people, not simply the most powerful.

Fifty countries met in San Francisco in 1945 to create an international organization that could help build a new world out of the wreckage of war. What united them was not so much a clear view of the future as a determination to prevent a repetition of the horrors and mistakes of the past.

The goal of the conference in San Francisco was aptly summed up in the phrase 'never again'. Never again should the world's leaders fail to prevent a global depression. Never again should they fail to stand up to aggression. Never again should they tolerate governments that assaulted the most basic dignities of their citizens. Never again should they squander the chance to create institutions that would make a lasting peace possible. It was these aims that led the delegates in San Francisco—and at the July 1944 United Nations Monetary and Financial Conference held in Bretton Woods, New Hampshire—to establish the key international institutions that became part of the post-war arrangements for global governance.

Few delegates in San Francisco questioned the state as such. What bad states had upset, good states could restore. Many of those with the requisite qualities of leadership and expertise had, after all, been drawn into the ever-widening web of state during the preceding thirty years. And the public-service mentality that had reached new heights during the war was now channelled into the construction of welfare states and the United Nations system.

Forty years on, the public sector has shrunk and service to the state has lost its exalted status. While leadership is once again urgently needed, it is leadership of a different character, in which reserves of commitment to public service are sought not only among politicians and civil servants but also in the voluntary sector, in private enterprise, and indeed throughout global civil society: leadership that represents all the world's countries and people, not simply the most powerful.

The concept of dispersed and democratic leadership should not be seen as contradictory. It draws its strength from society as much as the state, from solidarity much more than from authority. It operates by persuasion, co-operation, and consensus more often than by imposition and fiat. It may be less heroic, but it is the only form of leadership likely to prove effective.

The challenges facing the world today are vastly more complicated than those that confronted the delegates in San Francisco. They demand co-operative efforts to put in place a system of global governance better suited to present circumstances—a system informed by an understanding of the important transformations of the past half-century and guided by enlightened leadership.

CHAPTER TWO

VALUES FOR THE GLOBAL NEIGHBOURHOOD

The Preamble of the United Nations Charter pledged the resolve of the peoples of the world 'to practice tolerance and live together in peace with one another as good neighbours'. Those who drafted these words were not the first to hold out a vision of one world in which all people are neighbours. A similar ideal had inspired the League of Nations earlier in the century. And long before that, philosophers and religious and political thinkers had spoken of 'the family of man'.

The commitment to care for others, to the highest quality of behaviour among human beings, is for many cultures embodied in the metaphor of being a 'good neighbour'. As human social organization has evolved to encompass knowledge of, and loyalty to, wider and wider human groups, the scope of neighbourly duties has expanded. Even in 1945, few could envision the world as one neighbourhood. But the changes of the last half-century have begun to transform the incipient global neighbourhood into a reality.

NEIGHBOURHOOD REALITIES

Never before have so many people had so much in common, but never before have the things that divide them been so obvious.

The term 'global village' captured the impact of the electronic conquest of space. Technology, by telescoping distance and time, had made the world smaller.

Photographs from space confirmed the insignificance of terrestrial frontiers. But much has happened since satellites first girdled the globe, and advances in transport and telecommunications are only one set of factors making neighbours of far-flung people.

As noted in Chapter One, trade, industrial development, transnational firms, and investment also link the world's different parts much more closely than before in a multitude of ways. Few developments have conveyed the sense of global interdependence as strongly as the growing evidence that all depend on the earth's ecological resources and are vulnerable in the face of their degradation. A thickening web of interdependence requires countries to work together.

Indeed, in the global neighbourhood, citizens have to co-operate for many purposes: to maintain peace and order, expand economic activity, tackle pollution, halt or minimize climate change, combat pandemic diseases, curb the spread of weapons, prevent desertification, preserve genetic and species diversity, deter terrorists, ward off famine, defeat economic recession, share scarce resources, arrest drug traffickers, and so on. Matters requiring nation-states to pool their efforts—in other words, calling for neighbourhood action—keep increasing.

What happens far away matters much more now. Aerosol use in Europe can cause skin cancers in South America. A crop failure in Russia can mean more hunger in Africa. Recession in North America can destroy jobs in Asia. Conflict in Africa can bring more asylum-seekers to Europe. Economic difficulties in Eastern Europe can lead to xenophobia in Western Europe. By the same token, economic vigour in East Asia can protect employment in the United States. Tariff changes in Europe can ease pressure on forests in the tropics. Industrial restructuring in the North can reduce poverty in the South, which in turn can enlarge markets for the North. The shortening of distance, the multiplying of links, the deepening of interdependence: all these factors, and their interplay, have been transforming the world into a neighbourhood.

Movements motivated by a sense of human identity transcending national divisions are another mark of the world's evolution into a neighbourhood. These transnational movements—in working to emancipate women, to protect human rights or the health of the planet, or to bring about a world without nuclear weapons—have underlined the common humanity of the world's inhabitants. But these developments are not sufficient to make the neighbourhood agreeable to all who live here.

The global neighbourhood we have today is, like most neighbourhoods, far from ideal; it has many imperfections. Its residents are not all fairly treated; they do not have the same opportunities. Millions are so deprived that they do not even think they belong to a neighbourhood, as the tides of progress of recent decades have passed them by. If the communications revolution has touched them, it has served to confirm their sense of isolation. This reaction does not disprove the emergence of a neighbourhood, but it does pose a challenge to its governance to reduce alienation among neighbours.

Nor, at another level, does the world's becoming a neighbourhood mean that the nation-state is no longer relevant. But states, as well as peoples, are challenged to devise ways to manage their affairs—to develop new approaches to governance for the global neighbourhood in the interests of all. Much of this report is about how the world might make the shared neighbourhood a satisfactory home for all its citizens.

Neighbourhoods are defined by proximity. Geography rather than communal ties or shared values brings neighbours together. People may dislike their neighbours, they may distrust or fear them, and they

NEIGHBOUR-HOOD TENSIONS

may even try to ignore or avoid them. But they cannot escape from the effects of sharing space with them. When the neighbourhood is the planet, moving to get away from bad neighbours is not an option.

The emerging global neighbourhood is forging new bonds of friendship and interest, but it is also creating new tensions. Never before have so many people had so much in common, but never before have the things that divide them been so obvious. In a vast, uncrowded space, diversity often goes unnoticed. As people bump against each other more frequently, however, even minor differences become more evident and more contentious.

Multicultural communities are facing strains in many parts of the world. The partition of British India and the green line dividing Cyprus bear witness to the failure of the modern state to reconcile community and territory by substituting nationality for entrenched religious, ethnic, or linguistic sources of identity. But so, too, do riots in U.S. cities or the burnt-out homes of Belfast. And now many industrial countries face the challenges of a new multiculturalism fuelled by post-war migration. The more that people accept the logic of growing interdependence of human society, the more ready they will be to seek opportunities to overcome destructive notions of 'otherness' and 'separateness', and to find ways to work together.

The ferment rippling across the global neighbourhood is a consequence of several changes discussed in Chapter One, notably the end of colonialism and of the cold war. In an equally important transformation, the industrial age is giving way to an uncertain post-industrial age. Traditional economic relationships are being rearranged; services are replacing manufacturing as the lifeblood of advanced economies. Entire sectors are being made obsolete and jobs eliminated. But new economic niches are opening up for some people, just as old ones are closing for others.

Change of such magnitude creates stresses within society. Some arise as people confront a complex and uncertain future. Others are created by a clash between the familiar and the different. People are being forced to come to terms with new circumstances. Many find themselves living among people previously considered strangers—and they are being asked to behave differently in public, in the workplace, and in the home.

Some stresses arise because great transformations do not affect everyone equally. Change benefits some, but disadvantages others. It gives authority to groups previously on the margins of power, while weakening the authority of groups accustomed to being in the driver's seat. Society is enriched by the increasing freedom of women to control their own lives and to shape and participate fully in governance structures, but changing understandings of gender roles involve difficult abandonment of deeply embedded attitudes and social mores.

At the international level, the traditional great powers face the demands of the rest of the world for a greater say in global governance, and stresses could increase as those demands are pressed. Stress is also caused by corrupt, criminal, and self-serving forces that exploit the instabilities created by change in the global neighbourhood.

As the physical and other boundaries that have separated communities, cultures, and states are eroded by waves of intellectual and technological change, cherished notions of citizenship, sovereignty, and self-determination are being challenged. There is less ideological contention and less global confrontation in the world of the 1990s.

Yet it is not a unipolar world, but a more plural one. It has the potential to foster a range of cultures and sources of personal identity much broader than either the United States or the Soviet Union could easily tolerate during the cold war, least of all at home. There is less call than in the past for ideological uniformity and cultural policing. All this means that this is, or could be, a better world. But a world order geared to the needs of the global neighbourhood is not yet in place.

Given the unsettling trends, it is no surprise that so many parts of the world are in turmoil, that so many communities feel threatened, and that so many people seem to be searching for direction and meaning. This makes it difficult to reach agreement on common action among the world's many governments, institutions, and peoples. But it also creates opportunities and puts pressure on the world community to fashion global governance to new realities.

In this chapter we reflect on the norms and values that should guide the world, the ethics that should inform life in the global neighbourhood. The Commission has been convinced from the outset that whatever ideas it advances for institutional and other change must be grounded in values that speak to the tasks facing the contemporary world.

NEIGHBOUR-HOOD ETHICS

The quality of global governance will be determined by several factors. High among them is the broad acceptance of a global civic ethic to guide action within the global neighbourhood, and courageous leadership infused with that ethic at all levels of society. Without a global ethic, the frictions and tensions of living in the global neighbourhood will multiply; without leadership, even the best-designed institutions and strategies will fail.

Being global neighbours requires new ways of perceiving each other as well as new ways of living. Few recognize this better or acknowledge it as clearly as did Barbara Ward when she wrote in a 1971 paper to the Pontifical Commission on Justice and Peace:

The most important change that people can make is to change their way of looking at the world. We can change studies, jobs, neighbourhoods, even countries and continents and still remain much as we always were. But change our fundamental angle of vision and everything changes—our priorities, our values, our judgments, our pursuits. Again and again, in the history of religion, this total upheaval in the imagination has marked the beginning of a new life....a turning of the heart, a 'metanoia,' by which men see with new eyes and understand with new minds and turn their energies to new ways of living.

People have to see with new eyes and understand with new minds before they can truly turn to new ways of living. That is why global values must be the cornerstone of global governance. We believe that many people world-wide, particularly the young, are more willing to respond to these issues than their governments, for whom the short term in the context of political expediency tends to take precedence. People and governments alike need to pay greater heed to the interests of future generations, for whom this generation acts as trustee.

In our rapidly changing world, the standards and restraints provided by commonly accepted values and norms become ever more essential. Without them, it will be hard—if not impossible—to establish more effective and legitimate forms of global governance. These norms have to suit today's circumstances, which are radically different from those of previous eras in three important respects: the changing nature of violent conflicts in the world, which today often arise among people within states; the growing ability of private, independent actors both to provoke crises and to solve, or exacerbate, them; and the new understanding of the threats to the integrity of the planet and its life-support systems, and therefore to human survival.

As described in the remainder of this chapter, establishing an ethical dimension to global governance requires a threefold approach:

- Enunciate and encourage commitment to core values concerned with the quality of life and relationships, and strengthen the sense of common responsibility for the global neighbourhood.
- Express these values through a global civic ethic of specific rights and responsibilities that are shared by all actors, public and private, collective and individual.
- Embody this ethic in the evolving system of international norms, adapting, where necessary, existing norms of sovereignty and self-determination to changing realities.

NEIGHBOURHOOD VALUES

People should treat others as they would themselves wish to be treated.

We believe that action to improve global governance to cope with contemporary challenges would be greatly helped by a common commitment to a set of core values that can unite people of all cultural, political, religious, or philosophical backgrounds. These values must be appropriate to the needs of an increasingly crowded and diverse planet.

Despite the far-reaching changes outlined in Chapter One, states remain the single most important set of international actors. As long as this is true, traditional norms of interstate relations will provide a critical source of stability. But there is a need now to adapt some of these norms to new circumstances. It is fundamentally important that governance should be underpinned by democracy at all levels and ultimately by the rule of enforceable law (see Chapter Six).

In stable times, when the authority and capacity of established institutions is strong and secure, the fundamental values and principles guiding human behaviour are usually taken for granted. In unstable times, prevailing values are more likely to be doubted, questioned, or challenged. Paradoxically, then, values are often most in doubt when they are most needed. By providing a sense of direction, shared values can help people to see beyond immediate clashes of interest and act on behalf of a larger, long-term, mutual interest.

We believe that all humanity could uphold the core values of respect for life, liberty, justice and equity, mutual respect, caring, and integrity. These provide a foundation for transforming a global neighbourhood based on economic exchange and improved communications into a universal moral community in which people are bound together by more than proximity, interest, or identity. They all derive in one way or another from the principle, which is in accord with religious teachings around the world, that people should treat others as they would themselves wish to be treated. It is this imperative that was reflected in the call made in the UN Charter for recognition of 'the inherent dignity and equal and inalienable rights of all members of the human family'.

Respect for life and its corollary, non-violence, are vital to the well-being of any neighbourhood. Violence against persons negates the inherent dignity of all human beings. And its widespread use in diverse situations undermines humanity's claim to be civilized. Recent history is replete with instances of conflict and oppression in which human life has been treated with the utmost contempt and callousness. Extensive carnage, sometimes genocidal in intent and scale, has occurred in several parts of the world.

At a broader level, the security of people is imperilled by the culture of violence that has infected many societies, with a consequent loss of respect for human life. This trend is in some cases linked to political

RESPECT FOR LIFE

extremism of one kind or another, but elsewhere it is part of a breakup of the value systems that give stability to societies. The sanctity of life is a concept shared by people of all faiths as well as by secular humanists. Dealing with the political, economic, social, or other causes of violence and promoting the principle of non-violence are vital objectives of governance.

LIBERTY

We believe that all human beings are born equal in their right to human dignity and are entitled to certain basic liberties: to define and express their own identity, to choose their form of worship, to earn a livelihood, to be free from persecution and oppression, to receive information. Basic liberties also include free speech, a free press, and the right to vote. Without these, the world becomes a battleground of warring individuals and groups, each seeking to protect its interests or to impose its authority on others.

Next to life, liberty is what people value most. In its richest conception, liberty is all that enables people to choose the paths of their lives and to become whatever they can be. The rights and entitlements people actually enjoy across the globe fall far short of attaining liberty in this sense. Global governance is fundamentally concerned with enhancing rights, capabilities, and well-being.

People around the world have become more aware of the possible threats to their liberty from a variety of forces and circumstances. The threat could come from autocratic rulers, from political groups that try to cling to power unlawfully or to usurp power, from action to suppress or drive out ethnic groups (sometimes even those who constitute a majority within a country), or from the collapse of a state and the accompanying anarchy. Even where order prevails, liberty is threatened by deprivation, economic dislocation, oppression based on gender or sexual orientation, abuse of children, debt bondage, and other social and economic patterns. The threat could also be external, from a state that turns predator, or even from an enterprise whose activities overwhelm a local community or its traditional culture.

The threat to liberty in any part of the global neighbourhood needs to be seen as a threat to the entire neighbourhood. Action against attempts to violate the right to liberty is a common responsibility.

JUSTICE AND EQUITY

Justice and equity are essential human values. Respect for them is indispensable for peace and progress, as their absence can give rise to resentment and be destabilizing. Although people are born into widely unequal economic and social circumstances, great disparities in their conditions or life chances are an affront to the human sense of justice. Where large numbers of citizens are treated unfairly or denied their due, and where gross inequalities are not addressed, discontent is inevitable and conflict likely. When people lived in a less integrated world, the inequities that mattered were local or national. Today, with the enlarged reach of the media, global disparities have become increasingly obvious. There is also wider recognition that many inequities are caused or sustained by developments in other, once distant places.

A concern for equity is not tantamount to an insistence on equality, but it does call for deliberate efforts to reduce gross inequalities, to deal with factors that cause or perpetuate them, and to promote a fairer sharing of resources. A broader commitment to equity and justice is basic to more purposeful action to reduce disparities and bring about a more balanced distribution of opportunities around the world. A commitment to equity everywhere is the only secure foundation for a more humane world order in which multilateral action, by blunting current disparities, improves global well-being as well as stability.

Equity needs to be respected as well in relationships between the present and future generations. The principle of intergenerational equity underlies the strategy of sustainable development, which aims to ensure that economic progress does not prejudice the chances of future generations by depleting the natural capital stock that sustains human life on the planet. Equity requires that this strategy is followed by all societies, both rich and poor.

<table>
<tr><td>MUTUAL
RESPECT</td><td>Tolerance is indispensable for peaceful relations in any society. When it is transmuted into the more active attribute of mutual respect, the quality of relationships is distinctly raised. Mutual respect therefore offers a basis for making a plural society—which is what the global neighbourhood is—not only stable but one that values and is enriched by its diversity.</td></tr>
</table>

Throughout history, intolerance has tended to intensify in difficult or uncertain periods. Racial and religious extremism has shown a marked increase in many parts of the world recently. There have been virulent eruptions of ethnic animosities, and some nationalist movements have displayed xenophobic edges.

Neo-Fascist movements have appeared or gathered strength in some parts of Europe, and ethnic minorities have been early targets of their violence. Elsewhere, religious extremists have been ready to use violence to achieve their goals. Many civil conflicts have shown extreme levels of violence and brutality. Some assertions of particular identities may in part be a reaction against globalization and homogenization, as well as modernization and secularization. Whatever the causes, their common stamp is intolerance.

In several parts of the world, the resort to violence to achieve political ends has become the pattern. This has been most obvious in terrible civil conflicts, in such places as Afghanistan, Angola, Azerbaijan,

Bosnia-Herzegovina, Liberia, Mozambique, Rwanda, Somalia, Sudan, and Tajikistan, but it has also been evident in many societies where governments have used violence to suppress opposition or to forcibly incorporate unwilling groups.

The world community should reassert the importance of tolerance and respect for 'the other': respect for other people, other races, other beliefs, other sexual orientations, other cultures. It must be resolute in upholding these values and offering protection against the actions of those who would trample them. The guiding principle should be that all groups and individuals have a right to live as they see fit so long as they do not violate the coequal rights and liberties of others.

CARING

The quality of life in a society depends to a great extent on its members accepting a duty to care for their neighbours. Its sense of community and well-being are enhanced when more citizens are imbued by a spirit of care and concern for other citizens, whether deriving from African tradition, the Moslem obligation of hospitality, or the practices of other cultures.

Attitudes such as these generally lead a society to initiate action to alleviate distress and hardship and deal with problems of many kinds. The instincts of caring and compassion provide the impulse for humanitarian action—and for sharing with those less advantaged—that all societies need. In addition to motivating people to undertake voluntary action, the citizen's instinct of care can be a catalyst for action by official agencies.

The need for these qualities has deepened as the result of contemporary social trends that, while prominent only in industrial nations, have begun to show in other countries as well to varying degrees. These include tendencies towards looser family ties, more frequent marital breakup, a high incidence of single parents and elderly people in the population, and increasing anonymity in urban life.

In the global neighbourhood, the instinct of care must be given a global reach. Millions of people already demonstrate that they are moved by this when they help voluntary agencies that support anti-poverty projects or undertake humanitarian relief in different parts of the world. The ranks of those who are stirred by such instincts need to be enlarged. The task for governance is to encourage a sense of caring, through policies and mechanisms that facilitate co-operation to help those less privileged or needing comfort and support in the world.

INTEGRITY

Integrity is the basis of trust that is necessary in relationships among people and organizations as well as between them. Vital to the orderly functioning of any organization or society, it is of paramount importance in systems of governance at all levels. The quality of governance depends to a crucial degree on policy makers and those in positions of authority adhering to the highest principles and ideals.

The importance of integrity is underlined by the enlarging evidence of fraud and corruption of many kinds among persons in high positions in both public life and the private sector. Ranging from bribery to insider dealing to money-laundering, corruption is a form of social pollution that weakens democratic governance. People are its main victims, and it is their insistence on the highest standards of public and business conduct that can ensure that integrity prevails. The widest concern with standards of integrity and commitment to upholding them must be a feature of the global neighbourhood.

A GLOBAL CIVIC ETHIC

Over the long run, rights can only be preserved if they are exercised responsibly and with due respect for the reciprocal rights of others.

The realities of the emerging global neighbourhood require that, in addition to promoting the values just described, we should develop a global ethic that applies equally to all those involved in world affairs. Its efficacy will depend on the ability of people and governments to transcend narrow self-interests and agree that the interests of humanity as a whole will be best served by acceptance of a set of common rights and responsibilities.

The global ethic we envisage would help humanize the impersonal workings of bureaucracies and markets and constrain the competitive and self-serving instincts of individuals and groups. Put differently, it would seek to ensure that international society is imbued by a civic spirit.

An important consequence of the emergence of a global neighbourhood is that national civil societies have begun to merge into a broader global civil society. Groups of many kinds are reaching out and establishing links with counterparts in other parts of the world. Without the objectives and limits that a global ethic would provide, however, global civil society could become unfocused and even unruly. That could make effective global governance difficult.

During the past fifty years, the world has made great progress in elaborating universal human rights. This process began with the drafting of the United Nations Charter and has been furthered by the Universal Declaration of Human Rights; by conventions on civil and political rights and on economic, social,

RIGHTS AND
RESPONSIBILITIES

and cultural rights; by regional human rights charters; and by the Declaration on the Rights and Duties of States. Almost all governments have signed or subscribed to at least one of these treaties, conventions, or declarations. They provide an important starting point for a global ethic, but they need to be supplemented in two important ways.

First, as presently conceived, rights are almost entirely defined in terms of the relationship between people and governments. We believe it is now important to begin to think of rights in broader terms by recognizing that governments are only one source of threats to human rights and, at the same time, that more and more often, government action alone will not be sufficient to protect many human rights. This means that all citizens, as individuals and as members of different private groups and associations, should accept the obligation to recognize and help protect the rights of others.

Second, rights need to be joined with responsibilities. The tendency to emphasize rights while forgetting responsibilities has deleterious consequences. Over the long run, rights can only be preserved if they are exercised responsibly and with due respect for the reciprocal rights of others.

We therefore urge the international community to unite in support of a global ethic of common rights and shared responsibilities. In our view, such an ethic—reinforcing the fundamental rights that are already part of the fabric of international norms—would provide the moral foundation for constructing a more effective system of global governance. It should encompass the rights of all people to:

- a secure life,
- equitable treatment,
- an opportunity to earn a fair living and provide for their own welfare,

- the definition and preservation of their differences through peaceful means,
- participation in governance at all levels,
- free and fair petition for redress of gross injustices,
- equal access to information, and
- equal access to the global commons.

At the same time, all people share a responsibility to:
- contribute to the common good;
- consider the impact of their actions on the security and welfare of others;
- promote equity, including gender equity;
- protect the interests of future generations by pursuing sustainable development and safeguarding the global commons;
- preserve humanity's cultural and intellectual heritage;
- be active participants in governance; and
- work to eliminate corruption.

We believe this list of rights and responsibilities is the minimum basis for progress in building a more civil global society. In the final analysis, each individual and institution will have to decide exactly what is required to live up to these responsibilities. Over time, we hope that these principles could be embodied in a more binding international document—a global Charter of Civil Society—that could provide a basis for all to agree on rules that should govern the global neighbourhood.

The spread of democracy has been one of the most heartening trends of recent years. It is democracy that can ensure that a country's affairs are conducted—and its development directed—in ways that respond to the interests and wishes of the people. Democracy provides the environment within which the protection of

THE DEMOCRATIC TIDE

the fundamental rights of citizens is best safeguarded. It offers the most favourable foundation for peace and stability in international relations. Though democratic regimes may not all or always be virtuous, even recent history suggests that autocratic regimes are more likely to behave aggressively.

The recent tide of democratization has swept away many autocratic systems and several leaders who had clung to power for too long. Multiparty elections have been held in a large number of countries, allowing the public for the first time a real choice in who governs them. The implanting of a democratic culture is, however, not an instant or easy process. While many parties may emerge quickly and electors embrace their new opportunities with enthusiasm, the traditions of democratic behaviour and the institutions that support them take time to become established.

Elections are therefore only a first step on the democratic road, but they are a profoundly important one. The legitimacy of administrations depends on elections being free and fair—and being widely seen by electors to be so. International monitors observing elections, and pronouncing on their conduct, have been performing a useful service in many countries, with the UN, other

---

Democracy, Peace, and Development

Peace-building, as described in *An Agenda for Peace,* requires strengthening those institutions that do most to consolidate a sense of confidence and well-being between peoples. It is increasingly clear that the fundamental elements are to be found in democracy and development. Democracies almost never fight each other. Democratization supports the cause owf peace. Peace, in turn, is prerequisite to development. So democracy is essential if development is to be sustained over time. And without development there can be no democracy. Societies that lack basic well-being tend to fall into conflict. So three great priorities are interlocked.

—Boutros Boutros-Ghali, UN Secretary-General
An Agenda for Peace: One Year Later

---

international institutions, governments, and civil society contributing to the success of these exercises.

We welcome the efforts now under way to provide institutional support for the improvement and consolidation of the democratic electoral process worldwide. The experience of recent efforts to monitor elections and to train election officials points to the need to broaden the understanding of the norms, rules, and guidelines that apply to democratic processes. It is also necessary to strengthen national capacity to develop the full range of democratic instruments. Much research and analysis is needed. We believe that all those now involved in these efforts would benefit from closer institutional co-operation for the support of electoral processes.

As events in Haiti and Angola have demonstrated, international support for democratic transformation should not always end with the election returns. It needs to be sustained in some cases through a physical presence and almost always by support for long-term development.

The withdrawal of restrictions on political activity and free expression following the shift to democratic systems has in some countries allowed the emergence of movements that seek to deny the rights of others. Many newly created democratic systems have also to devise ways to reconcile conflicting demands and interests before they imperil national stability. Such difficulties are, of course, not exclusive to new democracies, and many countries with long democratic traditions have been troubled by the strains inherent in plural societies.

A wide variety of democratic constitutional models exists, and different models are suited to different traditions and social contexts. Although the winner-takes-all system of parliamentary democracy, for example, may have been successful in some countries, in others it clearly failed to ensure the rights of minorities or preserve national cohesion through conciliatory approaches. In this context, other constitutional models that have recently emerged may warrant serious consideration. In Francophone Africa, for example, some countries (Benin, Congo, Madagascar, Mali, Niger, and Togo) have recently developed the practice of holding a national conference in which all major political parties and forces are brought together to determine the political destiny of the country. This arrangement has worked well in ensuring a peaceful and consensual transition to multiparty democracy. In South Africa, the concept of a national compact has been carried a step further to include a power-sharing arrangement during a five-year transition period.

Whether through voting systems, coalitions, separation of powers, or other means, a way must be found within democratic systems for opposition voices to be heard and taken into account. Governments will govern, but governments-in-waiting need to be listened to even while they wait. Where, as in all too many countries, national reconciliation is a matter of pre-eminent need, creative approaches to power-sharing must be developed in the interest of good governance.

Centrifugal forces are not the only hazards for democracy. In a number of countries, democracy has suffered because the military has gained too dominant a position within the national polity. The countries where people have to put up with rule by soldiers are now fewer than they used to be. But even when soldiers are not in power, a high profile for the military, besides distorting the distribution of national expenditure and reducing the share devoted to development and other social purposes, can produce traits that undermine democracy and are hostile to a free society. The military ethos is inherently authoritarian and secretive. Particularly in developing countries in which the armed services is one of the few sectors offering stable, well-paid employment, the appeal of the soldier's uniform can be an unhealthy influence. The military's ascendance can be related in some cases to the instability arising from the action of dissatisfied minority groups. This further underlines the importance of strengthening the capacity of democratic systems to reconcile competing claims.

Societies in which there are deep and expanding social or economic disparities face enormous obstacles, whether in creating or maintaining democracy. Citizens who must struggle daily to meet basic needs and who see no possibility of improving their circumstances are unlikely to have either the interest, or the ability, to work on behalf of democratization. To be sustainable, democracy must include the continuing prospect of contributing to the prosperity and well-being of citizens.

As a result of the transformations of the past four decades, the participation of people in governance is now more critical than ever. Governments that do not have the active support of their people are finding it more and more difficult to survive. But democracy is not merely a matter of voting. It is a dynamic process, involving a commitment to democratic principles and institutions that meet the needs of citizens routinely and in times of crisis. Truly democratic institutions continuously engage people directly in a multiplicity of ways. The gap between governments and citizens needs to be narrowed. A viable democracy requires an active civil society. At its best, civil society is citizens acting in pursuit of a range of interests, many of which have implications for public policy. There is, at the same time, a need to ensure democratic functioning in the many institutions of civil society. Their leaders should be held to the same standards of accountability as political leaders.

Good governance requires good government. And government depends not only on state structures, but on political power. Political parties have key functions in a democracy. Yet in the debate about democracy and civil organizations, little attention is given to political parties. There is a widespread need to improve the way parties work, to attract more participants to the democratic process. To function, parties need resources; to avoid corruption, they should open their finances to public scrutiny. Political parties, a crucial part of national civil society, also have a role in the growing global civil society. Politics is vital for transforming values into action.

There is a symbiotic relationship between state, civil society, individual citizens, and democratic structures; together they set the framework and provide the substance of democratic governance. Not all democracies look alike, however. The form that a democracy takes is determined by a country's governing traditions and experience, by the economic and social conditions of its citizens, and by the nature of the democratic institutions that exist or emerge.

Nevertheless, there is a consensus that democracy, whatever form it may take, is a global entitlement, a right that should be available and protected for all. At the same time, some international standards are emerging with respect to democracy and to the systematic monitoring of compliance with democratic norms. The development of international human rights law and of procedures for international monitoring of elections underscores the links between national and international efforts to promote democracy.

The emergence of a global civil society is an important precondition of democracy at the global level, although it cannot guarantee it. More and more people are making connections across borders and developing relationships based on common concerns and issues: the environment, human rights, peace, women's roles, and many others. Advances in communications have greatly facilitated the process. The information and communication revolutions are helping to diffuse power throughout society, often transferring it from hierarchical structures to small groups, and increasing the ability of dispersed groups to communicate. Indeed, computer-based networking capabilities are giving new form and strength to civil society and facilitating partnerships with intergovernmental institutions.

It is easy to exaggerate the impact of these revolutions, however. An infinitely smaller percentage of the people in developing countries than in industrial ones is currently included in this process of interaction. The vast majority are currently left out. More significant, perhaps, this partial democratization of communications and information has been accompanied by the concentration of telecommunications and media power in the hands of a small number of private firms. Technological advance seldom unambiguously or permanently favours democracy over tyranny any more than it favours defence against attack. Yet the spread of the new technology has been so rapid that it is hard not to conclude that it will be generally used before long and that the net effect will be to favour democracy.

Corruption is a world-wide phenomenon affecting both the public and private sectors, compromising the processes of legislation and administration, regulation, and privatization. Corrupt dealings between the worlds of business and politics at very high levels have come to light in recent years in dozens of countries, both industrial and developing. The widening operations of international drug rings have been a fertile source of corruption in both drug-producing and consuming countries. The expansion in organized criminal activity, particularly evident in some former socialist countries, has been another. The Mafia's role in corruption on both sides of the Atlantic has been legendary.

In a number of developing countries, corruption flourished under despotic rulers as well as under

COMBATING CORRUPTION

democratic regimes. Vast sums that should have been in government treasuries to be spent on national objectives were siphoned off to be invested or banked abroad. The people of these countries were effectively robbed. The great powers that supported corrupt rulers in the full knowledge of their venality must share the blame. So must the banks that help stash away ill-gotten funds and launder the money of drug dealers and other criminals.

Most opportunities for significant corruption in developing countries arise in interactions between their politicians and officials and the business sector in industrial countries. The latter, which includes arms manufacturers, is too often ready to offer sweeteners to secure contracts and orders. The business community of the industrial world has not lived up to its responsibility for ensuring that its members follow ethical business practices.

The strengthening of democracy and accountability is an antidote to corruption. While they are no guarantees against corrupt practices, as so many democracies confirm, a free society with vigorous, independent media and a watchful civil society raises the chances of the detection, exposure, and punishment of corruption. Public servants who respect the highest traditions of service to the public are another defence against the spread of corrupt practices. While action within countries remains critical, there is much scope for co-operation among national law enforcement agencies, not only in such specific areas as drug trafficking but more generally in the fight against corruption world-wide. The need for early action against criminal syndicates, before they have time to entrench themselves, has been underlined by recent experience. It is also important that the privatization of state-owned companies should be carried out without any taint of irregularity, so that the process of economic reform, of which privatization forms a part, is not discredited.

In 1990, the South Commission, chaired by former Tanzanian President Julius Nyerere, addressed the issue of corruption in its report, *The Challenge to the South*. We endorse the points made there:

In the South, the excessive concentration of economic power in the hands of the government and the corporate sector, poverty, insecurity, and the underpayment of public personnel also account for some of these undesirable practices. So do corrupting influences from Northern sources related, but not confined, to obtaining profitable contracts and to the trade in arms and the illicit traffic in drugs.

Regardless of these factors, governments must bear a large part of the responsibility for corruption in the South. By and large they have not regarded its eradication as a priority, despite its acknowledged economic, social, and political costs. Higher standards of integrity in public life could do much to strengthen the people's confidence in governments and the sense of community and civic responsibility. The issue bears not solely on venality in the public sector, but on encouragement and facilitation of corruption within society through governmental mismanagement, authoritarianism, inadequate systems of control and public accountability, and militarization. The genuine democratization of political structures can go a long way to arresting these harmful activities. Sustained progress must rely on the effective functioning of democratic processes. It is also necessary to minimize the scope for discretionary controls in the management of the economy, thereby reducing the temptations for arbitrariness. Since discretionary controls cannot be dispensed with altogether, built-in safeguards must be provided to avoid their misuse by the authorities.

While a global civic ethic is needed to improve the quality of life in the global neighbourhood, effective governance also requires democratic and accountable

DEMOCRACY
AND
LEGITIMACY

institutions and the rule of law. In the past, governance and law used to be almost entirely national concerns. Democracy was defined primarily in terms of the role of national and regional governments, and the enforcement of the rule of law was seen as the responsibility of national courts. Today, this is no longer adequate.

As at the national level, so in the global neighbourhood: the democratic principle must be ascendant. The need for greater democracy arises out of the close linkage between legitimacy and effectiveness. Institutions that lack legitimacy are seldom effective over the long run. Hence, as the role of international institutions in global governance grows, the need to ensure that they are democratic also increases.

It is time to make a larger reality of that 'sovereign equality' of states that the UN Charter spoke of in 1945, but that it compromised in a later article in allowing a superior status to a few nations. Particularly in the context of the moral underpinnings of a new world order, nation-states and their people cannot but question the double standards that demand democracy at the national level but uphold its curtailment at the international level. There will always be differences of size and strength between countries, as there are between individuals within countries. But the principle of equality of status as members of the body politic is as important in the community of states as it is in any national or local community. The ethic of equality before the law is essential to guard against the temptation to authoritarianism—the predilection of the strong to impose their will and exercise dominion over the weak.

We do not imply that there is a need at the global level for a carbon copy of national democratic systems. There are differences between the two levels, but the norms of democracy must be pursued in both. The fiftieth anniversary of the United Nations is an appropriate time to reassert the primacy of the democratic principle. We address this question in Chapter Five when discussing the Security Council, and put forward there proposals for its reform. It arises as well in other institutional arrangements, such as the voting structures of the Bretton Woods institutions, for which we also recommend a more democratic basis.

Democracy has to do with the exercise of power and the recognition that imposition and coercion, however contrived, are unacceptable and in the end unworkable. Fifty years after the end of the conflict whose victors saw the need to assume special privileges and special responsibilities, the time has come for the world to advance towards more contemporary norms. As we approach the twenty-first century, there is no ideal more dominant than that of democracy. In many ways, the UN is a custodian of our highest ideals. We do a great disservice to its standing, and ultimately its capacities, if we make it an exception to that most basic principle, or if beyond the system itself we acquiesce in arrangements that diminish democracy at the level of the global neighbourhood.

The rule of law has been the ethical cornerstone of every free society; respect for it is at least as essential to the global neighbourhood as to the national one. Global governance without law would be a contradiction in terms. Its primacy is a precondition of effective global governance. In Chapter Six, we make recommendations for strengthening the rule of law world-wide.

ADAPTING OLD NORMS

Countries are having to accept that in certain fields sovereignty has to be exercised collectively.

Despite the use of the words 'we the peoples' in the opening line of the UN Charter, the post-war order was designed primarily to serve a world of states. Its architects assumed that states were the principal international forces. This assumption is reflected in the institutions they created and the norms they articulated.

In this respect, creating the UN system was simply a development in the continuing evolution of the system of international relations based on the sovereign rights of territorial states. This system was influenced most heavily by the development of the European state system, symbolized by the 1648 Peace of Westphalia. It took a long time to shift gradually from a Eurocentric order based on the primacy of great powers to a world-wide order supported by universal norms. The post–World War I Versailles Peace Conference of 1919 represented one phase in this shift, and the San Francisco conference in 1945 was a further step. Even now the shift is not wholly complete, but at least a system based on universal norms is in place.

Over the years, a large number of these norms have been defined, elaborated, and reiterated by a stream of declarations, conventions, and treaties. Two of central importance are sovereignty and self-determination.

SOVEREIGNTY

Sovereignty—the principle that a state has supreme authority over all matters that fall within its territorial domain—is the cornerstone of the modern interstate system. Three other important norms stem from this central principle. First, that all sovereign states, large and small, have equal rights. Second, that the territorial integrity and political independence of all sovereign states are inviolable. And third, that intervention in the domestic affairs of sovereign states is not permissible. Throughout the post-war era, these three norms provided a crucial source of international stability. Because they were widely accepted, overt aggression against sovereign states was remarkably rare.

And when it occurred, the international balance was heavily tilted against the aggressor.

These norms, and the claim that only the state could legitimately use force within its territory, also strengthened the ability of states to suppress dissenting voices. They served to increase the resources and support at the disposal of incumbent governments, while denying resources and support to dissidents. They have also restricted overt intervention by big powers in the internal affairs of small states, though they have failed to provide complete protection against intervention, much less subversion. Without these norms, the world would be much more insecure and less peaceful. Aggression and subversion would be far more common, and the small and weak constantly at the mercy of the big and powerful.

Sovereignty ultimately derives from the people. It is a power to be exercised by, for, and on behalf of the people of a state. Too often, however, this principle has been misused. In some cases, powerful countries have used their claimed sovereign right as a sword against weaker countries. In other cases, rulers have exercised their control of the instruments of government to usurp the prerogatives that flow from it. They have monopolized the benefits that derive from membership in the international community. They have used sovereignty to shield themselves against international criticism of brutal and unjust policies. And in its name they have denied their citizens free and open access to the world.

For these reasons, existing norms regarding sovereign equality, territorial independence, and non-intervention need to be strengthened in two ways. First, efforts must be made to ensure that they are universally enforced. Double standards must be eliminated: states should not be free to seek the protection that sovereignty affords at one moment and then ignore the limits it imposes at another. Second, ways must be found to ensure that those in power do not abuse sovereignty. The exercise of sovereign power must be linked to the will of the people. Unless the abuse of sovereignty is stopped, it will be impossible to increase respect for the norms that flow from it.

In an increasingly interdependent world, old notions of territoriality, independence, and non-intervention lose some of their meaning. National boundaries are increasingly permeable—and, in some important respects, less relevant. A global flood of money, threats, images, and ideas has overflowed the old system of national dikes that preserved state autonomy and control. The movement of people is still subject to rigid frontier controls, though these may sometimes be relaxed or overwhelmed when wars, famines, and other emergencies provoke people to seek safety. Territorial sovereignty is, however, under pressure from illicit crossborder movements, and there is concern in many countries that political or economic developments could add to these flows.

It is now more difficult to separate actions that solely affect a nation's internal affairs from those that have an impact on the internal affairs of other states, and hence to define the legitimate boundaries of sovereign authority. For example, changes in the interest rate policies of Germany, Japan, or the United States can have immediate effects on the national debt and employment prospects of countries all around the world; turmoil in Haiti and Russia can create economic, social, and political tensions in Miami and Berlin; environmental policies made in Washington can affect employment and pollution levels in Rio de Janeiro. Increasingly, countries are having to accept that in certain fields sovereignty has to be exercised collectively, particularly in respect of the global commons. Moreover, in today's world, most serious threats to national sovereignty and territorial integrity often have internal roots, and there is often criticism of other governments for wanting to stay aloof rather than for intervening.

For all these reasons, the principle of sovereignty and the norms that derive from it must be further adapted to recognize changing realities. States continue to perform important functions, and must have the powers to fulfil these functions effectively. But these must rest on the continuing consent and democratic representation of the people. They are also limited by the fundamental interests of humanity, which in certain severe circumstances must prevail over the ordinary rights of particular states.

Nothing brings this issue more forcefully to the fore than the question of 'humanitarian intervention'. Most threats to the physical security of people now arise from deteriorating situations within countries, from civil war and ethnic conflict, from humanitarian emergencies—natural or caused by humans—and, in extreme cases, from the collapse of civil order. Sometimes more than one of these factors could be present, or one could lead to another.

When there is human suffering on a large scale as a result of such factors, it inevitably provokes demands for UN action, notwithstanding the fact that such action would constitute external interference in the affairs of sovereign states. Small and less powerful states in particular have seen sovereignty and territorial inviolability as their main defence against more powerful, predatory countries, and they have looked to the world community to uphold these norms.

Where people are subjected to massive suffering and distress, however, there is a need to weigh a state's right to autonomy against its people's right to security. Recent history shows that extreme circumstances can arise within countries when the security of people is so extensively imperilled that external collective action under international law becomes justified. Such action should be taken as far as possible with the consent of the authorities in the country; but this will not always be possible, and we have put forward in Chapter Three proposals in this regard. It is important that any such action should be a genuinely collective undertaking by the world community—that is, that it should be undertaken by the United Nations or authorized by it and carried out under its control, as the UN so vigorously tried to ensure in the former Yugoslavia.

The United Nations may stumble and even fail from time to time, but so has every country that has ever assumed a role of leadership. In the global neighbourhood, a primary duty of everyone—states and people alike—is to support, not usurp, neighbourhood action. It is also essential that UN action should follow principled criteria. It should be consistent and even-handed; above all, it should not be unduly influenced by powerful nations, within a region or globally. An activist UN will not long survive as a legitimate and effective actor if it is used as a cover for the intervention of particular states.

The readiness of the Security Council to authorize UN action, including military action, in support of humanitarian purposes represents a proper and necessary evolution of the exercise of international responsibility. So far, the Charter has proved capable of accommodating it, albeit not comfortably or perhaps sustainably. This is a dimension of internationalism that must be developed with care and circumspection and within the framework of the constraints just mentioned. Ideally, humanitarian efforts undertaken by the UN will come to be seen as neighbourhood action motivated by the highest purposes of collective support for the security of people—of neighbours. And, as discussed in Chapter Three, it must be clearly authorized by the Charter and taken under it, not on an ad hoc or arbitrary basis.

The second core principle of the existing international order is self-determination. Not as venerable as sovereignty, it derives from the rise of democracy and the national idea, both of which contributed to the consolidation of divided European principalities into modern nation-states, the collapse of European empires in the Americas, and the breakup of the Habsburg and Ottoman empires.

The Versailles Peace Conference after World War I recognized the principle of self-determination, but it was not until the founding of the United Nations in 1945 that it became an effective norm equally applicable world-wide. Throughout the post-war era, self-determination was generally viewed as a right limited to territorially defined populations living under colonial rule. As such, it played a crucial role in the process of decolonization that has brought a succession of new sovereign states into being.

During the past decade, two kinds of developments have occurred that have forced the world to re-examine the issue of self-determination. The first was the breakup of countries, the two most dramatic being the Soviet Union and Yugoslavia. Both were multinational federations that had been held together by iron-fisted central governments. With the political cataclysms of the early 1990s, these governments lost both their legitimacy and their power—and the constituent national units were able to become independent states. Similar, albeit much more peaceful, negotiated separations occurred in Czechoslovakia and in Ethiopia, where there had earlier been a protracted conflict. While the violent and unsettling consequences of the Soviet and Yugoslav breakups have raised serious concerns about the exercise of the right of self-determination, it is arguable whether they involve any new issues of principle.

A much more far-reaching development is the growing assertion of a right to self-determination by indigenous populations and other communities in many parts of the world. In these cases, self-determination involves a complex chain of historical and other questions that go far beyond the issue of establishing a new state on the basis of a pre-existing territorial entity. Issues of identity, human rights, and empowerment that have little to do with previous boundaries are also involved.

Self-determination is a right of all nations and peoples, as long as it is consistent with respect for other nations and peoples. The challenge now is to find ways to define and protect this right in the environment of the global neighbourhood. It is becoming ever more difficult to resolve the problems raised by competing claims to self-determination on the basis of separate nationhood for each claimant. A process of territorial dismemberment could be set in motion that would leave much of the world far worse off and would greatly increase insecurity and instability. Moreover, redrawing maps will not succeed in reducing injustice and the risks of civil strife if the new states still lack workable formulas to reconcile conflicting claims to authority, resources, status, or land.

The problem is not made easier by the absence of any clear definition of what constitutes 'a people' or 'a nation'. It is time to begin to think about self-determination in a new context—the emerging context of a global neighbourhood rather than the traditional context of a world of separate states.

The demand for separation and the resort to violence in support of it often follow the frustration of constitutional efforts to secure less drastic changes. This points to the importance of governments being sensitive to the aspirations of ethnic or other groups that feel alienated or threatened. Most of the nearly 200 nation-states in the world consist of more than one ethnic group. There is consequently considerable scope for discord and conflict over the sharing of resources and authority and the policies that governments follow. But there is also a positive side to pluralism as manifest in several successful multiethnic states. Diversity need not become a cause for division. A challenge to governance is to make it a source of enrichment.

If tragedies are not to be multiplied one-hundred-fold, concern for the interests of all citizens, of whatever racial, tribal, religious, or other affiliation, must be high among the values informing the conduct of people in the world that has now become a neigh-bourhood. There must be respect for their rights, in particular for their right to lead lives of dignity, to preserve their culture, to share equitably in the fruits of national growth, and to play their part in the governance of the country. Peace and stability in many parts of the world could be endangered if these values are neglected. The world community needs to strengthen protection of these rights, even as it discourages the urge to secede that their frustration can breed. Governance in the global neighbourhood faces no stronger challenge.

CHAPTER THREE

PROMOTING SECURITY

The end of the cold war provides a new opportunity to make the world's collective security system effective and to adapt it to the broader needs of the security of people and of the planet.

Fifty years after San Francisco, the world needs to consider whether the UN Charter's provisions for maintaining peace should be revised, or if the need for change lies less in the mechanisms and procedures and more in the attitude of nations—not mending the machinery but minding how it is used. And what must the world community do to preserve peace not only among states but also within them?

There are no simple answers to these questions, but the Commission believes it is time to re-examine prevailing ideas of how to preserve peace and ensure the security of people, and of how to develop more effective means of preserving peaceful relations among states.

The task of ensuring peace and security is every bit as challenging today as it was in 1945. The alternative to a civilized international system, to a global neighbourhood living peacefully under common neighbourhood values with the help of effective collective mechanisms for common security, is too terrifying to contemplate. A second post-war failure to build an effective system of collective security would call into question our claim to be a humane society and an effective trustee for future generations.

THE CHANGED NATURE OF GLOBAL SECURITY

Global security must be broadened from its traditional focus on the security of states to include the security of people and the planet.

Rivalry has always been inherent among sovereign states. In the past, states' efforts to increase their own security by expanding their military capabilities and forming alliances with other military powers invariably threatened the security of other states. The struggle for national security was a perpetual zero-sum game in which some states won and others lost. To continue on this path is to court disaster.

In the twenty-first century, war between states is even less likely to produce winners. The world has become too small and too crowded, its people too intermingled and too interdependent, its weapons too lethal. Ballistic missiles, long-range aircraft, and weapons of mass destruction have made the security offered by national boundaries even more illusory. Efforts by great powers to preserve their military dominance will stimulate emerging powers to acquire more military strength. At the same time, emerging powers' attempts to redress the military imbalance can only prompt traditional powers to reinforce their capabilities. The results of such a vicious circle will be rising political tensions, wasted resources, or worse—war by accident or inadvertence.

Since the seventeenth century, international security has been defined almost entirely in terms of national survival needs. Security has meant the protection of the state—its boundaries, people, institutions, and values—from external attack. This concept is deeply embedded in international tradition. It is the reason the United Nations and other international institutions emphasized the inviolability of territorial boundaries and the prohibition of external interference in the internal affairs of sovereign states.

While these norms may have reduced the frequency of interstate aggression, they have also had other, less benign, consequences. The concept of state sovereignty in security matters has often provided the rationale for creating powerful national military systems, justified budgetary policies that emphasize defence over domestic welfare, and encouraged measures that severely restrict citizens' rights and freedoms.

Protection against external aggression remains, of course, an essential objective for national governments and therefore for the international community. But that is only one of the challenges that must be met to ensure global security. Despite the growing safety of most of the world's states, people in many areas now feel more insecure than ever. The source of this is rarely the threat of attack from the outside. Other equally important security challenges arise from threats to the earth's life-support systems, extreme economic deprivation, the proliferation of conventional small arms, the terrorizing of civilian populations by domestic factions, and gross violations of human rights. These factors challenge the security of people far more than the threat of external aggression.

As the face of global society has changed, so too has the nature of global security. Among the various concepts of security frequently used are common security, collective security, and comprehensive security. Common security was first spelled out by the Independent Commission on Disarmament and Security Issues, chaired by the late Olof Palme. The concept articulated by that Commission recognizes that lasting security will not be achieved until it can be shared by all, and that it can only be achieved through co-operation, based on the principles of equity, justice, and reciprocity.

> **Common Security**
>
> Our alternative is common security. There can be no hope of victory in a nuclear war, the two sides would be united in suffering and destruction. They can survive only together. They must achieve security not against the adversary but together with him. International security must rest on a commitment to joint survival rather than on a threat of mutual destruction.
>
> —Olof Palme, "Introduction"
> *Common Security: A Programme for Disarmament*
> Report of the Independent Commission on
> Disarmament and Security Issues

Collective security, as envisaged in the UN Charter, is based on the idea of members in a particular group renouncing the use of force among themselves while pledging to defend any member of the group attacked by external forces. It is inherently military focused. Comprehensive security, on the other hand, emphasizes changing the present military-based notion of security. Among its dominant ideas are co-operation, confidence-building, transparency, gradual disarmament, conversion, demobilization, and demilitarization. Recently, a new concept—human security—has received attention. This is a people-centred approach that is concerned not so much with weapons as with basic human dignity. As explained in the *Human Development Report 1994,* human security includes safety from chronic threats such as hunger, disease, and repression, as well as protection from sudden and harmful disruptions in the patterns of daily life.

While sympathetic to all these concepts and their implications, we have felt it appropriate to focus on the security of people and the planet, as defined in this chapter. We believe that the concept of global security must be broadened from its traditional focus on the security of states to include these other dimensions that are more relevant today.

The security of people recognizes that global security extends beyond the protection of borders, ruling elites, and exclusive state interests to include the protection of people. It does not exclude military threats from the security agenda. Instead, it proposes a broader definition of threats in the light of pressing post–cold war humanitarian concerns.

The Commission believes that the security of people must be regarded as a goal as important as the security of states. Ultimately, the two objectives are not in conflict: states cannot be secure for long unless their citizens are secure. Too often in the past, however, preserving the security of the state has been used as an excuse for policies that undermined the security of people.

Although Iraq's aggression against Kuwait reminds us that war between states is not extinct, in the years ahead the world is likely to be troubled primarily by eruptions of violence within countries. Civil wars, some of long standing, continue in such places as Afghanistan, Sudan, and Sri Lanka. The examples of El Salvador and Cambodia, of Somalia and Rwanda, and of Bosnia and Angola show how these conflicts can impose enormous hardships on massive populations for a long time.

As these examples show, in many countries the security of people has been violated on a horrendous scale without any external aggression or external threat to territorial integrity or state sovereignty. To confine the concept of security exclusively to the protection of states is to ignore the interests of people who form the citizens of a state and in whose name sovereignty is exercised. It can produce situations in which regimes in power feel they have the unfettered freedom to abuse the right to security of their people. There have also been civil conflicts in which the security of people has been extensively violated, with the parties in conflict showing scant respect for the lives of civilians.

Although it is necessary to continue to uphold the right of states to security, so that they may be protected against external threats, the international community needs to make the protection of people and their security an aim of global security policy.

THE SECURITY OF THE PLANET

The unprecedented increases in the scale and intensity of human activity since the Industrial Revolution, combined with equally unprecedented increases in human numbers, have reached the point where human impacts are impinging on the planet's basic life-support systems. Reductions in the ozone layer of the atmosphere are exposing humans and other forms of life to increased ultraviolet radiation. Vast increases in the amounts of carbon dioxide and other greenhouse gases being emitted to the atmosphere from human sources are affecting the atmospheric processes that determine the world's climate, giving rise to the prospect of climate change that could drastically reduce the habitability of the planet.

Species of plant and animal life are becoming extinct at rates far greater than experienced in the normal processes of evolution. Losses of forest cover and of biological diversity are changing some of the fundamental balances and resource systems essential to human life and well-being, including the carbon cycle, the capacity for photosynthesis, the water cycle, food production systems, and genetic resources.

The growing quantities of chemicals produced for human use, many of them not found in nature, ultimately reach the environment on a scale that is altering the chemical composition of the earth's waters, soils, and biological systems as well as its atmosphere. And the still huge arsenal of nuclear weapons as well as nuclear reactors built to produce power for peaceful purposes have a potential for release of radiation that could be pervasive and life-threatening.

Although scientific opinion is far from unanimous about the extent or the urgency of these and other risks, the consensus is that they are of an unprecedented nature and may threaten the continued capacity of the planet to support its human population. What is new about these hazards is that they pose a danger to the very survival, not just the well-being, of whole societies. In this sense, together with nuclear war, they constitute the ultimate security risk.

In confronting these risks, the only acceptable path is to apply the 'precautionary principle': even in the face of uncertainty about the extent or timing of environmental damage, prudent action is required when the outcome of continuing along the same path could be severe or irreversible damage. Action must be taken now to control the human activities that produce these risks so as to keep them within acceptable limits. In this, governments and citizens must be guided by the best available scientific opinion, but cannot afford to wait until the scientific evidence is complete.

One sobering fact is that all the deterioration and the risks perceived to date in respect of the planet's environment and life-support systems have occurred at levels of population and human activity much lower than they will be in the period ahead. World population is expected to double towards the middle of the twenty-first century before it stabilizes, and economic activity is likely to increase by a factor of four to five. Thus the measures required to avert risks must be put in place immediately and those already in place—the Framework Convention on Climate Change, the Convention on Biodiversity, and the protocol on ozone depletion and its amendments, to name a few—must be rapidly and substantially strengthened.

Fortunately, some of the most important steps that could be taken to ensure planetary security are those of a 'no regrets' nature—those justified as much on economic as on environmental grounds. A prime example is the need to become more efficient in the use of energy. The Electric Power Research Institute in the United States estimates that all that country's energy needs could be met without significant changes in life-style or quality of life with a 55 per cent reduction from current levels of energy use. Others believe that the reduction could be even greater. And the same would be true of virtually all industrial countries.

Energy efficiency is an economic imperative for developing countries faced with capital expenditures to satisfy growing energy needs that they simply cannot meet. And it is clearly in the interest of the industrial world to ensure that these countries have the financial and technological support required to meet these needs on the most environmentally as well as economically sound and sustainable basis.

PRINCIPLES OF SECURITY FOR A NEW ERA

All people, no less than all states, have a right to a secure existence, and all states have an obligation to protect those rights.

The world needs to translate these concepts of security into principles for the post–cold war era that can be embedded in international agreements. We propose that the following be used as norms for security policies in the new era:

- All people, no less than all states, have a right to a secure existence, and all states have an obligation to protect those rights.
- The primary goals of global security policy should be to prevent conflict and war and to maintain the integrity of the planet's life-support systems by eliminating the economic, social, environmental, political,

and military conditions that generate threats to the security of people and the planet, and by anticipating and managing crises before they escalate into armed conflicts.

- Military force is not a legitimate political instrument, except in self-defence or under UN auspices.
- The development of military capabilities beyond that required for national defence and support of UN action is a potential threat to the security of people.
- Weapons of mass destruction are not legitimate instruments of national defence.
- The production and trade in arms should be controlled by the international community.

Embracing these norms would go a long way towards responding to the most pressing security challenge of the twenty-first century: preserving and extending the progress made in securing states against the threat of war while finding ways to safeguard people against domestic threats of brutalization and gross deprivation and ensuring the integrity and viability of the life-support systems on which all life depends.

THE OBLIGATION TO TAKE ACTION

The line separating a domestic affair from a global one cannot be drawn in the sand, but all will know when it has been crossed.

We believe the international community has an obligation to take action in situations where the security of people is imperilled. In this respect, it is important to distinguish between humanitarian action at the level of the Security Council addressing the security of people, and action at the level of other UN bodies and specialized agencies as well as numerous organizations of global civil society.

The increasing resort to various types of humanitarian action in the post–cold war era has not always followed Security Council decisions or been primarily of a military nature. Several other bodies and institutions, both within and outside the UN, play a crucial part in providing security through their humanitarian and other activities. They do not necessarily rely on the Security Council for the right to take action.

The UN High Commissioner for Refugees (UNHCR) and the International Committee of the Red Cross, for example, have specific mandates, based on clear humanitarian and legal norms, to protect people in situations where their security is extensively imperilled. In recent years, UNHCR has become increasingly involved in providing assistance and protection not only to refugees but also to internally displaced persons. Requests for such UNHCR activity have come from the Security Council, from the Secretary-General, and from other UN organs. In addition, various human rights organizations play, or have the potential to play, an important role in promoting the security of people. In particular, the activities of the UN High Commissioner for Human Rights constitute an innovative contribution to the security of people.

The security of people is enhanced when humanitarian agencies carry out action not only to provide relief but also to ensure the basic human rights and security of all victims of conflict or other human-caused and natural disasters. The need for such action will increase if ethnic conflicts continue to proliferate.

A trend in the last few years has been a rise in the number of Security Council resolutions that link peacekeeping or enforcement action to the provision of humanitarian assistance. The numerous resolutions on the former Yugoslavia with respect to the creation of safe areas, the delivery of relief assistance, and the unhindered access of humanitarian agencies are a case in point. Security Council resolutions on Somalia, Rwanda, Liberia, and Georgia underscore the increasing linkage between military and political objectives and humanitarian ones. Within this context, there is a need to examine the complex and evolving relationship between humanitarian action supported by military force and under military command, on the one hand, and humanitarian action under civilian command. Military support, mostly in the field of heavy logistics, has been given to humanitarian operations to provide relief—for example, to Sarajevo and to refugee camps in Zaire. The miltary forces in these cases, while operating under UN auspices, remained under national command.

In most instances, humanitarian activities precede peacekeeping or enforcement action, and invariably continue thereafter. However, in order to carry out their tasks effectively, humanitarian agencies such as UNHCR must remain strictly neutral and impartial. In practice, it may often be difficult to draw a clear line between peacekeeping operations carried out by military forces and humanitarian activities. For instance, military force may be needed to open or secure an airport or land route for the transport of relief supplies used by humanitarian agencies. In conflict situations, military resources may be needed to augment the capacity of relief agencies. But if military involvement takes a partisan turn, or is perceived to be partisan, warring parties may consider or treat humanitarian assistance agencies also as parties to the conflict. Such developments raise fundamental questions for humanitarian agencies, which must maintain their commitment to the victims of conflict with impartiality and neutrality.

With respect to Security Council–based actions, we believe that a reformed Security Council (see Chapter Five) must develop a set of principles on UN responsibility for preserving global security and must work out means to respond to threats to peace, however they arise.

In interstate conflict, clear-cut aggression is relatively easy to define. But such situations are rare. In many cases, the identity of the aggressor is not obvious, and even the basic facts of the situation may be disputed.

A more difficult question is the right—and, even more, the obligation—of the United Nations to act in a purely internal context. Clearly, the international community should not meddle in countries' domestic affairs. We do not believe that Article 2.7 of the UN Charter, on non-intervention in domestic matters, should be treated lightly, or that the principle enshrined there should be overridden. We do think, however, that it is necessary to assert as well the rights and interests of the international community in situations within individual states in which the security of people is violated extensively.

It is possible, of course, for a domestic dispute in the global neighbourhood to assume such proportions that it endangers the peace of the neighbourhood itself. These cease to be matters 'essentially within the domestic jurisdiction of any state'. When the Security Council has determined the existence of a 'threat to the peace, breach of the peace or act of aggression', Article 2.7 does not prevent the application of enforcement measures under Chapter VII of the Charter. This determination can follow the Security Council's recognition that, in a particular case, the situation is not, or has ceased to be, an essentially domestic affair.

Non-Intervention

Nothing contained in the present Charter shall authorize the United Nations to intervene in matters which are essentially within the domestic jurisdiction of any state or shall require the Members to submit such matters to settlement under the present Charter; but this principle shall not prejudice the application of enforcement measures under Chapter VII.

—Article 2.7 of the Charter of the United Nations

Quite often, however, threats to the security of people that justify international action may not constitute threats to international peace and security. In some cases, the international community acts in response to humanitarian needs—as in Somalia, where there was no government to exercise sovereign functions, or in Rwanda, which was itself a member of the Security Council and wanted UN intervention. But this can put the practice of 'humanitarian intervention' on tenuous grounds. There will be situations when the international community will be hard put to stretch to purely intrastate situations Charter provisions designed for responding to interstate disputes and conflicts.

The Security Council is already empowered under international law to take appropriate action in certain extreme situations that imperil the security of people but do not involve an external threat. A provision for implicit reference to the Security Council is contained in the Convention on the Prevention and Punishment of the Crime of Genocide (which as of September 1994 had been accepted by 114 states), under which any party can request competent organs of the UN to take action against acts of genocide.

We are all for enlarging the capacity of the Charter by enlightened interpretation, but when that reading strains credulity, it may be unsustainable. There is an even more serious consideration, however. When the international community is dealing with an issue this sensitive, clarity is needed on both the nature and the limits of the authority to act. We believe a global consensus exists today for a UN response on humanitarian grounds in cases of gross abuse of the security of people. But if we seek to find a foothold for intervention on the basis of Security Council interpretation, what will limit such intervention save a self-denying ordinance of the Security Council itself? What, then, if it decides—under pressure from powerful members, for example—that there should be intervention in cases of human rights abuses or undemocratic practices or for other reasons but without there being a clear and generally acknowledged threat to the security of people?

If the Security Council is to disregard the prohibition against intervention in internal affairs that is enshrined in Article 2.7, it must do so in circumstances clearly defined by the Charter. It will, of course, always require a case-by-case judgement, but the judgement itself must be exercised within a circumscribed framework to which all have agreed. Thus we propose an appropriate Charter amendment permitting such intervention but restricting it to cases that constitute a violation of the security of people so gross and extreme that it requires an international response on humanitarian grounds. This would both strengthen the worldwide acceptance of the concept of the security of people and keep the evolution of humanitarian response to its violation within strictly observable limits.

The Convention on the Prevention and Punishment of the Crime of Genocide

Article II

In the present Convention, genocide means any of the following acts committed with intent to destroy, in whole or in part, a national, ethnical, racial or religious group, as such:

(a) Killing members of the group;
(b) Causing serious bodily or mental harm to members of the group;
(c) Deliberately inflicting on the group conditions of life calculated to bring about its physical destruction in whole or in part;
(d) Imposing measures intended to prevent births within the group;
(e) Forcibly transferring children of the group to another group.

Article VIII

Any Contracting Party may call upon the competent organs of the United Nations to take such action under the Charter of the United Nations as they consider appropriate for the prevention and suppression of acts of genocide or any of the other acts enumerated in article III.

Intervention is, of course, fraught with dangers. Outsiders may not fully understand the situation that necessitated the action; objectivity may not always be possible for long on the part of intervening forces; and intervention always has the potential to aggravate the problem. It is the danger of abuse of the right of intervention that has caused the world community to act only slowly on matters within the domestic jurisdiction of states. Any new step to legitimize intervention must be sensitive to the need to limit action strictly to cases in which the international consensus deems the violation of the security of people too gross to be tolerated. The principle of non-interference must be respected until such a consensus is reflected in the judgement of a Security Council reformed along the lines discussed in Chapter Five.

The line separating a domestic affair from a global one cannot be drawn in the sand, but we are convinced that in practice virtually all will know when it has been crossed. Amin's Uganda, apartheid South Africa, Khmer Rouge Cambodia, and the more recent situations in Bosnia, Somalia, and Rwanda are all examples of this. Few would dissent. Each case, none the less, calls for a specific judgement to be made.

We suggest that the following key question be considered: Given the sustained importance of the principles of sovereignty and non-interference in internal affairs, has the situation deteriorated to the point where the security of people has been violated so severely that it requires an international response on humanitarian grounds? If the Security Council answers affirmatively—as it could have in each of the cases just mentioned—then the Charter as amended would be no impediment to UN action, properly authorized and implemented under Security Council control.

Action, of course, does not necessarily mean an immediate resort to force. Authorization of action in the first instance would give legitimacy to a range of measures, most of them short of force.

We realize that this approach will allow UN intervention in domestic matters only when the situation has reached extreme proportions. This limitation is not only unavoidable, but also desirable. There are, moreover, factors that would mitigate the risk that this recommendation is too modest. First, the realization that sovereignty can no longer be used to shield gross violations of the security of people from international action should itself deter such violations. Second, non-governmental organizations (NGOs) would be able to help draw attention to situations within a country that threaten the security of people.

In Chapter Five, we recommend an institutional reform that would provide new global machinery through which warnings could be articulated: the creation of a Council for Petitions in which a new 'right of petition' could be exercised by non-state actors. In this way, situations endangering security within states could be brought to the attention of the United Nations and its member-states. The body entertaining the petition would determine if the situation poses or is likely to pose a threat of such proportions that it should be addressed by the Security Council.

We further recommend that the Charter amendment establishing the right of petition should also authorize the Security Council, if it determines that the situation endangers the security of people, to call on the parties to use one of the several means mentioned in Article 33 of the Charter for the pacific settlement of disputes. This article was intended for the settlement of disputes between states, but the methods are just as relevant for domestic disagreements.

The use of force would be authorized only if these means of peacefully resolving disputes failed and the Security Council determined that under the Charter amendment just proposed, such intervention was justified on the basis of the violation of the security of people. But even then the use of force would be a matter of last resort.

It is absolutely essential to cultivate an international environment in which the use of force remains the last possible means of resolving disputes, particularly when that action is being authorized on the basis of humanitarian considerations. Both ethical and practical considerations dictate an approach that elevates persuasion, conciliation, and arbitration above coercion, and non-violent coercion above the use of force. The international community must come to grips with this fundamental issue. The challenge is to find an acceptable basis for humanitarian action that respects the dignity and independence of states without sanctioning the misuse of sovereign rights to violate the security of people within a nation's borders.

The question we have proposed as the litmus test for Security Council action might have to be asked frequently in the future. If the global neighbourhood is to be a tolerable home for all its people, it has to be kept peaceful. And keeping the peace has to be a collective responsibility. The common security of its people depends on that responsibility being shouldered.

ANTICIPATING AND PREVENTING CRISES

The international community should improve its capacity to identify, anticipate, and resolve conflicts before they become armed confrontations.

A comprehensive preventive strategy must first focus on the underlying political, social, economic, and environmental causes of conflict. Over the long run, easing these is the most effective way to prevent conflict. Such a basic approach is also likely to cost less than action taken after conflicts have erupted. Preventing conflict in such strife-torn places as Angola and Somalia would have cost far less than dealing with the results now. Our recommendations in Chapter Four on economic and social issues and our observations in Chapter Two on the importance of shared values are an integral part of a comprehensive approach to creating a more secure world. Indeed, a declared objective of the United Nations at its founding was to establish social and economic conditions under which peace and security could flourish.

The many civil wars in different parts of the world, some of them of long duration, are evidence of the inability of the existing international security system to prevent conflict within states. If, as we propose, planetary security and the security of people are to become touchstones of security policy, mechanisms to relieve environmental degradation and prevent armed conflict within states must be developed and implemented. These should stress the prevention of civil conflicts as well as the resolution of those that have begun. Preventive action has so far received far less priority than efforts to stop civil wars.

One fundamental reason for the failure of the world community to prevent war is the unwillingness and inability of governments to respond to every crisis or threat of a crisis. To conserve resources, or to avoid difficult decisions about intervention, governments will often ignore the existence of a conflict that could threaten peace and security—until it has escalated into a deadly struggle.

The difficulty that most governments face in persuading people to support potentially risky operations before compelling evidence of a humanitarian disaster also stands in the way of preventive, early action. People throughout the world tend to be guided by the media—and they are predominantly Western media—in determining when a problem warrants international action. Television coverage of a situation has become, for many, a precondition for action. Yet for most commercial networks, the precondition for coverage is crisis. There has to be large-scale violence, destruction, or death before the media takes notice. Until that happens, governments are not under serious internal pressure to act. And by then, the international community's options have usually been narrowed, and made more difficult to implement effectively.

The media also have inordinate influence in shaping peoples' perceptions of the success or failure of international action. For example, television reports of the deaths of US soldiers in Somalia led Americans to see the mission as a failure and a mistake, and President Clinton, acceding to congressional pressure, decided to withdraw US forces over the next six months.

These problems make preventive action by the United Nations difficult. The world relies on an ad hoc system of international security that is driven by political considerations as they are perceived by the major powers. The results are erratic international security concerns and action.

Environmental deterioration, particularly in areas of pervasive poverty and recurrent drought, is a growing source of potential conflict. Natural cycles of drought rapidly turn into the human tragedy of famine when they occur in areas in which growing human and animal populations have already led to widespread destruction of tree and vegetable cover and deterioration of soils. This contributes, as it did in the famine in many parts of Africa of 1984–86, to large-scale movements of people within nations and across boundaries. Social breakdown and internal conflict in Somalia, Rwanda, and Haiti were undoubtedly exacerbated by environmental deterioration accompanied by mounting population pressures. These phenomena will, if unchecked, create on a much broader scale the underlying conditions that set the stage for future conflicts. And they can, by their very nature, only be addressed through preventive strategies.

The international community has an overriding interest in surmounting obstacles to preventive action. Over the long run, the success of efforts to eliminate nuclear weapons and other weapons of mass destruction and to demilitarize nations will depend on the international system's ability to prevent armed conflict—both among and within states. As long as there are significant threats of war, both civil and interstate, countries will be reluctant to limit their military options. Equally important, they will be predisposed to define their defence needs in maximum terms. As a result, it will be difficult to reduce the level of military preparedness and the threat of war.

As recent experience has demonstrated, it is increasingly difficult to obtain support for international intervention when there is a risk of casualties or major expenditures. Despite many examples of dedicated commitment on the part of service personnel who do become involved, this raises the possibility that the international community may stand aside as millions of people are brutalized by armed conflicts. Such a pattern is already beginning to be established, as was demonstrated by months of inaction over Rwanda. If this pattern continues, the world will become a cold and forbidding place, dispelling visions of a global community united in human solidarity.

Although preventive strategies must first focus on the underlying causes of conflict, it would be naive to believe that greater and better-balanced economic and social progress would be sufficient to ensure international security. There will still be a need to prevent and respond to armed conflicts. We therefore believe the international community should improve its capacity to identify, anticipate, and resolve conflicts before they become armed confrontations, and should develop criteria and capabilities for early intervention when armed conflicts arise. The preventive approach proposed here thus has two strategic objectives—anticipating crises before they erupt, and responding to crises early and rapidly. We have found it helpful to identify the possibilities available as steps on a ladder, ranging from early warning and fact-finding missions through dispute settlement and peacekeeping to coercive, peace enforcement actions.

The uneven and often inequitable impact of political, economic, and environmental change on different segments of a population often gives rise to violent conflicts. A root cause of many conflicts is poverty and underdevelopment. But not all development failures create security crises. A distinction must be made between the general conditions of poverty, inequality, and environmental degradation that may generate instability in the long term (and that must be addressed as part of a larger effort to promote sustainable development) and the specific developments, policies, or abuses that may precipitate conflict and lead to sporadic or sustained violence.

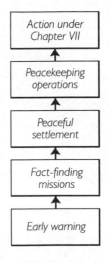

Clearly, the best solution to security crises is to remove or alleviate the factors that cause people, groups, and governments to resort to violence. Once violence breaks out, the international community's ability to act is limited. Only rarely, in circumstances of extreme humanitarian concern, is there likely to be a consensus for intervention. And even when such a consensus forms, insufficient resources can constrain action.

To remedy this situation, international and bilateral assistance policies, as well as those of civil society in general, should aim to address the alleviation of these root causes of violence. As noted earlier, we suggest in Chapter Five the creation of UN machinery for considering petitions from citizens or organizations that wish to draw attention to manifest injustices in certain fields. This would provide a mechanism to alert the world community to situations that could lead to humanitarian tragedies unless timely preventive action is taken. Public exposure will not guarantee that problems are resolved without resort to violence, but it could be a restraining influence. And it would formally raise the possibility of action by the international community through the United Nations.

<table>
<tr><td>EARLY
WARNING</td><td>

Early signs of impending crises may be seen in political and military developments as well as socio-economic and environmental factors. If such signs are to be spotted, and warnings given soon enough to be useful, the collection, analysis, and dissemination of information take on special importance. We propose that the UN develop a system to collect information on trends and situations that may lead to violent conflict or humanitarian tragedies.

</td></tr>
</table>

Early signs of impending crises may be seen in political and military developments as well as socio-economic and environmental factors. If such signs are to be spotted, and warnings given soon enough to be useful, the collection, analysis, and dissemination of information take on special importance. We propose that the UN develop a system to collect information on trends and situations that may lead to violent conflict or humanitarian tragedies.

For this to be effective, the United Nations must be able to benefit from information available to governments with extensive information-gathering capacities. All nations should share with the United Nations information on trends that may cause conflicts or tragedies.

Because of their work in the field and their close contact with local communities, some non-governmental organizations are often in a good position to alert the international community to potential conflicts. They should be encouraged to share their knowledge and insights with the United Nations. The regional and country representatives of UN agencies can also be monitors. We support the proposal for an NGO Early Warning Service, in which the United Nations would work with relevant NGOs to develop early-warning consultative and operational mechanisms.

Although the need for collection, analysis, and dissemination of information cannot be overemphasized, an even more important task is to initiate action on the basis of information providing early warning of possible conflicts.

Article 99 of the UN Charter empowers the Secretary-General to bring to the attention of the Security Council 'any matter which in his opinion may threaten the maintenance of international peace and security'.

The discharge of this responsibility clearly requires access to a regular supply of information, complemented by the capacity, when necessary, for on-the-ground verification. Fact-finding missions can help sift and assess information received; their presence in a country can also serve as a catalyst for conflicting parties, or potentially conflicting parties, to look for peaceful solutions. These missions are often welcome, as neutral third parties, in situations in which positions are getting rigid and political constraints make flexibility difficult.

We welcome the greater degree of freedom the Secretary-General now has in deciding to dispatch fact-finding missions, and hope that he will not be constrained. It is imperative that adequate resources should be available for deploying such missions. In some cases, these would need to set about their work with discretion, without drawing public attention. Their reports to the Secretary-General may be the basis for informal consultations in the Security Council. In other instances, open discussion in the Council may serve a useful purpose by giving the situation public exposure. Any ensuing action, of course, would be for the Council to decide.

RESPONDING TO CRISES

Military, political, development, and humanitarian work should be seen as complementary and mutually supportive.

The breakdown of the bipolar cold war system means that responses to security crises—both with preventive efforts and beyond them—have to come from a wider group of nations and organizations than before. The United Nations, particularly the Security Council, has the principal responsibility. But regional bodies and a wide range of civil society organizations are now in a position to play useful roles. Involving these groups can achieve a sensible division of labour and avoid overburdening the UN system.

Organizations of civil society have been responding to conflicts in several ways, undertaking humanitarian relief, mediation, refugee protection, and peace-building. Their activities now often extend beyond the mere provision of relief. For example, in Operation Lifeline in Sudan, some non-governmental organizations worked with UNICEF to persuade both government and insurgent forces to respect the right of the civilian population to receive humanitarian assistance.

It is often noted, however, that organizations of civil society are less active in the security and conflict area than in such fields as environment and development. This may often be because they are denied necessary access, or are offered no security guarantees for their personnel. The world community should recognize the important role—beyond humanitarian relief—that NGOs can play in situations of conflict. Access to conflict areas and international protection for humanitarian workers would be essential steps to promote the vital contributions of these organizations.

| PEACEFUL SETTLEMENT OF DISPUTES | Chapter VI of the UN Charter calls on those involved in a dispute to try to settle it peacefully, using a wide variety of methods. Too many disputes lead to violence, which is ultimately counter-productive and harms the interests of all parties and of ordinary people. The rule of law and the principle that aggression should not be rewarded need to be upheld. Along with the International Court of Justice (the World Court) at the Hague, the many other mechanisms for the peaceful settlement of disputes listed in the Charter represent an inadequately tapped resource. Both the Security Council and the Secretary-General should make more use of these. (See also Chapter Six.) |

Chapter VI—Pacific Settlement of Disputes

Article 33

1. The parties to any dispute, the continuance of which is likely to endanger the maintenance of international peace and security, shall, first of all, seek a solution by negotiation, enquiry, mediation, conciliation, arbitration, judicial settlement, resort to regional agencies or arrangements, or other peaceful means of their own choice.

2. The Security Council shall, when it deems necessary, call upon the parties to settle their dispute by such means.

Article 34

The Security Council may investigate any dispute ... in order to determine whether the continuance of the dispute or situation is likely to endanger the maintenance of international peace and security.

Article 35

1. Any Member ... may bring any dispute ... to the attention of the Security Council or of the General Assembly....

Article 36

3. [T]he Security Council should also take into consideration that legal disputes should as a general rule be referred by the parties to the International Court of Justice....

—Charter of the United Nations

In some instances, when parties to disputes are locked in frozen positions and movement is restricted by domestic political considerations, a move by the international community may be welcome. It could let the parties shift position without losing face. In other cases, international initiatives may be less welcome, particularly to a government that fears UN involvement could imply interference by other governments in what it regards as a purely domestic dispute. An NGO or even a highly regarded private individual may in those cases be able to help the parties agree to look for a peaceful solution.

There has been an increase in the number of organizations willing to offer their good offices in bringing together parties to disputes, or to work with others to look for solutions. There is a need now to take a pragmatic view of how positive efforts at peaceful conflict resolution are encouraged, and who brings them about. The problem, not the institutions or their mandates, should be the prime concern, and consideration of turf should not stand in the way of conflict resolution.

NEW ROLES FOR PEACEKEEPERS

The United Nations has become more active and its role more comprehensive as it deals increasingly with conflicts within states. It is also more exposed to scrutiny and to criticism. The UN is now commonly asked to reduce tensions between warring parties, encourage political reconciliation, and supply humanitarian assistance to affected civilian populations.

These roles are much more demanding than classical peacekeeping. This is obvious from a financial perspective—expenditures on peacekeeping have skyrocketed in the last four years.

The new role has also placed the UN in a more exposed position, both physically and politically. In the past, the UN was often not a relevant actor in difficult conflicts, particularly those that affected the major powers. Today, it is involved in many of the most complex conflicts, most of which are primarily internal in nature.

The new type of complex peacekeeping operations, with elements of the use of force, has also created new problems for the United Nations. We believe that two particular measures are needed to improve the situation.

First, the integrity of the UN command has to be respected. To increase the confidence of those who supply troops in the way an operation is carried out, much better mechanisms for sharing information and for consultations have to be worked out. UN resources for command and control of peacekeeping operations need to be strengthened. For each operation, a

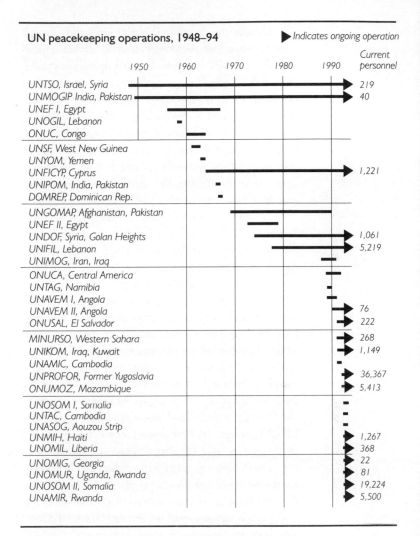

UN peacekeeping operations, 1948–94 ▶ *Indicates ongoing operation*

						Current personnel
	1950	1960	1970	1980	1990	
UNTSO, Israel, Syria						219
UNMOGIP India, Pakistan						40
UNEF I, Egypt						
UNOGIL, Lebanon						
ONUC, Congo						
UNSF, West New Guinea						
UNYOM, Yemen						
UNFICYP, Cyprus						1,221
UNIPOM, India, Pakistan						
DOMREP, Dominican Rep.						
UNGOMAP, Afghanistan, Pakistan						
UNEF II, Egypt						
UNDOF, Syria, Golan Heights						1,061
UNIFIL, Lebanon						5,219
UNIMOG, Iran, Iraq						
ONUCA, Central America						
UNTAG, Namibia						
UNAVEM I, Angola						
UNAVEM II, Angola						76
ONUSAL, El Salvador						222
MINURSO, Western Sahara						268
UNIKOM, Iraq, Kuwait						1,149
UNAMIC, Cambodia						
UNPROFOR, Former Yugoslavia						36,367
ONUMOZ, Mozambique						5,413
UNOSOM I, Somalia						
UNTAC, Cambodia						
UNASOG, Aouzou Strip						
UNMIH, Haiti						1,267
UNOMIL, Liberia						368
UNOMIG, Georgia						22
UNOMUR, Uganda, Rwanda						81
UNOSOM II, Somalia						19,224
UNAMIR, Rwanda						5,500

consultative committee should be set up, as was originally the case, including representatives of the countries that contribute troops. This committee, which
could be set up as a subsidiary organ under Article 29
of the Charter, should be consulted every time the
Security Council considers a renewal or a change of
mandate.

Second, the principle that countries with special interests in or historical relations to a conflict do not contribute troops to a peacekeeping operation should be upheld as far as possible. However, we recognize the need to discard the earlier view that the five permanent members of the Security Council should not play an active part in peacekeeping. Indeed, logistical support by major powers for UN operations (air transport, satellite communications, and so on) is not only appropriate, it will often be essential for effectiveness and the UN's own command-and-control.

The demands for UN peacekeeping have become so numerous that the capacity of the organization to respond has been hampered by the unwillingness of the member-states to provide needed resources. One way to deal with certain conflicts could be to delegate the actual implementation of an operation to a regional organization or arrangement, but to maintain Security Council control over enforcement action and its overall political leadership. This has already been done in some cases, but it could be developed further. Political authority must be maintained at the global level, to ensure international control over any given situation.

The Charter of the United Nations, in Chapter VIII, has several specific clauses about regional security arrangements. Its first article makes clear that nothing in the Charter precludes the existence of regional arrangements or agencies for dealing with matters on the maintenance of international peace and security. For several decades, cold war rivalry hindered cooperation between regional organizations and the UN under Chapter VIII.

Alliances such as the North Atlantic Treaty Organization (NATO), the Warsaw Pact, and the South-East Asia Treaty Organization were then unsuitable for a relationship with the UN. Other regional organizations, such as the Organization of American States (OAS), the Organization of African Unity, and the

Arab League, although modestly successful on a few occasions, were too loose and spread over too large an area to become forceful actors and to prevent or contain conflicts often dominated by competition between the superpowers. Even so, the role of some regional arrangements was by no means negligible in easing cold war tensions, as demonstrated by the Conference on Security and Co-operation in Europe (CSCE).

The end of the cold war opened up new possibilities for the involvement of regional organizations in responding to local conflicts in conjunction with the UN. We support the plea made by the UN Secretary-General in *An Agenda for Peace* for more active use of regional organizations under Chapter VIII, especially since the UN has become overstretched and overburdened. The contributions of the Association of South-East Asian Nations in Cambodia, the OAS and the Contadora Group in Central America, and the European Union (EU), CSCE, NATO, and the Western European Union (WEU) in the former Yugoslavia have pointed to a tremendous potential.

The relationship between the UN and regional organizations needs to be clarified in the light of recent experience. The conflict in the former Yugoslavia has led to a number of Security Council resolutions with explicit references to Chapter VIII and the active involvement of the EU, NATO, and the WEU. But there have been problems of co-ordination between the UN and regional organizations. Although some flexibility must be maintained, more structured mechanisms of co-operation are needed. For instance, standing arrangements between the UN and regional organizations, frequent high-level contacts, and common workshops, as well as harmonization of command procedures, should be initiated or further strengthened. In addition, co-operation should aim at a better exploitation of the potential of economic instruments, ranging from positive measures such as financial aid to sanctions.

For the United Nations to be effective in complex emergencies, its different roles must be played simultaneously as much as possible. Military, political, humanitarian, and development work should be seen as complementary and mutually supportive. Activities should not be put on a time axis starting with the role of the military and ending with development programmes.

<table>
<tr><td>

ACTION UNDER CHAPTER VII

</td><td>

During the last four years, the United Nations Security Council has gone through a hectic period. It has met almost continuously, and the veto has been used only once, on a marginal issue. The Council is now at last being used as a forum for dealing with situations that jeopardize international peace and security.

</td></tr>
</table>

The importance of the Security Council's special powers is seen not least in the frequent references to Chapter VII in its resolutions in recent years. This chapter deals with enforcement action—or, as its title reads, 'action with respect to threats to the peace, breaches of the peace and acts of aggression'.

The Security Council has taken an unprecedented number of decisions on enforcement action involving sanctions or the use of force during the past few years. In its new activist phase, the Council has also moved the UN in the direction of peace enforcement, placing the organization in a more vulnerable position, at risk of becoming a part of the conflict. One result has been a higher level of UN casualties than in previous peacekeeping operations. Negative reactions to casualties within countries contributing troops have made some governments reluctant to participate in UN operations.

The withdrawal of US troops from Somalia, together with those of several other nations, as a result of casualties in October 1993 demonstrates the difficulties of securing sufficient support for interventions that require large-scale troop and financial commitments, and that also carry the risk of casualties.

Sanctions Comprehensive sanctions against a country are a legitimate tool to bring about change, but they have many consequences. The effects of sanctions need to be thoroughly analysed by the relevant international organizations as well as independent institutions.

We recommend that the Security Council adopts a more precise and targeted approach to sanctions. An arms embargo is normally an early step in the Council's efforts to deal with a conflict. It can be a strong political signal to the parties to the conflict that the international community is watching developments carefully. Until now, the second step has normally been comprehensive economic sanctions. These often entail great risks for vulnerable groups. The political leaders or groups whom sanctions seek to influence are very often immune from their effects. Others, less culpable or wholly innocent, are invariably affected more severely. Also, sanctions tend to have an adverse impact on neighbouring countries. A more suitable second step, therefore, would be measures that are better focused on target groups. These could include action to stop certain types of economic transactions, to freeze assets abroad, and to suspend air links and other means of communications.

If these measures do not lead to the desired result, the Security Council could turn to comprehensive economic sanctions of the type in place in mid-1994 for Iraq and the former Yugoslavia. When doing so, the Security Council should consider also the following points.

- The Security Council should make provision, when sanctions are introduced, to ensure that humanitarian programmes are launched to help the most vulnerable groups.
- The present arrangements under Article 50 of the Charter for other countries to seek special assistance if they suffer from the effects of sanctions are clearly inadequate. The Security Council should be

able to recommend to the World Bank and other multilateral financial institutions that they give preferential treatment to such countries. The Sanctions Committee, which regularly is set up to decide on individual sanctions matters, should be given an additional mandate to follow this issue.

■ When comprehensive economic sanctions are being decided on, the Security Council should define, as clearly as possible, under what circumstances the sanctions would be lifted. This would make it possible to use sanctions to greater effect, allowing the lifting of particular sanctions to be presented as an incentive in negotiations.

Sanctions may prove less effective in certain situations than in others. Despite this drawback, however, we are convinced that sanctions are a legitimate and useful tool for inducing change.

The Use of Force The threat to use force is neither credible nor effective if there is no ability or preparedness to actually use it, as demonstrated by developments in Bosnia. The events in Somalia in 1993 contributed to a loss of faith in UN-led operations among some member-states, not least of which was the United States.

Obviously, plans for peace enforcement operations should be scrutinized more carefully in the future than was done in the Somalia case. Yet it is vital that the UN retains a capacity to act against aggression and to protect the security of people, as it tried to do in Somalia and Bosnia. All nations should be ready to make armed forces available to the Security Council, as envisaged under the Charter. It is commendable that some countries are taking steps in this direction, training special forces for UN service.

Although the command of large enforcement operations such as Desert Storm is likely to be delegated to one country or organization, it is also important that the UN Secretariat develop adequate facilities for command and control of smaller peace enforcement actions.

The Military Staff Committee was established under Article 47 of the Charter to 'advise and assist the Security Council on all questions relating to the Security Council's military requirements for the maintenance of international peace and security, the employment and command of forces placed at its disposal, the regulation of armaments, and possible disarmament'. A revitalized and strengthened Military Staff Committee could help by providing military information and expert advice to ensure that the Council's decisions on military intervention are based on authoritative, professional assessments.

Even if the United Nations enhances its capacity to enforce Security Council resolutions, 'coalitions' of countries may be formed to conduct certain UN enforcement operations. Groups such as those set up for the Gulf War in 1991 and for Somalia in late 1992 ensure that military capabilities, political support, and financial resources are mobilized in a way the UN cannot do at present. That inability of the United Nations is a matter for regret. It is a handicap that prevents the UN from living up to its full potential as outlined in the Charter.

But the establishment of coalitions also has a basis in the UN Charter. Article 48 states that '[t]he action required to carry out the decisions of the Security Council for the maintenance of international peace and security shall be taken by all the Members of the United Nations or by some of them, as the Security Council may determine'. What is essential is that the overall UN control be respected, even when a coalition command is set up, and that the Security Council determine whether any specific action should be entrusted to a coalition of countries.

The United Nations has, at present, no capacity to deploy immediately a well-trained force to carry out the mandate of the Security Council in the early stages of a crisis, before a situation gets completely out of control. Governments are understandably reluctant to commit troops rapidly for UN action, particularly in civil wars and internal conflicts, where the risk of loss of personnel is higher than in traditional peacekeeping operations. This has renewed interest in an idea originally raised in 1948 by Trygve Lie, the first UN Secretary-General. He called for the establishment of a small United Nations 'guard force' that would be recruited by the Secretary-General and placed at the disposal of the Security Council.

Lie's idea attracted no support at the time from the governments of the member-states. But today, when the Security Council is much more ready to agree on what should be done in a given crisis, this idea may be developed into an instrument that can help define how the Council's decisions can be implemented more rapidly and effectively.

In many of today's crises, it is clear that an early intervention could have prevented later negative developments, and might have saved many lives. The problem has been to find the capacity to deploy credible and effective peace enforcement units at an early stage in a crisis and at short notice. This underlines the need for a highly trained UN Volunteer Force that is willing, if necessary, to take combat risks to break the cycle of violence at an early stage. This would be particularly useful in low-level but dangerous conflicts.

Such an international Volunteer Force would be under the exclusive authority of the Security Council and, like peacekeeping forces, under the day-to-day directions of the Secretary-General. It would not take the place of preventive action, of traditional peacekeeping forces, or of large-scale enforcement action under

Chapter VII of the UN Charter. Rather, it would fill a gap by giving the Security Council the ability to back up preventive diplomacy with a measure of immediate and convincing deployment on the ground. It would provide the immediate spearhead and reconnaissance element for a later, much larger, operation, should that prove necessary.

Some objections have been raised to this proposal. It has been argued that such a force would give the Security Council or the Secretary-General too much power, that the idea raises the spectre of supranationality, that the volunteers would be viewed as mercenaries, and that it would be an expensive undertaking.

Maintaining a UN Volunteer Force—we envisage a strictly limited force with a maximum of 10,000 personnel—will involve expenditure probably beyond the UN's present system of government assessments. If so, this would rank high among the activities qualifying for financing under the system of automatic resources proposed in Chapter Four. Just as the UN cannot discharge its responsibilities if it is held hostage—as in Rwanda—to the hesitations of member-countries to provide forces even for fully authorized peacekeeping operations, so a UN Volunteer Force needed for rapid deployment would be hamstrung if it were subject to the uncertainties of national contributions, including the perennial problem of arrears. Outstanding leadership, high standards of recruitment and training, and dedication to the principles and objectives of the United Nations should help allay some of the other objections to establishing a Volunteer Force.

The words that President Roosevelt used in 1944 in presenting to the American public the case for an international organization with the capacity to enforce peace in the world are an effective argument for a UN Volunteer Force: 'A policeman would not be a very effective policeman if, when he saw a felon break into a house, he had to go to the town hall and call a meeting to issue a warrant before the felon could be arrested.'

The Force would not, of course, be a substitute for peacekeeping forces contributed by member-countries; indeed, peacekeeping forces will be crucial in the larger international role we envisage for the UN in preserving peace and security. Nor would it take the place of the understanding at San Francisco (although never implemented) that under Article 43 of the Charter, member-states would agree with the Security Council to hold national contingents on call for international duties authorized by the Security Council.

There are certain to be more than enough volunteers for an elite peace force of this kind. The problem would be to select, organize, and train the best of them, and then to develop a suitable command and support structure, along with valid rules of engagement and methods of operation. It will take awhile for such a force to become a working reality. At the same time, as its skill, experience, and reputation grew, its need to use force would probably decrease.

The very existence of an immediately available and effective UN Volunteer Force could be a deterrent in itself. It could also give important support for negotiation and peaceful settlement of disputes. It is high time that this idea—a United Nations Volunteer Force— was made a reality.

PAYING
FOR PEACE

In mid-1994, the United Nations was running seventeen peacekeeping or peace enforcement operations around the world. More than 70,000 soldiers were involved, and the cost of peacekeeping in 1993 was estimated at $3.2 billion. The peacekeeping budget of the United Nations showed a deficit of $1.6 billion in October 1994. Although peacekeeping expenditures have risen, an authoritative report on UN finances in 1993 reckoned that for every $1,000 that member-states spent on their own armed forces, they only spent $1.40, on average, on peacekeeping.

The demands on the United Nations to undertake peacekeeping and peace enforcement operations are steadily increasing. Several operations—in Namibia, in El Salvador, in Cambodia, on the Golan Heights—have been among the success stories of the United Nations. The UN's capacity to mount peacekeeping operations, as well as all forms of early, preventive action, is of the most fundamental importance to the future of the global neighbourhood. But the UN has not been given the resources needed to do the job—far from it.

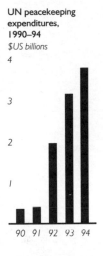

UN peacekeeping expenditures, 1990–94
$US billions

Expenditures on peacekeeping activities are a very inexpensive investment in human life, for their purpose is to prevent death and destruction. But finding the resources for peacekeeping operations is increasingly a problem. We propose that the international community prepare to make significantly increased funds available for peacekeeping in the next few years. This should be possible by using some of the resources that can be made available through a reduction of defence expenditures.

One way of dealing with these financial problems may be to integrate the costs of all peacekeeping operations into one single budget, shared by all governments. We therefore propose that the cost of peacekeeping operations, and of the facilities necessary to support them, such as command and control units, be progressively integrated into a single annual budget and be financed by assessments on all UN members.

To facilitate the rapid deployment of peacekeeping forces, a substantial peacekeeping reserve fund should be established.

ENDING THE THREAT OF MASS DESTRUCTION

The citizens of nuclear-weapon and threshold states would be immeasurably more secure in a world without nuclear or other weapons of mass destruction.

For three decades, the world has made substantial progress towards controlling the spread and use of nuclear and other weapons of mass destruction. Relevant international agreements now include the 1963 Partial Test Ban Treaty, the 1967 Treaty for the Prohibition of Nuclear Weapons in Latin America (the Treaty of Tlatelolco), the 1968 Treaty on the Non-Proliferation of Nuclear Weapons (NPT), the 1972 Anti-Ballistic Missile Treaty, the 1972 Biological Weapons Convention, the 1979 SALT II Treaty, and the 1985 South Pacific Nuclear-Free Zone Treaty.

In recent years, progress has been accelerated by the decisions of Argentina, Brazil, and South Africa to halt and reverse nuclear weapon development programmes; by the decisions of China, France, and South Africa to sign the Non-Proliferation Treaty; by the achievement in 1993, after decades of effort, of a global convention banning the development, stockpiling, and use of chemical weapons; by moratoria on nuclear-explosive testing being observed by four of the declared nuclear-weapon states; and by reductions in the nuclear arsenals of the United States and the former Soviet Union under the 1991 and 1993 Strategic Arms Reduction Treaties (START I and START II).

There are, however, several worrisome signs. They include the mid-1994 controversy about the inspection of North Korean nuclear sites, evidence that some scientists from the former Soviet Union are prepared to sell nuclear expertise on the open market, and the controversy about the conditions for and duration of extension of the NPT when it expires in 1995. In addition, some countries on the threshold of becoming nuclear powers, such as India, Israel, and Pakistan, are still not parties to the NPT.

The international community should reaffirm its commitment to progressively eliminate nuclear and other weapons of mass destruction from all nations, and should initiate a programme to make that goal a reality in ten to fifteen years. In the meantime, the processes of surveillance, monitoring, and reducing the use of weapons should be significantly strengthened.

ELIMINATING NUCLEAR WEAPONS

The end of the cold war provides a new opportunity to confirm this international commitment and begin to live up to it. As long as some states continue to retain nuclear weapons, and to insist that they are legitimate instruments of national defence, it will not be possible to establish effective, long-term controls on nuclear proliferation. As new global powers emerge, they are likely to insist on having the same rights of self-defence as others.

It is therefore imperative that all nations, especially existing nuclear powers, accept the principle of eventual elimination of nuclear weapons. More important, to build an equitable and universal nuclear non-proliferation regime, both the nuclear-weapon states and the threshold states must contribute to building a climate of confidence and openness. They should be prepared to take this step, since their citizens would be immeasurably more secure in a world without nuclear or other weapons of mass destruction.

The achievement of a nuclear capability—or steps taken towards it—need not be irreversible. Actions by Sweden in the 1950s, by Taiwan and South Korea in the 1970s, and by Argentina, Brazil, and South Africa since then demonstrate conclusively that nuclear weapon programmes can be reversed. A new commitment by the nuclear powers and other states to eliminate all weapons of mass destruction, combined with a concrete programme of action, could begin a process of negotiations and unilateral actions that could eventually bring about real nuclear disarmament. To work towards this goal, the international community should take four steps:

- the earliest possible ratification and implementation of existing agreements governing weapons of mass destruction (including the Chemical Weapons Convention; the START II Treaty, which would reduce US and Russian nuclear arsenals drastically; and the commitments by Belarus, Kazakhstan, and Ukraine to eliminate nuclear weapons and adhere to the NPT);

- the indefinite extension of the Non-Proliferation Treaty;

- the conclusion of a treaty to end all nuclear testing; and

- the initiation of talks among all declared nuclear powers to establish a process to reduce and eventually eliminate all nuclear arsenals.

It is now also necessary to begin thinking about the safeguards and disposal arrangements that would make the elimination of existing weapons in national arsenals possible. During the cold war, it was assumed that it was possible to build up excessive quantities of weapons and maintain control over them. Because of the eroding power of the state, however, control over weapons stockpiles is now more difficult. There are alarming possibilities if control is lost over nuclear weapons and their delivery systems. Independent organizations and scholars could take a lead in suggesting arrangements for the safe disposal of weapons, as in the recent report of the US National Academy of Sciences on disposition of plutonium from nuclear weapons. Gradual measures are no longer sufficient. With the radical changes in world politics of the past few years, there is an opportunity to realize the ultimate goal of a nuclear-free world.

The NPT is the cornerstone of the world's non-proliferation regime. In April 1995, a conference will be convened to decide on the length of its extension. No treaty is more important for continued progress towards the containment and reversal of nuclear proliferation than the NPT. All nations, whether or not they possess nuclear arms, stand to gain from its indefinite extension.

Indeed, failure to extend the NPT indefinitely could have three serious risks. First, the credibility of the non-proliferation regime could be seriously compromised. Second, it could lead to a rapid and uncontrolled proliferation of nuclear weapons that would greatly increase both the short-run risk of a nuclear accident and the long-run risk of a nuclear war. Third, it could cause the United States and other nuclear powers to undertake unilateral action to prevent proliferation.

Many non-nuclear-weapon states in the developing world are concerned that the NPT discriminates between states with and without nuclear weapons. In their view, nuclear powers have not fulfilled their part of the bargain that was struck in Article VI of the NPT that most nations would forgo nuclear weapons in exchange for the nuclear powers' pledge to pursue nuclear disarmament and provide peaceful nuclear technology.

The nuclear powers need to take additional steps to make the NPT more attractive to the non-nuclear countries in the developing world. All reasonable objections to extending the NPT without conditions or

---

The Nuclear Non-Proliferation Treaty

Article VI

Each of the Parties to the Treaty undertakes to pursue negotiations in good faith on effective measures relating to cessation of the nuclear arms race at an early date and to nuclear disarmament, and on a treaty on general and complete disarmament under strict and effective international control.

---

qualifications can be met through the adoption of a comprehensive programme to eliminate nuclear weapons from all nations on a specific time schedule, together with the conclusion of a comprehensive test ban. Additional reassurance would be a ban on the production of fissile materials for weapons use, an agreement on no first use of nuclear weapons, and a prohibition on deploying nuclear weapons on foreign soil.

| A BAN ON NUCLEAR TESTING | The establishment of a comprehensive nuclear test ban has long been seen as the premier symbol of a serious commitment by the nuclear powers to eliminate all such weapons. We hope that negotiations on such a ban will be concluded soon, ideally in conjunction with the 1995 Nuclear Non-Proliferation Review Conference. This international agreement is necessary if efforts to eventually eliminate these weapons are to succeed. |

Indeed, a comprehensive ban on testing is perhaps the most important arms control measure. No single act would symbolize more clearly the commitment of the international community to eliminate nuclear weapons. It would enhance the credibility of a commitment to the eventual elimination of nuclear weapons and remove a major impediment to the extension and strengthening of the NPT. In the long run, a ban on testing could also prevent the development of more sophisticated nuclear weapons or new military applications of sophisticated nuclear technologies. It would also make it more difficult for non-nuclear powers to develop these weapons.

A commitment to achieving such a ban is incorporated in the NPT, and this pledge provides an important part of the quid pro quo for the non-nuclear-weapon states to refrain from developing these weapons. For decades, the nuclear powers have danced around a comprehensive test ban, but they always stepped back when an agreement seemed feasible. With the end of the cold war, they no longer have an excuse.

Multilateral negotiations began in January 1994 at the Conference on Disarmament in Geneva. But there is no agreed time frame for concluding them. A failure to conclude a Comprehensive Test Ban Treaty soon could be a major setback for the effort to contain nuclear proliferation. Prospects for a successful negotiation of a Comprehensive Test Ban Treaty by April 1995 appear promising. We see three basic elements in any effective and comprehensive test ban.

- The international community must decide on institutional arrangements to ensure the safety of remaining nuclear explosives. For example, they should pursue comprehensive, reciprocal, and effective arrangements for monitoring warheads and fissile material that could protect them from the threat of 'loose nukes' and prevent the loss or theft of explosive materials from nuclear sites.
- Nations must establish a comprehensive and effective system of verification to monitor the ban on testing.
- The Treaty should have universal membership. It should thus include nuclear-weapon states, states with advanced nuclear capabilities, and all other states. In the short term, however, all actual and potential nuclear-weapon states should declare an immediate and unconditional moratorium on nuclear testing and refrain from using their existing stockpiles of weapons.

Regional agreements such as the Treaty of Tlatelolco, which established a nuclear-weapon-free zone in Latin America, represent effective, interim steps towards the total elimination of nuclear weapons. Similar agreements in other regions could contribute to the goal of a nuclear-free world.

In view of the practical difficulties involved in reconciling the vast differences in circumstances and

NUCLEAR-WEAPON-FREE ZONES

interests that exist between regions, an approach that combines a global declaration with region-by-region negotiations offers the best hope of creating a nuclear-free world. An agreement to create a nuclear-weapon-free zone already exists for the Southwest Pacific, but its implementation has been delayed by the objections of the nuclear powers, especially France, which has done tests in the region. All nations, particularly the nuclear-weapon states, should sign the protocols to the South Pacific Nuclear-Free Zone Treaty.

By working for agreement in other easy areas—such as Africa, where interstate rivalries are limited and no nuclear states now exist—it should be possible to develop precedents and pressures that make it easier to negotiate agreements in more difficult regions. Africa set a good precedent in April 1993 by convening a group of experts to draw up a draft treaty on the continent's denuclearization. The draft treaty is being drawn up with the aim of banning nuclear weapons and promoting peaceful uses of nuclear energy. Similar action should be encouraged in other regions.

Another area that could in particular benefit from such a zone is the Baltic Sea and adjoining region. An agreement for this region has long been proposed, but its conclusion was impossible during the cold war. Under General Secretary Gorbachev, the Soviet Union announced that it would no longer deploy new nuclear-armed submarines in the region. And with the withdrawal of the former Soviet forces from Eastern Europe, a nuclear-free region is in fact being created. This could provide favourable circumstances for negotiating a permanent ban on nuclear weapons in this region.

CHEMICAL
AND
BIOLOGICAL
WEAPONS

The threat of proliferation is not limited to nuclear weapons. The potential use and spread of chemical and biological weapons are also a major security concern.

Iraq's use of chemical weapons against Kurdish people reminded the world of the horrors of these weapons. In January 1993, more than 130 nations signed an agreement that prohibits the development, production, stockpiling, transfer, and use of chemical weapons. This is a momentous achievement. The Convention on the Prohibition of the Development, Production, Stockpiling and Use of Chemical Weapons and on their Destruction provides a means of ridding the world of one particularly abhorrent means of warfare by unconditionally outlawing an entire category of weapons of mass destruction and establishing an intrusive and highly complex implementation mechanism.

But the Convention still needs to be implemented. By its own terms, it will not enter into force until 180 days after ratification by the sixty-fifth state. As of November 1994, only sixteen states had ratified the Convention. Its procedures will be difficult to put into effect, and will require the co-operation of all nations. Although the Convention's implementation will be expensive in financial terms, the alternative is even costlier in both financial and human terms.

We hope that countries that have not yet signed the Convention will see the merit of doing so immediately, and we call on all nations to ratify the agreement before the end of 1995. The world should enter the twenty-first century free of chemical weapons.

The spectre of germ warfare that haunted hostilities in the Gulf conflict also sharpened the determination of the international community to tighten controls on the possibility of using biological and toxin weapons. The principal legal regime governing biological weapons is the 1972 Biological Weapons Convention. Together with the 1925 Geneva Protocol, this prohibits the development, production, stockpiling, possession, and use of biological and toxin weapons.

Unfortunately, neither the Convention nor the Protocol includes any verification procedures or sanctions. Under Article 10 of the 1972 Convention, however, parties undertake to facilitate, and have 'the right to participate in, the fullest possible exchange of equipment, materials and scientific and technological information for the use of bacteriological (biological) agents and toxins for peaceful purposes'. If this article is taken seriously, particularly by the scientific community, it would be an effective way to monitor both legal and illicit activity. Among other measures, the widest exchange of biotechnology is needed. States that have not yet ratified the 1972 Convention also should be induced to do so.

Chemical and biological weapons are directly linked in the public mind. We are convinced that, with the necessary political will, the world community can be rid of these weapons of mass destruction.

DEMILITARIZING INTERNATIONAL SOCIETY

All governments must jointly adopt a concrete goal for lower levels of defence spending.

When the cold war ended in 1989, it appeared reasonable to contemplate a serious, new look at prospects for demilitarizing international relations. Cold war rivalry—which had fuelled military budgets, powered the search for new weapons technologies, and fostered a reliance on military solutions to conflicts—was over, and it seemed that a new era of global harmony might be possible. That moment of euphoria was short-lived, however. Although the tide of democracy was rising, it could not stem the subsequent outbreak of a host of cruel and devastating civil conflicts. In 1991 and 1992, eleven major wars broke out and the human death toll in all twenty-nine of the ongoing wars reached 6 million, according to Ruth Leger Sivard.

None the less, despite continuing conflict and the emergence of new sources of global tension, the international security situation is changing in fundamental ways. As we have noted, security is no longer conceived solely in military terms; rather, it is a complex interweaving of economic, social, political, and military elements. Addressing interrelated, underlying issues in each of these realms is essential to lessening global tensions and, ultimately, to achieving significant arms reductions. At the level of the United States and Russia, a new focus on co-operation exists that must be encouraged for its own sake and for the context it provides for global co-operation. These governments are cutting back on weapons purchases and inventories; international agreements have been signed that will reduce arms, not merely control them; and, although the pace is slow, world military expenditures are declining and have been for several years. All these trends are encouraging and suggest that, despite current levels of conflict, there is a unique opportunity to make substantial progress in the demilitarization of global politics.

We call on the international community to redouble efforts to pursue demilitarization policies and programmes that are realistic, practical, well organized, and collaborative. Only then, and over time, will global security be significantly enhanced. We have already discussed issues related to reductions in strategic nuclear forces; military spending and arms transfers are the other essential aspects of demilitarization.

Statistical evidence for the last several years indicates that an overall global military contraction is under way. World military expenditures, which peaked in 1987 at about $995 billion (US dollars at 1991 prices and exchange rates), are declining. (See Table 3–1.) The drop that began with the end of the cold war was largely a result of budget cuts in the former Soviet Union; similar declines occurred in the West, although they were comparatively smaller. Nevertheless, although the pace is slow, there is a continuing decline.

MILITARY SPENDING

There are important exceptions to the general trend. Nations in the Middle East, along the Persian Gulf, and in South Asia continue to emphasize the need for large, modern armed forces and to spend at relatively high levels, even if current financial realities are causing some cut-backs of their plans. Nations in East Asia, where there has been very little fighting for many decades, are engaged in a major arms buildup. Almost every state in this region has been spending more on arms since the late 1970s, and many are building impressive defence industries that will create additional incentives for high military spending.

Recruiting, training, and equipping modern armed forces constitute very expensive burdens for nations all over the world. Most nations would like to see their resources used for more productive purposes. However, the long-term maintenance of military forces and defence industries during the cold war resulted in entrenched political, social, and economic systems. The reduction of armed forces and weapons production has adverse effects on these systems, resulting in unemployment and unrest. Many governments in

TABLE 3–1

Global Military Expenditures

(billions of US dollars, in 1991 prices and exchange rates)

Area	1987	1988	1989	1990	1991	1992	1993*	1994*
World	995	970	945	890	855	815	790	767
Industrial Countries**	850	835	815	760	725	690	669	649
Developing Countries	145	135	130	130	130	125	121	118

*estimates.

**including China.

Source: UNDP, *Human Development Report 1994* (New York: Oxford University Press, 1994).

OUR GLOBAL NEIGHBOURHOOD

developing and industrial countries are under pressure to slow or reverse decreases in military spending.

To counter these pressures, attention must be given to initiatives that offer incentives for reduced military spending and that support activities focused on the conversion of existing military resources. We advocate the design of a long-term global plan of action that would address the economic and social as well as the military aspects of demilitarization. Among the areas requiring attention are reallocation of financial resources, reorientation of military research and development, restructuring of industry, reintegration of military personnel into non-military jobs, reallocation of military installations, and alternative use or scrapping of surplus weapons.

To build on and accelerate current trends, we propose that all governments jointly adopt a concrete goal for lower levels of global defence spending. For example, we believe it would be feasible for governments to reduce their collective military spending to $500 billion by the end of the 1990s, compared with the $640 billion towards which they are now heading (again in 1991 prices and exchange rates), if an annual reduction rate of 3 per cent is maintained. In fact, we strongly advocate negotiations leading to an agreed percentage reduction over a defined period of time. A specific, detailed agenda must be developed to address the interrelated issues of disarmament and conversion and to illuminate the economic and social benefits to people and nations of a redirection in resources both human and financial.

The greatest levers on military spending are financial constraints. We propose that multilateral lending institutions and governments providing development assistance evaluate a country's military spending when considering assistance to it. Excessive military spending detracts from a nation's financial health and prospects for economic advancement. National and international aid-granting agencies must therefore use policy

Spending for war, spending for peace

$US, 1992

World total military expenditure *$815 billion*

UN peacekeeping expenditure *$1.9 billion* —

mechanisms to discourage defence spending, especially when it is disproportionate to expenditures on health and education. At the same time, the linkages between development assistance and military spending are complex, and require careful examination if policy conditionality is to be effective.

A DEMILITAR- IZATION FUND

To provide positive incentives for reductions in military spending, a Demilitarization Fund should be established to provide assistance to developing countries in reducing their military commitments. Created by agreement among participating governments, the fund could be managed by a multilateral institution, such as the World Bank.

The fund would focus on support of defence conversion activities in developing countries that demonstrate a commitment to reductions in military expenditures or armed forces to the minimum level consistent with their need for self-defence and contributions to peacekeeping. We believe the fund will add momentum to the current demilitarization trend by rewarding the efforts of developing countries to disarm and demobilize their armed forces and to reintegrate military personnel into civilian life through retraining for alternative economic opportunities and re-education for participation in civil society and democratic political life.

In many parts of the world, large standing militaries now serve no useful function. Instead of providing security, they often create serious threats to the security of people in their own countries. Despite this dawning reality, it is very difficult for governments to take unilateral steps to eliminate or even significantly reduce their militaries without positive reinforcement and financial assistance.

ARMS TRANSFERS

Arms transfers fell faster than global military expenditures after 1987, going from just over $70 billion to nearly $32 billion in 1993. (See Table 3-2.) The Gulf

War stimulated interest in arms purchases, and the United States, which had been behind the Soviet Union in the weapons trade, became the main recipient of a flood of new orders. By 1992, the United States was by far the leader in arms transfers world-wide, accounting for more than half of the global value of all agreements signed. By 1993, the percentage had risen even further to nearly 70 per cent, primarily as a result of high orders from Saudi Arabia and Kuwait.

The Third World continues to be the primary purchaser of arms. In 1993, the value of arms transfer agreements with the Third World constituted nearly 65 per cent of all such agreements world-wide. The decline in the total value of arms shipments arises from several factors, including limitations on funds to spend, the growth in indigenous arms industries, the loss of concessionary terms available during the cold war, and pressure from international agencies against military spending.

TABLE 3–2

Global Arms Transfer Agreements, by Supplier

(millions of constant 1993 US dollars)

Country	1987	1988	1989	1990	1991	1992	1993
United States	9,087	13,744	11,744	21,006	19,653	23,466	22,253
Russia/Sov. Union	30,750	24,755	17,952	13,121	6,356	1,837	2,800
France	4,428	2,511	5,096	3,781	3,663	4,389	1,100
United Kingdom	2,091	25,712	2,085	2,335	1,077	2,654	2,300
China	5,781	2,990	1,853	2,558	539	306	400
Germany	2,337	1,555	7,297	1,668	1,400	2,041	800
Italy	246	359	579	445	539	715	100
All Other Europeans	10,824	4,903	5,559	2,002	1,831	1,633	600
All Others	4,551	4,664	3,822	2,780	2,154	1,837	1,500
TOTAL	70,096	81,192	55,988	49,695	37,212	38,879	31,853

Source: Richard F. Grimmett, *Conventional Arms Transfers to the Third World, 1986–1993* (Washington, D.C.: Congressional Research Service, Library of Congress, 1994).

We propose that all arms-exporting countries, particularly the world's major arms suppliers, exercise restraint in weapons sales. In addition, we propose that the major military powers resume negotiations on guidelines for the export of advanced weapons. In 1992, the five permanent members of the Security Council signed an agreement on principles that should govern decisions on arms transfers. This was a positive step, and the signatories quickly began talks to define the constraints on arms sales more distinctly. These talks, unfortunately, came to an end that very year. They should be quickly resumed.

In addition, the reporting requirements of military and disarmament activities should be expanded at the international and national levels. We urge the continued discussion and development of institutions such as the UN Register of Conventional Arms (established in 1993) to increase transparency of arms transfers and nations' accountability for exports and imports of large weapons systems. There is also a need to study how transparency can be achieved in the transfers of dual-use components and technology.

Governments and citizens have grappled with the problem of arms transfers for decades. Currently NGOs in Europe and the United States are urging their governments to adopt a code of conduct that sets out guidelines to govern weapons transfers based on an agreed set of principles of behaviour. Under the code, governments would agree not to supply arms to countries that engage in aggression or violate human rights. The international community should also take steps to prevent the export or smuggling of arms to countries that are convulsed in internal conflicts, such as the former Yugoslavia or Somalia.

All states have a right to acquire arms for national self-defence, but the existing arms flows, by any reasonable standard, greatly exceed the defence needs of governments. Moreover, in many parts of the world, the easy availability of arms is fuelling local wars. It is also well known that the covert arms trade is making advanced weapons easily available to terrorists, drug traffickers, and other unconventional militias around the globe. But the biggest regular suppliers of weapons to the covert arms trade are not free-lancing private dealers, but governments themselves. Moreover, the greatly increased lethality of modern weapons has made the human toll of wars, even when only small arms and artillery are used, horrendous.

Efforts must be made to block those who ship arms into regions in trouble, particularly when they do so in violation of international sanctions. Greater resources could be devoted to enforcing sanctions, and the penalties for sanctions-breakers increased. In many cases, governments are believed to know who the major violators are. Such governments must recognize that weapons exported from or through their countries may ultimately be used for purposes other than those for which they were intended. Those who violate arms embargoes imperil the security of people. They should not enjoy immunity.

To strengthen regulation in this area, we recommend to states the immediate negotiation and eventual introduction of an international convention on curtailment of the arms trade. This convention must build on work already under way in national parliaments, international organizations, and private institutes and NGOs. It should make the voluntary reporting requirements under the existing Arms Register mandatory. It should also prohibit or heavily circumscribe the financing or subsidization of arms exports by governments. The conclusion of a convention on curtailment of the arms trade will go a long way towards demilitarizing international society.

The talks on arms transfers in 1992 concentrated on weapons incorporating advanced technologies. Exports of advanced aircraft and other high-technology

LAND-MINES AND SMALL ARMS

weapons can complicate relations between states, de-stabilize the military balance in a region, and lead to a greater risk of war. But it is land-mines, small arms, and artillery that cause the most casualties. Given the carnage caused by land-mines in so many parts of the globe in recent years, it is long past time for the international community to curtail sales of these weapons.

A typical anti-personnel mine is a harmless-looking plastic object that fits easily in the palm of a hand. Yet the human and financial cost of their use is almost unimaginable.

Since 1975, it is estimated, land-mines have killed or injured more than 1 million persons, the vast majority of them civilians. An estimated 100 million anti-personnel land-mines lie scattered in more than sixty countries. Another 100 million mines are believed to sit in stockpiles, ready for use. The cost of an anti-personnel land-mine may be very low: less than $3. But cleaning them up costs between $300 and $1,000 per mine, using local deminers. The current annual rate of deployment is at least 1 million mines; during the same period, only 100,000 mines are cleared.

The social and economic consequences of the proliferation of land-mines are thus staggering, and the problem is growing. So much suffering has been

---

The Impact of Small Arms

[Those] who have died in war since [9 August 1945] have, for the most part, been killed by cheap, mass-produced weapons and small-calibre ammunition, costing little more than the transistor radios and dry-cell batteries which have flooded the world in the same period. Because cheap weapons have disrupted life very little in the advanced world, outside the restricted localities where drug-dealing and political terrorism flourish, the populations of the rich states have been slow to recognize the horror that this pollution has brought in its train. Little by little, though, recognition of the horror is gaining ground.

—John Keegan, *A History of Warfare*

---

inflicted by them in recent years that the world should finally be ready to consider effective means to curtail the production, sale, and use of these weapons. We endorse the proposal for a world-wide ban on the manufacture and export of land-mines.

The world can no longer talk merely about the demilitarization of international relations. What is needed is demilitarization of international society. Militarization today not only involves governments spending more than necessary to build up their military arsenals. It has increasingly become a global societal phenomenon, as witnessed by the rampant acquisition and use of increasingly lethal weapons by civilians—whether individuals seeking a means of self-defence, street gangs, criminals, political opposition groups, or terrorist organizations.

An emphasis on the security of people requires the world to address the culture of violence in everyday life, which is a major source of insecurity today for people everywhere around the globe. This culture of violence—as vivid in daily life, particularly against women and children, as it is on television screens—infects industrial and developing countries, and rich and poor alike, even if in different ways. Every effort must be made on the local and community level as well as at the international level to reverse this trend and to sow the seeds of a culture of non-violence.

We strongly endorse community initiatives to protect individual life, to encourage the disarming of civilians, and to foster an atmosphere of security in neighbourhoods. All have a role to play, including television, the cinema, and other media. The task of promoting security in the global neighbourhood will be immeasurably harder if in societies around the world a culture of violence is on the rise and personal insecurity is pervasive.

INCULCATING A CULTURE OF NON-VIOLENCE

Summary of Proposals in Chapter Three

Security for a New Era

1 The security of people and the security of the planet should be goals of global security policy, along with the security of states.

2 The Charter of the United Nations should be revised to allow the Security Council to authorize action in situations within countries, but only if the security of people is so severely violated as to require an international response on humanitarian grounds.

Anticipating Crises

3 The preventive approach to security should be strengthened, with the UN improving its capacity to anticipate and resolve crises and to respond early to armed conflict.

4 The United Nations should develop a more comprehensive system to collect information on trends and situations that may lead to violent conflict or humanitarian tragedies; all states should share with the UN information on such trends and situations.

5 Adequate resources should be provided to enable the Secretary-General to make full use of fact-finding missions as part of efforts to promote peace and security.

Responding to Crises

6 Both the Security Council and the Secretary-General should make more use of the mechanisms for peaceful settlement listed in Chapter VI of the UN Charter.

7 In peacekeeping operations, the integrity of the UN command should be respected, and consultative committees should be formed for each operation, which should include countries providing troops.

8 The Security Council should use a more precise, targeted approach to sanctions.

9   All nations need to live up to their obligation under the UN Charter to make armed forces available to the Security Council.

10 The Military Staff Committee provided for in the UN Charter should be revitalized to provide military information and expert advice to the Security Council.

11 A United Nations Volunteer Force should be formed and be available for rapid deployment under the authority of the Security Council.

12 The international community needs to make significantly increased funds available for peacekeeping operations.

13 The cost of peacekeeping operations should be progressively integrated into a single annual budget, and financed by assessed contributions by all UN members.

THE THREAT OF MASS DESTRUCTION

14 The international community should reaffirm its commitment to eliminate nuclear and other weapons of mass destruction from all nations, and initiate a programme to achieve that goal in ten to fifteen years.

15 The Nuclear Non-Proliferation Treaty should be renewed for an indefinite period.

16 Negotiations on a comprehensive ban on the testing of nuclear weapons should be successfully concluded in conjunction with the 1995 Nuclear Non-Proliferation Review Conference.

17 Nuclear-weapon-free zones should be created as a means of confining the spread of nuclear weapons.

18 The Biological and the Chemical Weapons Conventions should be signed and ratified immediately by all nations that have not already done so, and their provisions rapidly put into effect.

DEMILITARIZATION

19 Demilitarization should be given increased priority by the international community.

20 Governments should jointly adopt a concrete goal for lower levels of global defence spending.

21 A Demilitarization Fund should be established to help developing countries reduce their military commitments.

22 States should undertake early negotiation on a convention on the curtailment of the arms trade that should, among other things, make the reporting requirements under the existing Arms Register mandatory; meanwhile, arms-exporting countries should exercise restraint in arms sales.

23 There should be a world-wide ban on the manufacture and export of land-mines.

Managing Economic Interdependence

In the last fifty years, the structure of global economic governance has been extended, repaired, and adapted in the face of enormous technological, economic, and political change. This chapter reviews the underlying driving forces now bearing down on the structure of governance, evaluates the basic framework of multilateralism, puts forward a proposal for strengthening it through an Economic Security Council, and reviews in some detail the specific strengths and weaknesses of current rules and institutions in relation to trade, investment, international finance, development, and the environment.

CHALLENGES TO GLOBAL ECONOMIC GOVERNANCE

Stability requires a carefully crafted balance between the freedom of markets and the provision of public goods.

The international community today faces enormous challenges in dealing with economic governance—challenges related to the growing interdependence of economies and civil society, the continued impoverishment of much of the world and the unused human potential that entails, and the increased realization of the threats to the environment and thus to planetary survival, as discussed in Chapter Three.

While the world has become much more highly integrated economically, the mechanisms for managing the system in a stable, sustainable way have lagged

GROWING
INTER-
DEPENDENCE

135

behind. Today's much higher level of economic integration and resulting interdependence are in part due to improved communications. When the post-war system of global governance was being conceived and negotiated, television, computers, and international telephone systems had barely been introduced.

The conduct of business, methods of production, tastes, and life-styles have since changed out of all recognition. Contemporary advances in multimedia communications and information processing will contribute even further to the shrinkage of distance and acceleration of change. One remarkable manifestation of this interconnectedness is the spread, at enormous speed, of computer networks such as Internet, which now provide millions of users with instant communication.

The possibilities created by technology have been magnified by the remorseless logic of economic specialization and scale. Trade has consistently grown more rapidly than global output. Capital flows have grown even faster. During the last decade, foreign direct investment has been growing four times as fast as world trade. In some industries—cars, electronics, information processing—production is so globalized that it is no longer possible to pinpoint or measure nationality in any meaningful way. The Ford Motor Company, to cite but one example, has evolved from a predominantly US company with some overseas subsidiaries serving local markets to an integrated operation around regional subsidiaries that in Europe serve the Single Market and that produce a 'world car' through co-ordinated operations.

The last two years have seen a veritable explosion of portfolio investment by institutional investors—insurance companies, pension funds, unit trusts—in 'emerging markets' as stock markets become truly global in reach. People can trade in the world's leading currencies twenty-four hours a day and use a growing variety of financial instruments. In the field of finance, national frontiers have little meaning; 'the end of geography' is approaching.

That all this global economic integration has come to pass is in part a tribute to the relative order and stability of post-war economic governance, as well as to new technologies. Enormous opportunities are being created for societies and individuals to advance. But there are also imbalances and risks.

As economies become more interdependent, it is not only the opportunity for wealth creation that is multiplied, but also the opportunity for destabilizing shocks to be transmitted from one country to another. International co-operation has forestalled or mitigated some shocks (such as action taken after the 1987 stock market crash), but others (the debt crisis of the 1980s, for instance) have been allowed to gather momentum and inflict economic damage and social pain. No satisfactory mechanism exists to anticipate or respond promptly to future global shocks. The International Monetary Fund (IMF), which should be playing a major role in countering destabilizing shocks, is constrained by limited resources.

Both the dynamism and the instability of the process of global economic integration are linked to the fact that it largely originates in the private sector. Future stability requires that a carefully crafted balance be struck, nationally and internationally, between the freedom of markets and the provision of public goods. The pace of globalization of financial and other markets is currently outstripping the capacity of governments to provide the necessary framework of rules and co-operative arrangements to ensure stability and prevent abuses of monopoly and other market failures. National solutions to such failures within a globalized economy are severely limited.

Private capital flows to developing countries have increased sharply, but they are going to only a few regions

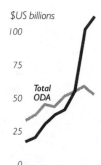

Net private capital flows to developing countries

Regional distribution of private capital flows to developing countries, 1990–92

Yet the structures of global governance required for pursuing public policy obligations in an interdependent world are underdeveloped. The multilateral trade regime of the General Agreement on Tariffs and Trade (GATT), for example, is only just beginning to negotiate agreements on cross-border flows generated by services and information-based industries, though these have been a major phenomenon for a decade. Much is being done to establish new structures of governance at a regional level, as in the European Union, but even this could not prevent the European Monetary System from being severely destabilized by large-scale capital movements.

A further concern is that the integration of markets does not necessarily occur harmoniously. Different systems of commercial law-making, tax, social welfare, bureaucratic decision-making, corporate governance, labour law, and much else have a bearing on how firms compete with those from other countries through trade and direct investment. Without good, clear rules that are widely accepted, there is 'systems friction' based on a sense of unfairness or incomprehension.

Growing economic interdependence brings in its wake freer trade in 'bads' as well as goods. International drug traffic, for example, now dominates the economies of a significant number of countries; it may even be worth more than trade in foodstuffs. Trade—illicit or licit—in arms, waste disposal, and human traffic, as in prostitution, have all become big global businesses.

Governments have learned that command-and-control systems of economic management do not work. But they have yet to develop—especially at a global level—effective, alternative tools of governance. With the agreement at Marrakesh to establish a World Trade Organization (WTO), there is at least the hope that such tools can now be fashioned.

As noted earlier, a sophisticated, globalized, increasingly affluent world currently co-exists with a marginalized global underclass. The post-war system of economic governance has seen—and facilitated—the most remarkable growth in economic activity and improvements in living standards within human history. Despite an increase in population from 2.3 billion to 5.5 billion, per capita incomes on average are now around three times the level in 1950. Many indicators of social progress—infant mortality, literacy, life expectancy, nutrition—have improved significantly, at least in terms of global averages. When Britain became the first country to industrialize in the late eighteenth and early nineteenth centuries, it took six decades to double living standards; now China, among other countries, is accomplishing the same feat within ten years.

At the same time, people are increasingly aware—through better communication—of the global problem of continued poverty. The number of absolute poor, the truly destitute, was estimated by the World Bank at 1.3 billion in 1993, and is probably still growing. One fifth of the world lives in countries, mainly in Africa and Latin America, where living standards actually fell in the 1980s. Several indicators of aggregate poverty—1.5 billion lack access to safe water and 2 billion lack safe sanitation; more than 1 billion are illiterate, including half of all rural women—are no less chilling than a quarter-century ago. The conditions of this 20 per cent of humanity—and of millions of others close to this perilous state—should be a matter of overriding priority.

The challenge of global development has changed in several respects since it was analysed by, among others, the Pearson and Brandt Commissions. First, the old division between industrial and developing, North and South, is becoming blurred, though there are still some striking imbalances; rich countries account for more than 80 per cent of world trade, 85 per cent of direct foreign investment in the 1980s, and 95 per cent of all research and development. There are different Souths and different Norths, reflecting varied experiences of development and growth, internal disparities of income and opportunity, and different country sizes and economic structures. Although it is a caricature to talk of the Asian development miracle and the African development disaster, for example, these areas have had very different experiences.

Second, there is the fall-out from the ending of the cold war. Russia and other former Communist countries of Central and Eastern Europe have embarked on one of the most ambitious and difficult economic transformations in history. If the process is successful, it will provide a major stimulus to the growth of the world economy. If it fails, the consequences could be catastrophic: a collapse of orderly government in these countries, several of whom still have stockpiles of nuclear weapons.

The challenge posed to global economic governance by this transformation is considerable: the need to incorporate some thirty new countries into global and regional institutions and trading rules; the demand for large amounts of additional official capital to support adjustment and to facilitate private capital flows under conditions where the problems are enormous and largely unprecedented; the dismantling of vast and technically sophisticated arms industries while safeguarding the livelihoods of millions employed in them. It is clear that enormous hardship is being endured by some. But from Eastern Europe and to a lesser degree Russia there are encouraging signs that private-sector growth is beginning to replace a contracting state sector.

One of several wider implications is the end to the 'cold war' of ideas. Instead of polarized and unproductive conflict between opposed ideological systems, there is a much greater degree of consensus on economic policy questions. Some continuing disagreement about the appropriate roles of the public and private sectors is inevitable. But many countries are finding wide agreement on the need to draw in a balanced way on the energies of a profitable private sector, global markets, and competition as well as the need to use the powers of the state to provide security, a regulatory framework for competition, a good environment, and a sense of equity and social cohesion. The painful experience of getting this balance badly wrong earlier should now facilitate development.

A further change is taking place in industrial countries. They are collectively slowing down, and not just because of the current recession. Various factors are at work, including the ageing of the population and the problems of adjusting to a service-based, post-industrial society. These trends have good and bad implications for developing countries. Positively, there should be less competition for scarce resources, notably capital for investment. But by the same token, low-growth conditions in rich countries mean a weaker demand for goods that developing countries export.

The crisis of unemployment and the associated evils of growing poverty and social deprivation in many industrial countries may also create a political environment where there is less willingness to adjust quickly to new sources of competition. 'Cheap' imports and migrant labour are often made the scapegoat for unemployment.

One of the greatest ironies of the current scene (and, potentially, one of the greatest future dangers) is that just when developing and former Communist countries discover the benefits of liberalization and greater openness, rich countries may turn in on themselves. A central challenge for global governance will be to prevent this dangerous situation from creating new fissures between and within countries.

UNUSED HUMAN POTENTIAL	A major failure of past development in rich and poor countries alike is that very large numbers of people have been unable to realize their potential.

A major failure of past development in rich and poor countries alike is that very large numbers of people have been unable to realize their potential. Unemployment, discrimination against women or minorities, poor facilities for education or health, slum conditions in crowded cities, and other similar phenomena are found to varying degrees throughout the world. They not only affect the security and well-being of people, they are themselves obstacles to development. Economic policy, however well conceived, does not itself ensure the social progress and better standards of life in larger freedom held out in the UN Charter.

The failure to integrate social policy, in the widest sense, into the economic policy framework has led countries down economically wasteful paths. Western Europe, for example, is losing what a tenth or more of its labour force could produce as it idles in unemployment, with devastating effects on individuals, families, and communities. While the root causes of joblessness persist, support for the unemployed makes ever larger demands on national budgets, creating deficits that compound economic problems. Large numbers of people are pushed out of the work-force to languish on the margins of society.

In Africa, Latin America, and Eastern Europe, underfinanced structural adjustment programmes have often neglected the social implications of austerity measures. Though macroeconomic stability and market liberalization are clearly necessary objectives, the failure to anticipate and counter the severe stresses on society and the cutbacks in long-term investment in human development have set back the long-term prospects for economic progress and weakened political support for continued adjustment.

The most pervasive denial of human potential is found in the discrimination that women suffer worldwide. Society benefits hugely from the economic contribution of women, although this is seldom recognized. Thus, half the world continues to be systematically—though in varying degrees—denied their full rights as human beings, with stultifying consequences for them and at great cost to society, which is denied the many additional contributions they can make. Awareness of these issues was greatly sharpened by the International Conference on Population and Development in Cairo and will be again at the World Conference on Women in Beijing in 1995. There is now wide awareness that gender sensitivity must be introduced into the conceptual, decision-making, and operational stages of all multilateral and government agencies, and in Chapter Five we recommend some ways to achieve these objectives.

Social policy is a matter not only for national but also for global governance. Different societies have different preferences for—among other things—income distribution, welfare provision, cultural diversity, worker protection, and structures of education. None the less, societies increasingly interact and cannot function in isolation. Failures of social development resulting, for example, in involuntary mass migration cannot be confined within national borders. The World Summit for Social Development in 1995 will define more concretely what the priority areas for common action are in the social policy field.

The *Human Development Report* of the UN Development Programme (UNDP) and UNICEF's 'Adjustment with a Human Face' campaign have helped considerably in bringing social concerns into economic policy. And although the recent Group of Seven (G7) Jobs Summit in Detroit in 1994 had no concrete results, it helped direct attention not just to the plight of the long-term unemployed in G7 countries but to

Women remain far behind men in education

Women's literacy rate as a percentage of men's 1992

Adult literacy

Girls' enrolment as a percentage of boys' 1990

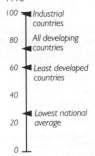

Secondary school enrolment

the 800 million or more workers world-wide who live in poverty because of unemployment or underemployment.

THE ENVIRONMENT

One of the truly momentous changes of recent years—and a change that could not even have been envisaged by those who designed the post-war global economic system—is the growing awareness of the importance of the physical environment and the extent of the threats now posed to vulnerable ecosystems. This has forced governments to face up to the extent of the interdependence of their countries. The UN system deserves credit for having helped to create this awareness, with the 1972 Stockholm Conference being a seminal event. The 1992 Earth Summit in Rio left an agenda of great political weight.

Growing awareness of global environmental threats has nudged governments into devising co-operative (albeit weak) forms of governance to address the overfishing of oceans, the extinction of certain species, the threat to Antarctica from commercial development, the depletion of the ozone layer, and the risks of climate change caused by the build-up of greenhouse gases in the atmosphere. (See also Chapter Six.)

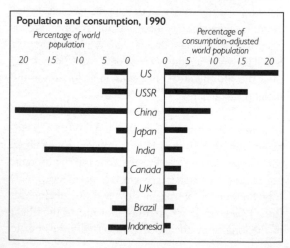

Population and consumption, 1990

Percentage of world population

Percentage of consumption-adjusted world population

20 15 10 5 0 0 5 10 15 20

US
USSR
China
Japan
India
Canada
UK
Brazil
Indonesia

Links Between Consumption and Population Growth

In debates [on sustainable development], it is often asserted that developing countries with large populations pose a greater threat to the world environment than developed countries with smaller populations. However, it is well known that developed countries have higher levels of consumption than developing countries and that consumption exerts pressure on the environment.

The conclusions obtained from the estimates of population adjusted by consumption seriously question the assumption that countries with larger populations pose a greater environmental risk. Sustainable development is based on the premise that there has to be a balance between population and consumption within the overall limits imposed by nature. Therefore, it becomes clear that not only population but also consumption has to be reduced if sustainability is to be achieved.

Consumption-Adjusted Population, Selected Countries, 1990

(million)

Country	Population	Adjusted Population
China	1,139	9,329
India	853	3,907
Soviet Union	289	16,828
United States	249	22,993
Canada	27	3,159

—The Earth Council, 'Consumption: The Other Side of Population for Development', presented to the International Conference on Population and Development, September 1994

Environmental stresses arise from an imbalance between what people consume and what natural systems can provide. Human impact on the biosphere is essentially what people use and waste. Some 80 per cent of that consumption is what is thought of as prosperity—wealth creation and enjoyment by some 20 per cent of the world's people. Those disparities become important when environmental sustainability requires restraint on consumption at a global level, including greater efficiency in the use of resources, as is the case for carbon emissions.

There is also a strong relationship between environmental stress and poverty. So far the impacts have been localized, such as microclimatic change and flooding resulting from deforestation caused by subsistence agriculture. But there are already examples of large-scale environmental refugee movements—in the Horn of Africa and from Haiti—that have wider implications.

Economic growth and the multiplication of population will eventually create a world economy many times larger than today's. The concept of 'sustainable development' defined by the World Commission on Environment and Development (the Brundtland Commission) provides a framework of policy within which strong growth, necessary to overcome poverty, can be achieved while adapting economic policies to take full account of environmental considerations. Major changes in economic practices will have to occur.

Even then, there will be considerable pressure on some fragile ecosystems, and some scarce environmental resources—such as fish stocks, tropical forests, and watersheds—are currently being used at an unsustainable rate. These will have to be shared and managed equitably to prevent overuse. The high consumption levels of these resources need to be reduced without any slackening of poverty alleviation. The failure to establish a common approach can have disastrous consequences.

| GLOBAL DECISION-MAKING | At a global level, what model of decision-making should an emerging system of economic governance adopt? It will have to draw on lessons from regional and national levels and from business organizations where inflexible, centralized command-and-control structures have been shown to be unsustainable. Multilayered decision-making systems are emerging that depend on consultation, consensus, and flexible 'rules of the game'. Intergovernmental organizations, however, still face |

OUR GLOBAL NEIGHBOURHOOD

basic questions as to who should set the rules and according to what principles.

One particular challenge is the growing number of countries. Some fifty countries were involved in founding the UN and the Bretton Woods institutions—the IMF and the World Bank. The end of colonialism and, more recently, the breakup of the Soviet empire added many new nations, with the total participating countries now approaching 200. They want not just statehood but a voice in international economic decision-making. Global economic integration and interdependence have to accommodate, and be accommodated in, a post-imperial world of formal political independence.

There is an inevitable tension between the democratic ideal of universal participation and the need for speedy, efficient decision-making, as well as between the respective claims of statehood, population, and wealth. The tension has increased as the number of states has grown while global economic decision-making, far from reflecting a polycentric world, has become concentrated in the hands of the United States, Europe, and Japan—with just over 10 per cent of the world's population.

This concentration of decision-making is reflected in the voting arrangements of the Bretton Woods institutions. Even more important, it is also a factor in the exclusivity of such groups as the G7. And major powers dominate the negotiating processes of GATT, where all parties are nominally equal but actually very unequal. The countries that benefit from these inequalities would never accept such undemocratic arrangements in their own societies, and, in part at least, their economic strength derives from that rejection.

Whatever the democratic legitimacy of current intergovernmental arrangements for global economic governance, a fresh approach to the question is required by the shifting centre of gravity of the world economy. Taken as a whole, developing economies have been growing more rapidly than Western industrial ones during the last three decades, with Asian developing countries growing much more rapidly. The share of output accounted for by members of the Organisation for Economic Co-operation and Development (OECD) has shrunk to barely half, once we take account of the underlying purchasing power of economies measured at comparable prices. The world's ten biggest economies on a purchasing power parity basis include China, India, Brazil, and Russia, with Mexico, Indonesia, and the Republic of Korea not far behind.

Yet none of these participate in the Group of Seven, all are under-represented in terms of votes in relation to their population and economic weight in the Bretton Woods institutions, and China and Russia are not yet members of GATT. It is a matter of common interest that the major players in the global economy be fully involved in decision-making on common problems.

But in focusing on intergovernmental relations, it is necessary to bear in mind that the traditional role of nation-states is evolving. There are powerful forces making for greater decentralization of decision-making.

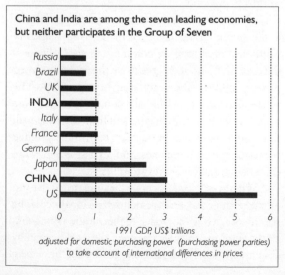

China and India are among the seven leading economies, but neither participates in the Group of Seven

1991 GDP, US$ trillions
adjusted for domestic purchasing power (purchasing power parities)
to take account of international differences in prices

Nationally centralized, top-down systems, exemplified by the former Soviet Union, have collapsed. Large states are under growing pressure to decentralize to provinces and local government just as companies are having to devolve management responsibility. In areas such as Western Europe where stronger regional institutions are being created, there is a vigorous debate about 'subsidiarity'—the allocation of responsibilities to the lowest level appropriate among global, regional, national, and local authorities. Global economic governance has to recognize this diffusion of decision-making, while acknowledging that there is still a compelling need for an overall framework of rules and order.

THE CASE FOR MULTILATERALISM

The time is now ripe—indeed, overdue—to create a global forum that can provide leadership in economic, social, and environmental fields.

Historically, global governance has occurred without global institutions. The nineteenth century was a time of deepening integration and unprecedented expansion of trade, investment flows, and migration of people. Some world-wide governance was partly provided by the exercise of dominion through empires, especially Britain's. It was politically stable, but it lacked consent and was ultimately unsustainable. It also depended heavily on self-regulated markets that were prone to crisis, drawing states into more active management of their economies. This in turn contributed to destructive economic nationalism and indirectly to the major twentieth-century conflicts.

There is no case and no call for a return to a system like that of the nineteenth century. Without strong international rules, however, the most powerful countries will act unilaterally, or try to control the system, which makes rules-based processes all the more crucial. Migration, for instance, is one area where policy is overwhelmingly unilateral. No desirable system of governance can be based on the capacity of strong nations to coerce weaker ones, which is the inevitable consequence of the unilateral projection of power in economics as much as it is in the military sector.

The rules and sense of order that must underpin any stable and prosperous system can be described as international 'public goods'. It is in their nature not to be provided by markets or by individual governments acting in isolation.

Most governments accept responsibility for the provision of public goods such as policing and justice, financial stability, or environmental protection; to do otherwise would be to abandon essential functions of a state. The same responsibility applies—but is less readily acknowledged—at an international level. Among the basic international public goods that global economic governance should provide are:

- systemic financial stability: a stable monetary system, a capacity to deal with major systemic slumps and shocks, and prudential regulation of international financial markets;

- the rule of law: for an open system for trade, technology transfer, and investment, with mutually acceptable dispute settlement machinery;

- infrastructure and institutions: common standards for weights and measures, time, and many technical specifications, and agreed systems to manage and maintain freedom of the seas and commonly used networks for aviation and telecommunications;

- environment: through protection of the global commons and the required framework of policy to promote sustainable development; and

- equity and social cohesion: through economic cooperation in its widest sense, including international development assistance and disaster relief.

The growing interdependence of the global economy and environment increases both the benefits of providing these international public goods and the penalties for neglecting them. None the less, some governments are reluctant to accept the sharing of national sovereignty that must occur for strong multilateral rules and institutions to function. The struggle to place GATT rules above unilateral trade policy, the marginalization of the IMF from the management of the international monetary system, the continuing struggle to maintain and increase flows of concessional resources through international institutions, and the virtual exclusion of the UN from a central role in the field of global economic governance: all these attest to this reluctance.

A workable system of international economic governance is not solely based on global arrangements. Many tasks can be carried out between neighbours. So far, only the European Union has created both a durable system of regional trade liberalization and a strong commitment to political co-operation, but others may well follow. Regional integration is currently receiving much attention elsewhere, especially in the Americas and South-east Asia, though it has made little progress in Africa and South Asia.

REGIONALISM AND INFORMAL MULTI-LATERALISM

Some issues are best dealt with regionally rather than globally (localized spillovers of pollution, for example). Regional economic groups can also contribute to burying historic enmities through developing closer economic and political linkages, realizing economies of scale, developing common infrastructure, and pioneering new methods for deepening integration in advance of progress at the global level. As noted, the concept of subsidiarity being vigorously debated in Europe provides a framework for allocating responsibilities between institutions of global, regional, national, and local governance in an efficient way.

For regional institutions to form building blocks for global economic governance rather than exclusive 'blocs', they should also be open—both in offering membership on the same terms as existing members and in regard to market access. There is a fine line between the degree of exclusivity needed to create a regional identity and that which creates division. The European Union has many features of openness, especially now that it is being enlarged; but some other features, such as the Common Agricultural Policy, are protectionist and divert trade. The advocates of 'fortress' Europe are a minority, but they are not insignificant. Although regional arrangements can strengthen global economic governance, the wrong kind of regionalism can weaken it.

Much governance can and does informally take place through groups of countries such as the G7, the OECD, or the Commonwealth. The G7 is a significant development and its role is discussed further later. The OECD has played a major role in developing principles to govern the behaviour of international investment, environmental management, and export credit. And it is now reaching out to a wider number of countries through enlargement and dialogue.

Several functional, specialist institutions should also be mentioned, such as the International Telecommunications Union (ITU), the International Maritime Organisation, the Bank for International Settlements (BIS), and the Paris Club. ITU has responsibility—now shared with GATT—for creating a regime of global governance for the rapidly expanding, interconnected network of telecommunication, multimedia, and information technology systems. BIS provides the world's financial system with an underpinning of co-operative supervision. In these quiet, unspectacular ways, a system of global governance is being put in place, albeit on a piecemeal basis.

Global governance is not, however, only a public sector activity. Multinational companies account for a substantial and growing slice of economic activity. Some centrally important industries—notably the complex of activities variously described as telecommunications, information, or multimedia; automobile production; banking and other financial services—are being developed largely through private companies that operate on a multinational basis. Their concerns are necessarily with the totality of their business operations rather than with any one country. We discuss later in this chapter the checks and balances that have to be established to ensure that business operates, at a global level, within a wider framework of social responsibility.

Finally, there is what might loosely be called international civil society including non-governmental organizations (NGOs), international humanitarian agencies such as the Red Cross and Red Crescent, voluntary rule-making bodies such as the International Standards Organisation, and groups of scientific professionals such as the International Council of Scientific Unions.

These structures often have the great merits of flexibility, responsiveness, and enthusiasm. They will rightly play a growing role in governance. They can, however, become self-electing and exclusive. Fewer than 15 per cent of NGOs registered with the UN Economic and Social Council (ECOSOC) are from developing countries. Although NGOs are of inestimable value in establishing governance in the widest sense, they cannot be expected to substitute for effective intergovernmental structures.

AN APEX BODY: AN ECONOMIC SECURITY COUNCIL

Rationale The international community has no satisfactory way to consider global economic problems in the round and the linkages between economic, social, environment, and security issues in the widest sense. The boundaries between issues of trade, competition policy, environment, macroeconomic policy, and social policy are increasingly blurred. Neat functional segregation of problems no longer works, and traditional institutional arrangements no longer suffice. As noted, global interdependence is growing, driven by powerful technological and economic forces. Political structures that can articulate a sense of common interest and mediate differences are not keeping pace at national and—even more—at a global level.

The Group of Seven is the nearest the world comes to having an apex body concerned with the global economy. It has some claims to success, such as preventing the 1987 stock exchange crash from producing a deep deflationary shock. But it is neither representative of the world's population as a whole nor very effective. The G7 represents only 12 per cent of the world's population. By excluding China and India, it can no longer even claim to represent the world's major economies. The development issues that concern most of humanity have low priority on its agenda. Looking decades ahead, it will become more and more anachronistic that non-OECD economies that account for a large and growing slice of the world economy are not represented in the main body with an overview of international economic issues.

More governments are involved in discussions within the 'theme debates' of ECOSOC and the UN General Assembly. But so far the UN has not provided a satisfactory forum for practical, well-focused international economic discussion. Nor do the Bretton Woods institutions pay much attention to the UN. Meetings fail to attract ministers, let alone senior economic ministers, and have little impact. All too often the UN is dismissed as a 'talking shop'. The UN has not been given the chance to do the sustained, high-level economic work required to make an impact on decision makers.

For reasons of realism, attention has switched instead to the Bretton Woods institutions. Some imaginative ideas were put forward in the 1980s for using their Interim and Development Committees as vehicles for global economic dialogue. Although the Bretton Woods institutions have substantial economic expertise at their disposal and are operationally important in particular aspects of global economic governance, their perspective is necessarily a partial one.

Another route that has been tried is North-South dialogue, as in the Conference on International Economic Co-operation in 1975 and, following the proposal of the Brandt Commission, at the meeting of twenty-four Heads of Government in Cancun in 1981. These attempts at dialogue have not encouraged either industrial or developing countries to continue on that line.

But circumstances have changed. There is now little ideological disagreement; most developing and former Communist countries are no less committed to liberalization of markets, private investment, and openness than industrial ones are; the groups of countries are more varied and less confrontational; and new areas of mutual interest (notably global environmental issues) provide a stronger driving force for discussion.

The time is now ripe—indeed, overdue—to create a global forum that can provide leadership in economic, social, and environmental fields. It would be more broadly based than the G7 or the Bretton Woods institutions, and more effective than the present UN system. While not having authority to make legally binding decisions, it would gain influence through competence and relevance, and acquire the standing in relation to international economic matters that the Security Council has in peace and security matters.

We propose the establishment of an Economic Security Council (ESC). The idea is not original—others have made similar proposals—but we have formulated it in terms we believe have the best prospect of early implementation and a successful outcome.

Aims   The proposed Economic Security Council would have the following tasks:

- to continuously assess the overall state of the world economy and the interaction between major policy areas;
- to provide a long-term strategic policy framework in order to promote stable, balanced, and sustainable development;
- to secure consistency between the policy goals of the major international organizations, particularly the main multilateral economic institutions (the Bretton Woods bodies and the proposed WTO), while recognizing their distinct roles;
- to promote consensus-building dialogue between governments on the evolution of the international economic system, while providing a global forum for some of the new forces in the world economy— such as regional organizations.

The increasing limitations of current structures, such as the G7, make it likely that the need for a more representative and effective forum will be widely recognized, even by governments that have in the past shown little enthusiasm for an enlarged economic role for the United Nations. In particular, no major new bureaucratic apparatus is being suggested for the ESC, and it would work closely with the Bretton Woods institutions, not in opposition to them.

The work of the Council could indeed facilitate the effectiveness and authority of the IMF and World Bank, which have traditionally taken their cue from the Group of Seven. The industrial countries may wish the G7 to continue as a forum. But the IMF and Bank would be better able to proceed in implementing strategies and policies for stabilization and adjustment if they also had at their disposal the conclusions of a more representative body.

Agenda The ESC would exist to give political leadership and promote consensus on international economic issues where there are long-term threats to security in its widest sense, such as shared ecological crises, economic instability, rising unemployment, the problems of transformation in the former Soviet Union, mass poverty, or lack of food security. It would be concerned with the overall state of the world economy and with the promotion of sustainable development. The context of its functions would be the evolution of a long-term strategic policy framework and securing consistency between the policy goals of the major international organizations.

The ESC would be concerned with policy issues, but it would have deliberative rather than executive functions. It would not be responsible directly for the work of UN agencies, the Bretton Woods institutions, or the proposed WTO, but it would certainly influence them through the relevance and quality of its work and the significance of its membership.

We do not envisage the ESC primarily as a crisis management forum. Its primary task would be to look at the main trends in the world economy and to give signals that could guide the global community. It will also have a role in responding to acute crises, since it is often these events (the oil shocks, the near breakdown in trade negotiations, the debt crisis, and the collapse of the Soviet Union) that have triggered the need for leadership and fresh thinking.

One of the most valuable roles of the ESC could be in addressing international problems for which there is no clear institutional mandate or several overlapping ones. The Council could not usurp the functions of established institutions, but it could clearly identify responsibilities and ensure that procedural and bureaucratic difficulties do not stand in the way of responding to the compelling need for multilateral action. The ESC would also be the appropriate forum for studying proposals for financing international public goods by international revenue raising, as discussed at the end of this chapter.

The agenda of the ESC would be set by its members, but other states and institutions should be able to add items to the agenda, in order to ensure that issues beyond those raised by its limited membership can be addressed. We suggest that the Economic Security Council meet twice yearly, but additionally as required to galvanize co-operative activity.

The meetings should be held once a year at the level of Heads of Government and otherwise at Finance Minister level. Other ministers, for example Trade Ministers, would be involved as appropriate. A supporting infrastructure would be needed of official representatives to ensure that ministerial discussions are properly prepared and followed through.

It would, however, be the spirit rather than the formalities that would decide its success. Long ministerial speeches for the record would quickly devalue the discussions; sharp, informal exchanges would enhance them.

Structure and Membership   For the ESC to be effective, it has to be practical and efficient, and therefore small. And it must be able to capture the priority attention of key economic ministers in major countries. The various possible approaches include building on the authority of the Security Council by giving it an economic dimension, and establishing a distinct body within the UN family structured like the Security Council but independent of it.

On balance, the Commission favours the latter approach. As a distinct body it would be better able to assume a new mandate including an overarching role extending to the international financial institutions and the WTO. Unlike the current Security Council, the ESC would work by consensus, without vetos. Moreover, the short-term character of the Security

Council's decision-making and its preoccupation with peace and security matters make it an inappropriate model for the ESC, which will be more concerned with the evolution of policies and rules.

Various legal options are available for establishing the ESC within the overall UN structure, including a UN Charter amendment. But our proposals do not turn on technical considerations of how the ESC can be implemented.

A variety of criteria would have to be satisfied for membership. First, the world's largest economies would be represented as of right; the gross domestic product (GDP) numbers based on purchasing power parity now used by the UN and Bretton Woods institutions would be an appropriate reference point for this.

Second, there would also have to be balanced representation between regions; a constituency system would provide for this and for participation by some smaller states. Third, there should be enough flexibility to allow for the possibility that where member-states have produced strong regional organizations—notably the European Union but also emerging groups such as the Association of South-East Asian Nations and MERCOSUR—these can participate on behalf of all their members. Finally, the ESC should be no larger than the reformed Security Council proposed in Chapter Five (twenty-three members). But there is no point in being over-prescriptive here about the details of membership; it is more important that the broad criteria are met.

However the proposal is implemented, the concentration of responsibility in the hands of a relatively small ESC does raise the question of how the broader membership of the UN can be heard in matters on the ESC's agenda. Increasingly, constituency systems and rotation and consultation mechanisms are used to ensure participation by all member-states. In the near term, the relationship between the General

Assembly and the ESC would have to be defined. In Chapter Five, we have more to say on this, including a proposal to discontinue ECOSOC. However, the reform we propose is primarily designed to fill a gap in governance not taken care of anywhere else.

Institutional Support   We have emphasized the need for intellectual leadership from the ESC. An imaginative and probably unconventional approach is required to service it. The Secretariat and research capacity should be of high professional quality. Staff would include recruits from outside the UN system, drawing on the experience of multilateral institutions and the creativity of business, academia, and NGOs in a wide variety of countries. Some would be seconded on a short-term basis from other organizations.

The primary qualification would be a capacity for strategic thinking on economic, social, and environmental issues. It might be possible to use some of the research resources of UNCTAD and also to make some cross-appointments with the Bretton Woods institutions, but we are sensitive to the need to maintain vitality and avoid institutional staleness. One option to keep the institution efficient and alert to outside ideas would be to invite competitive bidding from UN and private agencies for any significant piece of work done on the ESC's behalf.

Quality leadership would be essential to the success of the new body. To be credible, it would need someone of stature and independence, functioning at a level second only to the UN Secretary-General. We suggest, therefore, that the direction of the ESC Secretariat should be among the functions of a new Deputy Secretary-General for International Economic Co-operation and Development.

Working with Other Institutions   A key objective in the design of the ESC would be to bridge the gap between the various international economic institutions. This does not mean there has to be centrally co-ordinated direction of all the world's institutions of economic governance under one umbrella. That would be neither feasible nor desirable. What is required is agreement on goals, roles, and mandates. The rest would flow from good communication and mutual respect. The heads of the IMF, World Bank, and the new WTO should be invited to report to the ESC on a regular basis. Other institutions—in particular the Commission on Sustainable Development (CSD), given its comprehensive mandate for development and the environment—should also be asked to report on specific matters (along with the reformed Trusteeship Council, which we see as having a mandate for the global commons).

At a practical level, the ESC and its staff would expect to work closely with staff from the Bretton Woods institutions and the GATT/WTO, breaking down the institutional isolation that currently exists, as well as with bodies such as the International Labour Organisation (ILO), to underline the social dimensions of its functions.

The international community is best served by a plurality of institutions with a diversity of approaches and functions rather than by attempts to create a monopoly of wisdom. Yet since we are suggesting that a new body be set up, it is only fair to ask whether others might now become superfluous. International institutions cannot simply assume an indefinite existence. Nor can they be dispensed with casually, of course, and an effective ESC is only one of several actors relevant to their future.

The Development and Interim Committees of the Bretton Woods institutions address in a deliberative way some of the issues that would be put before the ESC. And they have a similar audience, in particular Finance Ministers. So some rationalization of effort here is called for. If the ESC proves to be more purposeful in its discussions, governments may want to consider whether it is necessary to continue the work of the Development and Interim Committees.

The establishment of the ESC could also be an opportunity and a catalyst to take a hard look at the economic work of the UN that is now scattered among a variety of institutions—ECOSOC, regional commissions, UNCTAD, and specialist bodies. The UN's economic work is fragmented and regrettably does not at present carry great authority. Evidence that the UN system is willing radically to rationalize and focus its activities would add greatly to its credibility and to the willingness of member-states to have international economic issues discussed within the system.

We expect the ESC gradually to emerge—on merit—as the focal point for global economic governance, and as a forum that both industrial and developing countries would find useful. The world badly needs an apex body for consideration of economic and related issues. We are not dogmatic about its form. We have offered one approach—an Economic Security Council—and explained why it commends itself to us. There could be others. The design is less important than the concept. Without a representative high-level body developing an international consensus on critical economic issues, the global neighbourhood could become a battleground of contending economic forces, and the capacity of humanity to develop a common approach will be jeopardized. Time is the enemy of such reform: problems are mounting, but the institutional capacity to handle them is standing still.

RULES FOR TRADE AND INTERNATIONAL COMPETITION

Multilateral negotiating processes let weaker members of the international community operate in a rule-based system rather than one controlled by raw power.

Economic interdependence is producing in many sectors a global market-place in which production is located where costs are lowest, relative to particular markets, and where capital (but not labour) flows freely to maximize returns. Global governance lags well behind this business reality. Public policy on foreign investment and competition is still predominantly a national concern, although the European Union (EU) has developed regional mechanisms, and the UN and OECD have tentatively established codes of conduct.

The main instrument of global governance in trade-related issues is the GATT. Its mandate has been largely confined to trade in a limited range of mainly manufactured goods, and traditionally governments have sought to use its machinery to open up international markets essentially to benefit their national exports.

Intercompany Trade and International Trade

The way international trade is traditionally seen and measured ignores the existence of multinational firms. For example, trade figures exclude the sales overseas of domestically based companies that have invested abroad. If they are recalculated on the basis of ownership, a radically different picture emerges, as the following table shows.

International Trade, 1991
(billion US dollars)

Sales	Conventional Method	Alternative A	Alternative B
US sales to foreigners	581	632	498
Foreigners' sales to US	609	608	334
Net balance	−28	+24	+164

The two alternatives are different ways of calculating the balance.

Sources: Alt. A from S. Landefeld, O. Whitchard, and J. Lowe in *Survey of Current Business*, December 1993; Alt. B from J. Duncan and A. Gross, *Statistics for the 21st Century* (New York: Dun and Bradstreet Corporation, 1993).

The conclusion is not that the alternatives are better for the United States but that policy makers in all countries should be careful about rushing to conclusions (and retaliatory trade sanctions) on the basis of apparent surpluses and deficits.

But emerging patterns of international business have produced a set of economic relationships that are radically different from traditional trade patterns. A substantial percentage of trade now occurs between affiliates of the same companies. In 1990, the overseas production of firms ($4.4 trillion) exceeded the value of world trade as conventionally defined ($3.8 trillion). One practical consequence is that a country with a 'trade deficit' may actually have a 'trade surplus' if the overseas operations of companies based there are taken into account. The affiliates of US companies abroad sell twice as much as the United States exports.

In a world in which interdependence through investment and trade is growing, the ability of firms to compete and to gain access to overseas markets is affected by many factors, including—but not primarily (except in a few areas such as agriculture and textiles)—tariffs and quotas. A wide range of what used to be considered purely national concerns are now seen as affecting competitiveness: nationally created technical and product standards, different approaches to social provision and labour markets, competition policy, environmental control, investment incentives, corporate taxation, and different traditions of commercial and intellectual property law, of corporate governance, of government intervention, and of cultural behaviour.

| TRADE AND THE WTO | The issue confronting governments is how to provide a framework of rules and order for global competition in the widest sense. GATT has emerged as the main forum for addressing these concerns, although the economic environment facing GATT (and its successor, the WTO) is very different from when it was established. |

GATT has considerable strengths and weaknesses as an instrument of governance. Its strengths include a track record of presiding over successive rounds of multilateral negotiations that, through reciprocal bargaining, have liberalized much of world trade and facilitated five decades of trade expansion. The latest of these—the Uruguay Round—has yet to be implemented, and is too new to be evaluated properly. But at the very least it has forestalled some potentially debilitating trade conflicts and opened up such areas as agriculture and services to progressive liberalization.

GATT has also provided a rule-based system to settle disputes and govern trade behaviour, including a greater transparency in trade measures. Through the principle of non-discrimination, it has tried to protect weaker parties in trade negotiations from bullying by the strong. All who join theoretically have equal status (unlike in the Bretton Woods institutions), although in the past the major economic powers have written the rules and dominated the negotiations.

Its weaknesses include a restricted mandate: GATT has never addressed the problems of trade in raw materials, including energy products. Massively distorted and highly protected agricultural trade regimes were not addressed until the Uruguay Round. Nor was trade in services included, though it is now 20 per cent of the total in value terms. Even within manufacturing, trade in some important sectors, such as textiles, steel, and aircraft, has been managed in ways that make a mockery of the spirit and often the letter of GATT. Membership has been incomplete because of the absence of state trading countries. The process of making GATT/WTO a truly global body must be completed through the early admission of Russia, Vietnam, China, and others as their trade policies become more open.

A further limitation is that negotiating processes have been cumbersome, long-winded, and confrontational. One of the fundamental problems is that negotiations rest on reciprocity, with an underlying

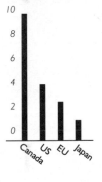

Trade effects of Uruguay Round tariff reductions

Estimated percentage increase in imports from developing countries

premise that granting improved access to imports is a 'concession' that others must match. This is at variance with the idea accepted by a growing number of governments that trade liberalization in fact benefits the liberalizer. It has, however, produced a mind-set that is conducive to protectionism and trade conflict and ill suited to many of the new, procedural issues. The Uruguay Round took a decade and almost ended in acrimonious disaster.

Even when GATT negotiations have been successfully concluded, many developing countries have felt marginalized from the process, which is still monopolized by the United States, the European Union, and Japan (plus, arguably, Canada), especially in the crucial concluding phase. This invidious position originates in part in developing countries being regarded as 'free riders' during regional bargaining, a result of having sought special and differential treatment.

In recent years, however, many of them have radically liberalized their trade and foreign investment regimes and have been pressed by industrial governments to make concessions on services and intellectual property rights (although the last is of questionable relevance to trade liberalization). In return, they have received only limited and grudging improvements in access to markets in sensitive sectors. They face trade barriers estimated to cost them twice the value of all aid. Whether they offer reciprocity or not, most developing countries discover that the current multilateral negotiating process is very unequal.

Despite these deficiencies, multilateral negotiating processes at least let weaker members of the international community operate in a rule-based system rather than one controlled by raw power. Yet even this is threatened by a re-emergence of unilateralism in trade. Hot on the heels of the conclusion of the Uruguay Round, the United States threatened Asian trading partners with the use of Super 301 powers—a markedly punitive provision of US trade law under which sanctions will be invoked if unilateral trade demands are not met. Although this has so far been a threat only, the very concept negates the whole spirit of multilateralism.

A key test of the post–Uruguay Round regime will be whether it can restore faith in multilateralism and the rule of law. And in particular whether the World Trade Organization will be able to gather to itself the necessary authority to outlaw protectionist and domineering behaviour and ensure that the strong as well as the weak observe the rules.

We welcome the prospect of early implementation of the Uruguay Round agreement, and we urge legislation to enact it. Particularly important is the establishment of a WTO to provide a stronger and more permanent successor to the GATT, as a forum for equitable dispute settlement, for further liberalization, and for curbing the use of protectionist and discriminatory measures. Its establishment will be a crucial building block for global economic governance. And there is still considerable scope for improvement as the rules of operation of the WTO evolve.

The momentum of the Uruguay Round must be maintained and, in particular, industrial countries should recognize the importance of quickly dismantling barriers to the exports of developing and former Communist countries. The commitments to reduce protection in textiles and agriculture are particularly crucial, though they are limited in scope and lack urgency. There are, none the less, some short-term losers among developing countries from the GATT agreement—notably African countries, from higher world food prices—and action should be taken through compensatory finance to cushion them.

The new GATT powers in the Uruguay Round agreements require greater transparency and conformity to multilateral rules, but they need to be supported

Towards a Strengthened Multilateral Trade Regime

From ITO to WTO—Evolution of an Idea

The World Trade Organization has had a long gestation. An International Trade Organisation was first proposed in the US House of Representatives by Cordell Hull during World War I. The idea was advanced at the World Economic Conference in 1927 and at the Seventh International Conference of American States in Montevideo in 1933.

In the 1941 Atlantic Charter, President Roosevelt and Prime Minister Churchill proposed a new initiative that would further the access of 'all states, great or small, victor or vanquished, ... to the trade and raw materials of the world which are needed for their prosperity'. Then the first meeting of ECOSOC in 1946 called for a conference on Trade and Employment, and the preparatory committee for that recognized the suggested charter for an International Trade Organisation.

The Havana Conference concluded in 1948 with an agreement between fifty-three countries. The Havana Charter subsumed the General Agreement on Tariffs and Trade signed in October 1947 (which extensively cut trade barriers and discrimination but also dealt with employment, development, restrictive barriers, and commodity agreements), and established an International Trade Organization. But the Charter lapsed when the United States failed to ratify it.

At the conclusion of the Uruguay Round of GATT in 1993, and then finally in Marrakesh in April 1994, the community of nations agreed to establish a World Trade Organization, entering into force on 1 January 1995, to implement the Uruguay Round, provide a forum for negotiations, administer the new mechanisms for dispute settlement and trade policy review, and coordinate with the IMF and the World Bank for greater coherence in global economic policy-making.

by stronger governance at a national and regional level. We recommend that governments adopt decision-making structures, like those in Australia and Canada, that require full public examination of the benefits and costs of trade restrictions for the community at large.

The underlying objective of the WTO is to create a comprehensive framework of rules governing the trading system in its widest sense including, as stated in the WTO treaty, the objective of sustainable development. Inevitably there will be frictions as common rules are established between countries with widely different levels of development and systems of government. In the long run, however, there should be no conflict between free trade and the ambitions of sustainable development and improved social standards, since as countries develop they will naturally wish to adopt higher standards.

There is a worrying trend in some industrial countries of invoking threats against what is described as 'social' or 'environmental dumping' by developing countries when in fact those making the threats are less concerned with human dignity or the security of the planet than with protecting their own uncompetitive industries. The accusations of unfair trade against countries with lower social and environmental standards are too often founded either on ignorance of the realities of poverty in developing countries or on outright self-interest. Trade negotiations should not be used to impose the standards of industrial countries on their trading partners.

There is, however, a shared and legitimate interest in raising standards, including social and environmental standards, everywhere as part of the process of development, and we would urge that this necessary work, which enjoys wide support, is not undermined by threats of trade restrictions. For economic growth to raise the living standards of the poor and be environmentally sustainable, trade has to be open and based on stable, multilaterally agreed rules.

We recognize, moreover, that there are some genuine areas of overlap between the concerns of other multilateral agencies and those of the GATT/WTO, and that mechanisms to reconcile them are needed. There are, for example, normative systems in the social and environmental fields as expressed in the ILO-sponsored conventions, the new agreements from the Earth Summit, and elsewhere.

In order to avoid conflict between countries regarding the overlap between trade and other concerns, there is need for intensified dialogue and better methods of conflict resolution. The WTO and, as we have proposed, the Economic Security Council, are appropriate fora. An example of the issues to be resolved are the implications of some new international environmental agreements incorporating trade-restricting provisions—to stop trade in toxic substances, for instance, or in substances such as chlorofluorocarbons that threaten the global environment, or to help save certain species from extinction. In the future, it will be necessary to consider from a trade standpoint much more radical ideas arising from the concerns about global warming, such as carbon taxations and traded permits. One of the early priorities of the WTO will be to ensure that action can be taken to protect the global environment in a way compatible with the principles of non-discrimination and transparency, and not as a cover for protectionism.

In other contexts, there are demands to use trade-restricting measures to enforce universally agreed human rights or labour standards. Trade sanctions against specific human rights abuses, as with South Africa, have in the past enjoyed overwhelming support in the international community. Some cases—the use of slave and prison labour for exports, for example—have long been recognized as exemptions from GATT protection, though GATT has never aspired to create rules enforcing moral values as opposed to trade rules.

We share the concern about serious breaches of core conventions of the ILO, in particular those on freedom of association, the right of collective bargaining, and the bans on forced labour and child labour. It would, however, be quite inappropriate and potentially damaging for the WTO to become an enforcement agency of labour standards. It would be more appropriate to reinvigorate the ILO and strengthen its dispute-settlement procedure. Trade measures should be part of the remedy only in really extreme and predefined cases.

Trade liberalization can proceed fastest in a regional context. In many respects, groups such as the EU have been pace-setters, and its recent adoption of the mutual recognition principle could establish a secure basis for deeper integration that combines the need for common minimum standards within an integrated market with the wish of individual countries to

---

Regionalism

Trade within regions, loosely defined, accounts for half of all world trade; the EU alone accounts for a third. The desire for regional integration is reflected in the many attempts to create regional unions in Africa, the Americas, and the Middle East, even though only a few have survived as functioning organizations.

Regionalism has nevertheless been promoted for a variety of reasons, some of which have endured better than others: closer political integration to overcome past animosities; common security concerns; gains from accelerated trade liberalization from more efficient resource allocation, economies of scale, and 'dynamic' effects of competition; shared infrastructure and institutional costs; and stronger bargaining power in trade and other international negotiations.

Two opposing views are heard on the compatibility between regionalism and global integration. One is that regionalism is leading to new or stronger trade barriers and a neglect of multilateral processes, and, because it is inherently discriminatory (favouring members over non-members), weakening global non-discriminatory rules. The other view is that some activities are best carried out at regional as opposed to global or national levels (known as the subsidiarity principle). Further, regionalism enables states to make advances in co-operation and liberalization in ways that provide a building block for global initiatives.

There are few examples in practice of multilateralism being undermined. The Uruguay Round was completed alongside parallel advances in regional integration in the EU and North America. There are also examples, especially in the EU, of regional integration being a pioneering experiment for global liberalization agreements (as with services).

set their own standards and rules in many fields. But there is still a danger of inward-looking protectionist blocs. Restrictive regional rules of origin and the extensive use of anti-dumping action are warning signs. The WTO should set out clearer guidelines that define and encourage open regionalism.

The WTO and advanced regional groups such as the EU will increasingly be faced with the issue that will dominate the international economic agenda in years to come: how to create rules for deep integration that go way beyond what has traditionally been thought of as 'trade'.

Rules for Foreign Investment   The number of transnational corporations is now estimated at 37,000 world-wide. These companies control a third of all private-sector assets and have sales of $5.5 trillion, comparable to the US gross national product (GNP).

Foreign investment is growing much faster than trade. Most countries are liberalizing in both respects, and many developing countries have reversed their earlier antipathy to foreign investment, recognizing it may be a source of scarce capital as well of management and technology. Private investors are beginning to respond to the improved investment climate, though most of the interest has been in Asia, especially China, followed by Latin America and Eastern Europe, with very little in Africa. Direct and portfolio foreign investment is now filling the gap in private flows to most developing countries created by the collapse of bank lending after the debt crisis.

If flows of private equity capital are to grow and spread on a sustainable, long-term basis, there must be a balance of rights and obligations between host countries and investors. Investors are looking for non-discriminatory national treatment, which allows them to compete as equals with domestic investors. For their part, host countries can reasonably expect responsible behaviour by investors. There is, however, a danger that some private firms will follow anti-competitive restrictive practices to restrain trade and make monopoly profits unless there are mechanisms to enforce competition. Strategic alliances are being formed in some industries, which can be a cover for monopolistic practices. Consumers everywhere, and small or poor states with little bargaining power, are always the victims of monopolistic capitalism and have the most to gain from a strong multilateral regime enforcing competition internationally as well as nationally.

The UN Restrictive Practices Code is a useful but limited step. The WTO should adopt a strong set of competition rules and we suggest that a Global Competition Office be set up, linked to the WTO, to provide general oversight of national enforcement efforts and to resolve inconsistencies between them.

The globalization of business also requires rules of behaviour going beyond competition policy. Abuses such as corruption are common. Although some companies have high ethical standards, others hide malpractice behind commercial secrecy. Corruption is a large, deeply corrosive phenomenon in many societies. Often it stems from over-regulation, but even where obvious temptations are removed, all societies require constant vigilance. A strong deterrent to corporate corruption is public exposure and publicity. For this reason we support Transparency International and other NGOs committed to combating corruption in international business transactions by mobilizing awareness of the dangers and monitoring abuse.

Governance would be strengthened through multilateral agreements that define minimum standards of corporate behaviour. It is in no one's interest that standards of safety are allowed to slide to the level that allowed the Bhopal disaster. There are areas in which international agencies set the necessary standards; the agreed certification of standards for pesticide use is a good example of this principle at work.

Previous attempts to negotiate an overall UN code failed in more confrontational times. But now there is a high degree of convergence of attitude and common interest in creating a regime that supports business but outlaws abuses. (The United States, for instance, now seeks a multilateral code to curb corrupt practice.) The WTO and the UN together should negotiate a strong code for international investment, drawing on the considerable success of the OECD in achieving a voluntary code amongst its member-states. There is a good deal of scope for even further collaboration between governments on, for instance, monitoring illegal overseas bank accounts and fraud. And beyond governments, there are roles for the non-governmental sector, as shown by Transparency International.

In addition, we are attracted to the proposal whereby an international organization—probably the WTO, if it is able—negotiates a set of rules for investment and gives accreditation, for a modest fee, to transnational companies that accept the basic principles of good conduct as enshrined in the code just discussed. The scheme would be an incentive to companies wishing to achieve a degree of international status, and may help to screen out some fly-by-night operators. Responsible transnational companies—the substantial majority—should welcome an explicit global agreement that recognizes their property and certain other rights.

Rules for Global Communications and Networks An emerging issue of great importance is the regime of global governance that will apply to the rapidly expanding and increasingly complex and overlapping fields of telecommunications and multimedia.

The communications technologies that will shape the way people work, do business, shop, learn, travel, relax, and manage personal relationships are evolving with great speed. They are being developed and applied through interconnections between firms in what

The communications explosion

1983-93
message minutes
(Index 1983=100)

300

International telephone traffic

200

100
1985   1990

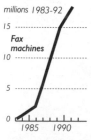

millions 1983-92

15

Fax machines

10

5

0
1985   1990

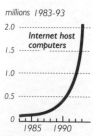

millions 1983-93

2.0

Internet host computers

1.5

1.0

0.5

0
1985   1990

used to be distinct industries—telecommunications, television, entertainment, computing, aerospace, even railways and electricity—and their identities are becoming increasingly blurred.

Major technological choices are opening up: fibre-optic cable versus wireless communications; digital versus analogue systems; high- and low-altitude satellite communications. Now possibilities are emerging in the form of multimedia communications (such as telephones that can send visual images) and interactive networks (when television is no longer passive but responds to audience participation).

The outlines of future communications systems can now be discerned, but the precise shape will depend to a considerable degree on the process of market competition and regulatory structures at global as well as national levels. The position is similar to—although happening much faster than—communications competition in the nineteenth century, when rail, canals, roads, telephones, and shipping responded at different speeds to new technological possibilities and the demands of the new industrial age.

In response to these new possibilities, the leading telecommunications companies are moving quickly to cement alliances across industrial and geographical frontiers or to achieve economies of scale, producing the largest corporate mergers and take-overs yet seen.

The process of technological change and commercial response will be heavily influenced by government policies of privatization, regulation, and deregulation. So far, regulatory activity is taking place overwhelmingly at a national level. This applies also to the ambitious attempts to create 'information superhighways' in the major industrial countries. Most countries have evolved systems based on national telecommunications and broadcasting monopolies. But there are enormous global implications.

Rapid rise in TVs and radios in developing countries

Units per 1,000 inhabitants in developing countries

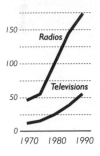

The International Telecommunications Union plays a respected but low-key role in standards harmonization and technical assistance to developing countries. But its way of operating was built on co-operation between national monopolies: a world that is now disappearing. GATT, which provides rules for competition, has had a minimal role in the sector so far. Overall, global governance in this area is highly underdeveloped and could soon be overwhelmed by the pace of technical change and commercial development.

Even at a regional level, the EU's integration effort lags way behind that in other sectors in part because of a tradition of nationalized monopolies. The highest priority should be given to examining how an appropriate system of global governance can be created for overseeing the 'global information society' through a common regulatory approach.

At this stage it suffices to sketch some of the problems such a system would have to deal with. One is competition. At present, the main task facing governments is to open up protected national monopolies to competition. But in the longer term, the main issue will be large global companies and alliances that may be able to exercise monopolistic control over information flows. This is a particularly sensitive subject in the media field, where a handful of companies now dominate satellite television channels. It is of vital importance that the WTO should create an agreed set of rules providing for market access in a more liberalized global telecommunications regime and taking account of the need to ensure competition.

A second concern is allocating some globally scarce resources, such as radio wavebands and satellite slots (though technological change is alleviating constraints in both). Multinational co-operation is key to achieving an effective and equitable regulatory structure that takes into account countries with currently underdeveloped technology. One way to reconcile these objectives would be to auction licences to use scarce resources, giving poor countries a preferential allocation that they can sell or lease if they do not use it.

New technological options are eliminating some access problems. These are, however, only the more tractable aspects of access. The poor have no access to information superhighways since they lack both the vehicles—the personal computers, telephones, and modems—and the education and skills required to drive on them. Larger developing countries, such as China and India, are beginning the process of leap-frogging into the new age using a combination of indigenous technological capacity and foreign investors as network providers. But many countries will require a great deal of assistance to manage this process without being marginalized or exploited. It is important, too, that they are able to play an active part in the standard setting process, which will affect future generations if not the current one.

A third question relates to trade in less desirable goods. Already the flow of information on Internet, for example, is being polluted by computer pornography. It is doubtful how much governments can block these new channels of communication even if they want to. But there is an urgent need for common understanding on what can and should be regulated at an international level.

Primary Commodities   For many countries, the debate about trade liberalization and market access is somewhat academic since their exports are overwhelmingly of primary products. In general, manufacturing exports are now worth more to developing countries than raw materials, including oil. But that partly reflects depressed commodity prices and, for a large number of small and low-income states, raw materials still dominate exports. Chile, an early convert to liberal economic reform and with a sophisticated economy, has developed a wide range of non-traditional exports during the last twenty years. But at the start of the 1990s, copper still accounted for 50 per cent of Chile's exports.

Diversification into manufacturing is not easy or necessarily efficient. The limited direct investment flowing to Africa is overwhelmingly in oil and mining and, to a smaller extent, in plantation agriculture. This is not inherently undesirable. Some countries (Australia, Canada, and, in part, the United States) have grown rich on the back of commodity exports; others (Malaysia, Botswana, and the Gulf states) have developed quickly from raw material exports.

Still, commodities present special problems, notably instability in earnings. Rich countries may have little interest in supporting commodity agreements to keep prices steady—though they have been happy enough to tolerate cartels in such processed commodities as aluminum when it suited them and to operate policies of agricultural support for their own farmers that openly violated the principles they commend to others.

The case for concentrating on market-friendly earnings stabilization rather than commodity price regulation has been essentially won. But this has not been reflected in a degree of support for the IMF's Earnings Stabilization Facility that would make it a major force helping the low-income countries that are the main victims of erratic movements in commodity prices and earnings. If the facility were strengthened to include interest subsidies for low-income countries, it would help those in greatest need of assistance but least able to afford loan financing on commercial terms.

In an era of rapid technological change, new uses for primary commodities and the development of synthetic substitutes make the roller-coaster of international commodity markets an even harder ride for the many specialized communities that depend on them.

Concentration and specialization give mining and farming communities a power and an inflexibility that will not easily accommodate market prescriptions. This presents a major strategic challenge to global governance.

It will require the combined resources of giant corporations, community leaders, states, and international organizations to ensure that urgently needed gains from new materials and energy technologies are neither denied to the world by a resurgence of defensive protectionism nor effectively wiped out by losses to traditional producers of products as varied as sugar and rubber.

THE IMF AND GLOBAL ECONOMIC STABILITY

Despite the emotions aroused by IMF conditionality, the problems now often lie with the workings of the global international economic system as a whole.

Fifty years ago, the establishment of the Bretton Woods system created rules for exchange rates and payments, along with two new institutions—the IMF and the World Bank—to oversee economic co-operation. We shall look at these institutions separately and in different contexts, though in some respects—notably structural adjustment lending—their roles overlap considerably.

Within the last twenty years, there has been a globalization of private financial markets, which is in part a product of the confidence engendered by the post-war order. The ease of movement of large financial flows—which now far exceed trade in terms of their impact on currency markets—generates opportunities for a more efficient use of capital. But it also exposes individual countries, and the world economy as a whole, to greater instability. At the same time, major countries are

EVOLUTION
OF THE SYSTEM

less committed to intergovernmental economic co-operation.

This process of integration has raised questions about the role of the IMF, which was originally set up primarily to maintain a system based on fixed but adjustable exchange rates. In its early years, the organization was important in helping countries with adjustment pressures under this system. The abandonment—and practical difficulty—of exchange controls has led to major exchange rates now being predominantly determined by market sentiment, except where constrained (and only with difficulty) by a commitment to overall policy convergence, as in the embryonic European Monetary Union.

Financial markets will often, but not necessarily, help correct major imbalances. There have also been prolonged periods in which currencies are heavily over- or undervalued in real terms, with serious side-effects, as with the growth of protectionist sentiment in the United States when the dollar has appreciated strongly.

A related feature of the world economy is that liquidity has been, in effect, privatized through international capital markets. The IMF's reserve currency—Special Drawing Rights (SDRs)—currently accounts for only a very minor part of world liquidity. Responsibility for maintaining levels of national liquidity consistent with an expanding real economy rests with central banks, which are increasingly seen (certainly in the United States, Japan, Germany, and France) as independent of their governments as well as of each other. What remains of international macro-economic management is occasional conversations among G7 governments, when exhortations over imbalances are made.

A further weakness of the current system is the underlying asymmetry between countries that can maintain adequate external liquidity (or solvency) only by borrowing from the IMF—since they have lost, or never gained, access to private capital markets—and countries that have no need of Fund financing. The last rich country to be forced to borrow from the IMF was the United Kingdom, almost two decades ago. Countries with recurrent budget deficits or current account deficits have been able to finance them by domestic or foreign borrowing in capital markets. The United States has had the unique luxury of being able to borrow in its own currency abroad and then devalue its repayment obligations. Surplus countries such as Japan have faced only the indirect pressures of an appreciating real exchange rate. Eventually, market forces exert their inevitable pressure. But major countries have often been able to adjust at a leisurely pace, ignoring the effects of their policies on others; a notable example is the high global long-term interest rates generated by large US government borrowing to bridge its persistent budget deficit.

Asymmetry of treatment results in instability for the world economy and disproportionate pressure on the weakest economies to adjust. The IMF has increasingly shifted from its original central role to one of ensuring that borrowers in developing and former Communist countries meet strict and politically demanding conditions to obtain balance-of-payments financing (and with it, the seal of approval to attract other official and private flows).

Yet many IMF programmes in recent years have failed to achieve even these objectives. The IMF has increasingly shouldered the responsibility for balance-of-payments financing in low-income countries, especially in Africa, that have deep-rooted problems associated with depressed commodity earnings, external debt, serious domestic policy failures, often serious problems of political instability, and the accumulated problems of economic decline. The conventional tools of fiscal and monetary stabilization and exchange rate adjustment have worked slowly, if at all, in these countries. Despite a longer-term approach to adjustment and the offer of loans on concessional terms under its Structural Adjustment Facilities, the results of these IMF programmes are often disappointing.

A related problem is the very uneven responsiveness of the international economic system to major shocks. Where the interests of the G7 have been seriously engaged, shocks have been dealt with quickly and effectively. The 1987 stock market crash did not have the same dire consequences as in 1929 because authorities in major countries acted quickly and in concert to inject liquidity into their economies. They did not act with the same urgency after the onset of the debt crisis. Four to five years passed before debt reduction was added to the menu of options, and even today relief is grudging and has not gone far enough.

Debtor countries were required to reduce imports (and growth) and run a trade surplus in order to make net transfers to their creditors. Painful adjustment would have been required in any event. But the lack of external financial support and more generous debt relief made adjustment much more painful and protracted than it need have been. As a consequence, many countries in Africa and some in Latin America are still struggling with the aftermath of the debt crisis.

Not only debtor countries suffered from the 'lost decade for development'. Asymmetric adjustment—involving enforced contraction by the debtor countries but no compensating macro-economic policy action by creditor countries—has introduced a deflationary bias into the world economy. Growth and employment in the rich world have been less than they would have been if developing countries had been able to expand at rates closer to their productive potential.

REFORMING THE SYSTEM

In a world of globalized private capital markets, it is not possible or desirable to recreate a system of fixed exchange rates and strong public-sector control over the international monetary system. The market genie has already escaped from the bottle. But there are important tasks to be performed by the IMF or any other custodian of the international financial system, and these are growing in urgency.

System Instability and Prudential Regulation
The current international system has the advantage of flexibility, but it also has some considerable deficiencies that reform of the international economic system needs to address. The most serious of these is the threat of instability in a highly integrated and mutually dependent system that relies almost exclusively on governments' self-discipline and the corrective mechanisms of markets.

The international monetary system's dependence on private capital markets exposes it to the risk of a collapse of confidence in the system as a whole. Economic history is littered with financial crashes, and a major global banking collapse was averted in the 1980s only because developing-country debtors were coerced into maintaining interest payments, thus forestalling large-scale bank insolvencies. Growing financial interdependence increases the risk of panic spreading if the system gives way at one of its weakest points. It is not possible to predict where lightning will strike next, but worries over the markets in some of the new financial instruments, such as derivatives, are a salutary warning of future storms that could threaten the system. It is also necessary to take account of some new destabilizing factors such as the role played by large sums of drug money.

Global banking supervision is currently the responsibility of central bankers meeting under the auspices of the Bank for International Settlements in Basel. Their efforts to strengthen the liquidity of banks around the world through capital adequacy ratios have had a far-reaching effect on banking behaviour. Global securities markets are the responsibility of another informal group, the International Organisation of

Securities Commissions. It is probable, but not certain, that these networks are the best defence against system failure. One important task for the proposed ESC is to maintain overall surveillance—not to interfere in the workings of these co-operative supervisory structures, but to investigate whether they are adequate and appropriate. And to act in time if danger threatens.

Adjustment and the IMF   There will be a continuing need for far-reaching adjustment, particularly in deficit and seriously indebted developing and former Communist countries that cannot cover deficits by borrowing from the market.

In some cases, adjustment has been harsh and resented, since it has stemmed not primarily or only from domestic policy failures but from external shocks and from the failings of other countries that have not come under the same pressure to adjust. Where we part company with some critics of the international economic system is in making the IMF a scapegoat for failures that lie elsewhere. Although there are legitimate criticisms of particular Fund programmes, many of these relate to experience of insensitive application of conditionality in the past. Despite the emotions aroused by IMF conditionality, the problems now often lie with the workings of the global international economic system as a whole rather than the IMF.

Some borrowers—most recently India and Mexico—have had a satisfactory and businesslike relationship with the Fund. And most of the IMF's clients now welcome its assistance and wish there were more of it. They see the problem as being essentially one of lack of external resources to cushion the impact of adjustment. The social costs of adjustment then become too high to justify politically.

In many countries, a political consensus for necessary adjustment can be achieved provided there is a realistic time frame and the prospect of an early recovery in living standards supported by adequate external finance. Where policy reform is too abrupt and harsh and where it relies too much on adjustment rather than supporting external finance, programmes are likely to lose public support and fail, as many have in Africa.

Fulfilling this role effectively requires ample financing for adjustment. The particular need is an enlargement of the IMF's capacity to provide balance-of-payments support to finance cyclical deficits and shocks, for example through low-conditionality compensatory finance, with concessional financing through a window for low-income countries.

International Economic Co-operation The most single serious deficiency in the IMF at present is that it has drifted too far from its original role in having oversight of the international monetary system and a capacity to ensure that domestic economic policies in major countries are not mutually inconsistent or damaging to the rest of the international community.

There are some specific implications. The first is in relation to exchange rates. The flexible rate system is not working as well as it should. There is too much volatility and serious misalignment of important exchange rates. Although there are good technical ideas in circulation for trying to manage exchange rates within broad bands, the essential point is that major countries have to develop the habit of closer consultation on macro-economic policy leading to convergence. Here, the European Monetary System, despite its recent difficulties, has much valid experience since it has already achieved a remarkable degree of convergence particularly in anti-inflation and monetary policy.

We would also like to see the IMF have a greater capacity to support nominal exchange rates, where these are not fundamentally overvalued, in the interests of exchange rate stability. The recent introduction of a mutual currency support mechanism within the North American Free Trade Agreement (NAFTA), in parallel with continued attempts to stabilize nominal rates within the European Monetary System, suggests an awareness of the advantages of stability. The rationale is just as valid at the global as at the regional level. Concrete progress could be made at regular meetings of the relevant authorities including Central Bank governors, under IMF auspices, to ensure that monetary and fiscal policies are consistent.

Second, and related, the Fund should play a more active and high-profile role in the surveillance of policy in major economies, including regular, detailed peer reviews of macro-economic policies by members of the international community, both industrial and developing. Although surveillance is already a part of the Fund's mandate, the asymmetrical treatment of borrowing countries is a deep-rooted problem. It can be addressed in part by giving the IMF more effective say in the management of major economies, which would occur if there were at global level the same kind of commitment to policy convergence as exists within the EU.

Third, the effectiveness and credibility of the Fund would be enhanced by increasing the issue of SDRs. A growing world economy requires constant enlargement of international liquidity. Although some countries have objected, on general anti-inflation grounds, to a large, general issue of SDRs, many countries simply do not have easy access to private capital markets for liquidity. Managing Director Michel Camdessus has called for a new issue of SDRs, a topic taken up by many countries at the IMF meeting in Madrid in October 1994. The strong stance taken there by developing countries—rejecting a proposal for an SDR issue that they saw as too restricted—heralds a new approach to international economic management issues. The IMF is being forcefully supported to play a larger role by developing countries, which see it as a means to achieve a stronger rules-based system of global governance.

The IMF and Development The IMF has increasingly become the lender of last resort for countries, especially in Africa, with desperate difficulties of external insolvency, extreme poverty, and adjustment. The IMF's role has as a consequence increasingly overlapped with the World Bank's International Development Association (IDA). It is to the credit of the IMF that it has managed to transform itself from an intimidating ogre to a welcome source of concessional assistance.

The IMF should not, however, be more closely integrated with the World Bank to become, in effect, a development agency. This would not merely confuse the roles of the institutions. It would take the IMF in totally the wrong direction. The Fund has a valuable role in financing developing countries, a role that has been strengthened by the Enhanced Structural Adjustment Facility (ESAF), which lends on highly concessional terms to low-income countries. It could do more in this area and reconsider the practice of imposing market-related charges, to allow for a greater degree of concessionality in reverse proportion to the capacity to pay; its main long-term role, however, should be what its founders intended: to provide oversight of the international monetary system as a whole, not just of its most indigent members.

Decision-Making Many of the problems in the international monetary system stem both from lack of will to adjust rapidly and radically in major industrial countries and from an underrepresentation of the poor in global economic governance. This problem can be realistically addressed in several ways.

We have already recommended an Economic Security Council to take an overview of the global economy. Second, the decision-making structures of the Bretton Woods institutions have to be reformed. For one thing, their work and decisions need to be more open and transparent. Furthermore, they need to be more democratic in the sense of moving away from the strong dominance of a small number of powerful economies. The most obvious way to do this is for quota weights, which govern how many votes member-countries have and therefore their responsibilities and privileges, to be adjusted to reflect economic reality.

It was always the intention that the number of votes should reflect economic weight. This should mean, in practice, using GDP figures based on purchasing power parity rather than conventional GDP, a change that would generally benefit developing countries. At present, the new GDP and GNP per capita measures are being used by some to argue that certain countries are not poor enough to qualify for aid. But the corollary—that they have sufficient economic importance to qualify for enhanced voting rights—is being avoided.

The Interim Committee has played a useful role in providing ministers with an opportunity to discuss financial issues in between annual meetings. We can see the Economic Security Council taking on many of its functions. But some reform of the Committee is desirable for its own sake and to set precedents for the ESC: to stop formula ministerial speeches (which can instead be automatically accepted for the record); to reduce the size of delegations; and to create subcommittees to advance serious technical discussion.

DEVELOPMENT ASSISTANCE AND THE FIGHT AGAINST POVERTY

In too many nations, the benefits of growth are very unevenly shared, and many people are left out or even victimized by the process of modernization.

In reviewing the Bretton Woods institutions, we identified two separate strands: the post-war commitment to provide international monetary stability, and support for development. The latter, in its critical phases, involved post-war European reconstruction and now involves post-Communist countries, but is primarily concerned with developing countries.

There is now considerable experience of different approaches to development. This is not the place to try to advance thinking on the underlying causes of poverty and its remedies. It is, however, significant that there is a broad consensus on many of the elements: a strong, long-term commitment to high rates of saving and investment; maximization of the opportunities potentially available through an outward-looking trade regime; release of the private sector from bureaucratic controls; an understanding of the importance of environmental sustainability; financial stability; and a strong social dimension to policy, emphasizing education (especially of women), health, and family planning.

The current broad consensus on the elements in successful development and transformation provides an opportunity that did not exist when the world was ideologically polarized, a chance to try a co-operative approach to development resting on an implicit contract whereby governments receiving aid dedicate themselves to long-term development, and the donor community honours pledges to give financial support.

This is not to say that the process of development and the elimination of poverty are easy. But the path followed by some countries, especially in East Asia, has provided hope that, with political will, rapid growth can be achieved and combined with successful reduction of poverty. The 'information revolution' is creating enormous possibilities for the poor as well as the rich to achieve access to knowledge that can raise living standards and improve the quality of life, provided people can be educated and trained to make use of it.

But in too many nations, the benefits of growth are very unevenly shared, and many people are left out or even victimized by the process of modernization.

The pressures are to achieve international competitiveness and to give high rewards to scarce capital and human knowledge. This may lead to a widening of the rich-poor divide within societies unless governments are exceptionally sensitive and committed to ensure that all have access to productive assets, land, and education.

Combating poverty calls for good governance and a commitment to development at a national level combined with a supportive international economic environment. The central problem is how improved global governance can help countries, mainly but not entirely in Africa, where poverty has been increasing. Even where there is tangible progress in raising living standards, as there is in the Indian subcontinent and South-east Asia, hundreds of millions are still marginalized and desperately poor. The challenge posed by mass poverty has too often been seen in terms of development assistance, particularly multilateral aid. This remains a crucial and underresourced component, but it must be complemented by others, notably market access for labour-intensive exports. Nothing, however, can replace in importance the domestic, political commitment to overcome poverty.

DEVELOPMENT AND AID: RETHINKING THE PRINCIPLES OF GOVERNANCE	Official aid programmes are currently under growing pressure in many countries. So-called aid fatigue is invoked to explain why the rich world is barely able to achieve (and with increasing difficulty) even half the 0.7 per cent of GDP target for official development assistance (ODA). By 1993 aid levels had fallen to 0.29 per cent, the lowest level since the targets were set.

Several reasons for aid fatigue are cited. First, some relatively rich countries are preoccupied with domestic problems. It does require some political courage to send money abroad when people in your own country are poor, homeless, and unemployed. Yet this problem is perhaps exaggerated. The response to charity appeals during many emergencies reveals deep wells of human solidarity to be tapped.

Second, aid has had a very bad press, with programmes being attacked from all sides by people worried about waste, corruption, human rights abuses, and neglect of the environment in recipient countries. Serious evaluation of aid programmes shows that the complaints are often exaggerated or simply wrong, but enough flawed programmes exist to sow serious doubts in the minds even of the committed. There are complaints on the other side about the expense of foreign experts.

Third, donors have often used aid programmes to promote exports or security priorities. Half of the rather meagre US aid budget, for example, goes to Egypt and Israel. Where self-interest overwhelms altruism, the cynicism in donor and recipient countries alike is not surprising.

The case for large-scale concessional aid remains compelling for countries that cannot raise enough private capital to sustain development and that are committed to using external support for genuine development purposes. For this reason, we fully back the 0.7 per cent target for ODA. Yet we recognize that some of the traditional mechanisms and motives for aid have to be rethought. For most developing countries, trade—and, in particular, market access to industrial-country markets—will be far more important than aid. Official assistance can only be a supporting, complementary feature of this process, not an alternative. But it can, in certain situations, mean the difference between sustainable development and continuing poverty, and even between life and death.

Although arguments about quality and targets remain relevant, the world is moving to a new concept of what aid should be about, a new philosophy of aid. It has several elements. One is the idea of solidarity between people, which may be lost in aid that is simply a transfer from bureaucracy to bureaucracy. Associated with that idea is the notion of active participation by people within the recipient country in the design and implementation of projects.

On the donor side, it means capitalizing on and learning from the experience of small-scale but cumulatively large programmes by NGOs, especially those with an innovative quality. There are many examples— from craft development in Mexico to energy efficiency in Jamaica—of how NGOs have made a major contribution on the ground. We strongly support ideas for the automatic 'gearing' of NGO aid—practised in a number of donor countries—with a fixed proportion of official aid to increase the scale of the former and the effectiveness of the latter.

Another strand in the new philosophy involves changing the relationship between donor and recipient governments from charity and dependency to interdependence and shared contractual obligation. The idea that aid is a form of intergovernmental charity will have to give way to the concept of aid as a form of payment for services rendered, where, for instance, developing countries act as custodians of rare species and biological diversity and as managers of tropical forests.

One political mechanism suggested to capture a new approach based on mutual interests is a system of contracts between donors and recipients, whereby a package of aid and debt relief is negotiated in return for a variety of environmental services. Clearly, such ideas need to be treated with care since the contracts are not being struck between equals, are non-binding, and could be a vehicle for insidious forms of control. None the less, the idea should be looked at carefully in the light of the experience of a few countries (such as the Netherlands and Norway) that are experimenting with it.

The World Bank and Other Multilateral Development Agencies The World Bank group— particularly its soft-loan agency, IDA—is a key player in the global struggle against poverty because of both its ability to mobilize, co-ordinate, and channel resources effectively and its intellectual influence on policy. There is, however, a need to rethink the Bank's role. The growing importance of small-scale NGOs working with the poor has called into question the effectiveness of a big international institution in the area of social policy and grass-roots poverty programmes. And the increasing role of the private sector internationally—through capital markets and direct investment—and domestically in developing countries has raised the issue of how needed the Bank is as a financial intermediary, and whether a public-sector agency lending to the public sector is appropriate in a more entrepreneurial environment.

In addition, there have been some damaging attacks on the Bank. The institution has indeed made mistakes in the past, just as all private companies and public agencies do. But its overall record in producing a good social return on its investment in development is impressive, and its staff are generally respected for their professionalism. It deserves continued strong backing.

Moreover, we unequivocally support the idea of the Bank continuing to play a major role in concessional aid financing. Many low-income developing countries will not for many years be able to obtain commercial financing for investment on the scale required to lift them out of poverty. For them, IDA is a crucial support and all the more useful for being free of the distorting influence of procurement tying and political strings associated with bilateral aid.

Yet the Bank is struggling to put together the three-yearly replenishment of IDA and get donors to honour their undertakings. At present, a decline in real resources is threatened. The limited resources available are one reason that some low-income countries have been prematurely 'graduated' from IDA, obliging them to borrow on commercial terms and creating debt-servicing problems. It has also led to stringent treatment of countries eligible for IDA support.

But the IDA resource problem is perhaps a symptom of deeper difficulty. The World Bank suffers from the general problem of aid fatigue in the rich world and from a diversion of resources from multilateral to bilateral or regional aid. The transformation in Eastern Europe, important as it is, is also making additional demands on donor resources. Attention and competence have been reoriented to these acute needs at the expense of the long-standing needs of developing countries. This has also affected the Bank.

One of our main concerns from a governance standpoint is to find a way to avoid the periodic haggling over IDA replenishment, which is invariably vulnerable to passing political moods in key industrial countries. IDA, as the most important single source of concessional financial help for the poorest countries, could benefit from the long-term commitment implied in a system of automatic financing. Various mechanisms for this are discussed at the end of this chapter.

The governance issues concerning the World Bank's aid role are not, however, simply about money. Transparency, local ownership and capacity building, participatory methods of working with national and local governments, and the guidelines for aid effectiveness drawn up by OECD's Development Assistance Committee all apply to the Bank as well as to other development institutions.

A further issue for the Bank, in its role of financial intermediary, is how far to detach itself from 'graduating' middle-income countries. Private loan capital is often freely available to creditworthy developing-country borrowers, generally at cheaper rates and without the conditionality attached to Bank loans. Yet there is still a major role to be played by the Bank. The big infrastructure projects—power, roads, telecommunications—now opening to the private sector are often unlikely to get off the ground without the technical and policy support, guarantees, and cofinancing of a body such as the Bank. Many countries, moreover, are not clear-cut 'graduating' countries, but need a blend of aid and finance on commercial terms.

Furthermore, there is no reason why the World Bank should not use its good standing in markets to relax its current conservatism over lending in relation to its equity base. This would allow it to raise more money to lend on commercial terms to successful middle-income countries, diversifying the sources of finance these countries can draw on. Such an expansion would not make any demands on industrial-country shareholders of the Bank, whose contribution is in the form of uncalled callable capital. A continued large and growing role for the International Finance Corporation is another way in which successful development can be supported by working with the grain of markets and in support of them.

Co-ordination Where donor agencies duplicate each other's activities, there is clearly a need for co-ordination. World Bank Consultative Groups and UNDP-led Round Tables have greatly improved the quality of aid. The co-ordinated effort of the World Bank to mobilize additional resources for development assistance and debt relief to support adjustment in Africa was successful as far as it went.

Excessive co-ordination between multilateral agencies has, however, a corresponding danger of cross-conditionality between the various agencies. In general, there is benefit in multilateral pluralism—encouraging a variety of multilateral agencies to offer different kinds of assistance rather than channelling aid and conditionality through one source in the name of co-ordination. For example, the IMF's ESAF and the soft-loan facilities of regional banks can mobilize additional financial flows and offer a distinct perspective. But we are aware of the strong arguments for aid co-ordination, and realize that difficulties can arise when, for example, the new concern for 'social' projects leads both the World Bank and regional banks to chase the same projects.

A further consideration is that some countries feel more comfortable working with UNDP than with the Bretton Woods institutions. And although UNDP can offer no finance, its role as an interlocutor can be useful provided there is a co-ordinated approach. On balance, the co-ordination argument must be given great weight because of the scarcity of resources.

Rationalization is also needed in shifting the emphasis in aid from bilateral to multilateral flows. Bilateralism has frequently degenerated into promoting exports, which is economically inefficient, corrupting, and makes aid less rather than more appealing to domestic constituencies. The value of aid would be increased significantly if bilateral donors untied it (see Table 4–1) and let recipients use funds to buy from the cheapest source through internationally competitive tendering. The key requirement is for bilateral programmes to reinforce and not undermine multilateral assistance.

Widening the Development Constituency For a number of countries, aid is likely to be for many years one of the main ways to escape from a low-income, low-savings, low-investment trap. Demand for aid from these countries greatly exceeds donor supply. Conditionality is the rationing device. Although continued exhortation to rich countries to meet aid targets is an obvious starting point, it is no substitute for a politically realistic strategy to mobilize aid flows and to demonstrate value for money.

In addition to the approaches just suggested, several other steps are important. First, the donor base has to be widened. This is primarily a question of

TABLE 4–1
Development Assistance, Bilateral and Multilateral, from Selected Countries, 1991*

(percent of total aid)

Country	BILATERAL			MULTILATERAL	
	Untied	Partially Tied	Tied	Non-EC	EC
Australia	8	-	55	37	-
Canada	27	15	23	35	-
France	35	3	40	10	12
Germany	32	-	38	14	16
Italy	4	-	56	25	15
Japan	66	6	11	17	-
Netherlands	39	27	3	21	10
Sweden	62	-	12	26	-
United Kingdom	16	-	41	20	22
United States	61	10	17	11	-

* Rows may not total 100 due to rounding.

Source: Alexander Love, *Development Co-operation: Aid in Transition* (Paris: OECD, 1994).

'levelling up' the contributions of OECD donors. If the United States, United Kingdom, and Germany were to match the efforts of Norway or the Netherlands, total aid would more than double. Already, non-OECD countries make a useful contribution to IDA and to the IMF's Enhanced Structural Adjustment Facility, and we urge middle-income and large low-income countries to help countries less well placed than themselves.

In the long term, Russia and countries in Eastern and Central Europe could be prominent in the donor community. One reason for timely and generous help to these countries is that in time they will be able to help countries poorer than themselves.

NGOs can also make a valuable contribution, both through additional finance and through careful attention to attacking poverty and building up local institutions. We deal with this dimension in more detail in the next section.

Second, we endorse the recent recommendations on aid effectiveness of OECD's Development Assistance Committee and the World Bank, which underline the importance of local ownership of aid processes and of predictability and stability. Immense resources of human energy and resourcefulness remain to be tapped, provided aid programmes are carefully designed to ensure local participation and self-help. One mechanism to keep this priority in sight is for agencies to carry out a 'social audit' of their programmes.

Third, the process of development and the causes of poverty are still imperfectly understood. To enhance understanding of this complex process, regional centres of excellence for development studies should be established in the developing world. These should be fully independent of governments and donor agencies, and should be the source of world-class research and policy advice.

Finally, the entirely proper focus of aid on the poorest people and the poorest countries should not detract from the problems of countries that, through successful development, are emerging from the extremes of poverty but are by no means affluent. Quite apart from unmet need, it is crucial to the political psychology of development—and of aid—that success should be seen to be rewarded and reinforced.

| NGOS AND ECONOMIC DEVELOPMENT | There has been a surge in the number and participation of non-governmental organizations, from both North and South, in development-related activities, and also a recognition that sustainable development cannot be achieved solely through government action or market forces. Active partnerships among the main sectors of society—government, business, and organized citizenry—allow the complementary skills of each to be mobilized. Developing such partnerships is not easy |

because of the diverse nature of NGOs; they range from small grassroots citizen associations to larger public assistance contractors, specialized membership organizations, and groups that straddle the public-private domain or are, in effect, instruments of government. The development-focused organizations that emerged in the early post-war period were largely based in the North; in the 1970s, such groups began to appear in the South. By the end of the 1980s, NGOs of both kinds had become significant in development.

Most development assistance funds are provided from government to government, but a significant portion is channelled today through non-governmental bodies. Moreover, private donor organizations invariably work through NGOs: the sums they provide are, of course, much smaller than those spent by governments.

Although much international aid is given to improve welfare or provide relief, there is a growing appreciation of the importance of economic activities that enable people to help themselves in the long run. Thousands of non-governmental enterprises now work for economic empowerment. They use local resources, build on local skills, and encourage the creation of indigenous institutions—private banks, philanthropic bodies—to sustain self-help.

NGOs often have direct knowledge of local needs and opportunities. Partly because they are small, flexible, and independent, they can also test innovative ideas and act as pioneers or catalysts for government or business action. The scaling-up potential and policy relevance of NGOs are further assets. Many groups are making their own international connections and taking part in building global networks of citizens' interests.

The growing reliance on non-governmental organizations and institutions as partners with government and business in achieving economic progress is leading to more participatory development. Involving agents

NGOs in Development

Development Alternatives (DA), India

This Indian NGO now employs 300 scientists, engineers, managers, and social scientists to promote environmentally sound development and mass deployment of appropriate technologies. DA seeks to combine academic research, the social goals of voluntary agencies, and the policy impact associated with government.

DA develops inexpensive technologies to enable the poor to improve housing and sanitation and to increase income while conserving natural resources. These have included a manually operated mechanical press to make mud bricks that do not require firing, so saving firewood and topsoil; a mechanical loom that can double productivity; inexpensive roofing tiles; and a wood-conserving cookstove. These and other technologies are manufactured by Technology and Action for Rural Advancement, DA's sister organization, and through franchising arrangements.

Through its work with state and local governments in India and its many international links, Development Alternatives can disseminate the result of its work widely. DA staff serve on several influential official bodies, including those developing India's Eighth Five-Year Plan.

Instituto Nacional de Biodiversidad (INBio), Costa Rica

Linking conservation research with sustainable economic development, this Costa Rican NGO is preparing a total inventory of the country's biological resources. An important aim is to develop new sources of chemical compounds, genes, and other products.

Under a 1991 agreement between INBio and Merck Corporation, a US company, the chemical make-up of Costa Rican plants is being studied to identify medical potential. Merck provided an initial commitment of $1 million for conservation and the training of scientists. In turn, INBio-trained 'parataxonomists' provide Merck with samples from the forests to test. If a medicinal source is discovered, Merck will develop and test the drug; Costa Rica will get a perpetual royalty on sales.

Chemical prospecting is rapidly gaining attention from large corporations and development banks. The INBio-Merck agreement is an example of the kind of mutually beneficial collaboration that can be established.

of civil society leads to programmes and projects that are more focused on people and more productive.

A false sense of complacency has enveloped the developing-country debt problem. The reduction of the debt-servicing burden owed to banks by some middle-income countries (but by no means all of them) has been widely taken to imply that the problem is solved. But the position for many low-income debtors—involving mainly debt owed to governments and official agencies—is still desperate despite repeated initiatives to write off a sizeable chunk of their debt.

More than twenty African countries have debt burdens regarded by the World Bank as unsustainable. (In 1991, the discounted present value of their debt service was more than 200 per cent of exports.) Whatever process was originally at fault for the situation, it is simply unreasonable and unrealistic to demand that the debt be serviced. For countries where the ratio is 1,000 per cent or more, such as Mozambique, Sudan, and Somalia, the position is almost surreal as the compounding of interest pushes servicing obligations to stratospheric levels. The predicament of many of these countries is so dire that even the full application of the debt reductions currently on offer would bring only six of the twenty-one countries most severely indebted in 1991 into the sustainable category.

A severe penalty is incurred by these low-income debtors as a consequence of unsustainable debt. In some cases, notably Nigeria, the cash-flow implications mean imports are severely squeezed. Another consequence is the loss of access to trade credit or an increase in its cost. And key government officials are absorbed for long periods in debt renegotiation rather than domestic policy issues. Domestic and foreign investors are discouraged by the prospect of resources for development being swallowed up in debt service.

Low-Income Debt

For many low-income developing countries, the 'debt crisis' was not a historical event in the 1980s; it is a live and growing problem. Between 1980 and 1992, the ratio of debt service to exports for middle-income countries fell from 24.9 per cent to 18.4 per cent as a combination of debt rescheduling and export growth gradually eased the problem (with some exceptions, such as Côte d'Ivoire).

But for low-income countries, the situation deteriorated badly—with debt service ratios going up from 11.8 per cent to 24.5 per cent, excluding China and India. Many countries, especially in sub-Saharan Africa, have simply been unable to pay their debt service, and large arrears have piled up: $10.1 billion for Sudan; $4.5 billion, Nicaragua; $3.4 billion, Nigeria; and more than $1 billion for Egypt, Madagascar, Mozambique, Myanmar, Somalia, Tanzania, Yemen, and Zambia.

For many of the most serious cases, there are deep structural weaknesses, including poor infrastructure and undiversified exports, and the long-term consequences of war and civil war.

It was recognized in 1988 that the position was unsustainable in a number of cases; debt reduction was offered in the Paris Club as one of a series of alternatives (the 'Toronto terms'). These were further enlarged in 1991 (the 'enlarged Toronto terms'), involving a 50 per cent forgiveness of the present value of debt-service payments. An alternative approach advocated by the UK Chancellor of the Exchequer became known as the 'Trinidad terms', which were more concessional for some debtors.

In parallel, some donors offered to write off past debt arising from official development assistance. Even when the most generous contribution is considered, however, some countries retain very high debt-service obligations (such as Guinea-Bissau, Sierra Leone, Somalia, Sudan, and Uganda), and more comprehensive relief is clearly necessary.

The remedies lie in strong domestic policy reform allied to radical debt reduction. In two areas, improved processes could alleviate a problem that, by wide international consensus, should have been dealt with long ago. The first is for the World Bank and other multilateral agencies to be much more sensitive to debt-servicing difficulties in terms of their own loans. The second is a more radical approach to debt relief. At the very least, the undertaking to provide 'full Trinidad terms' should be honoured. And it is almost certainly necessary to go further for countries that are, in any meaningful sense, bankrupt.

A case can also be made for having a formal status akin to corporate bankruptcy, whereby a state accepts that its affairs will, for a while, be placed under the management of representatives of the international community and a fresh start is made, wiping much of the slate clean. There are also cases of countries being offered far-reaching and consolidated approaches to debt relief—such as Indonesia in the 1960s and more recently Mexico and Poland—that have subsequently advanced as a result of pursuing policies consistently supportive of development, but without the burden of a large overhang of debt. That model could be more widely emulated.

The ability of some of today's developing countries to achieve rapid growth is in large measure due to their having successfully made use of new technologies. Access to technologies that raise the productivity of traditional farming and other activities while being appropriate to environmental conditions and the availability of labour is crucial to development. This can be achieved in a variety of ways—from direct foreign investment to the transfer of publicly available scientific knowledge. The decision of large numbers of developing countries to liberalize their foreign investment regimes is prompted in significant measure by the belief that this will facilitate technology transfer.

Although more is now being done in terms of South-South technology co-operation, there is some concern in developing countries that the transfer of technology is becoming more difficult, partly because R. & D. on the most advanced technologies—in information, biotechnology, and new materials—is overwhelmingly

TECHNOLOGY FOR DEVELOPMENT

concentrated in rich countries. An estimated 97 per cent of R. & D. on these frontier technologies takes place in industrial countries.

The issue of technology for development is of crucial importance, but it has slipped out of focus and has no single international agency giving it concentrated attention. It should have priority attention on the agenda of the new Economic Security Council.

At the national level, an important component of good governance is for governments, working with the private sector and scientific communities, to develop a capacity for anticipating the long-term impact of technical change on their societies and the necessary adaptations—for education and training, for example—required.

RESPONDING TO DISASTER

Emergency appeals for help in response to disasters usually evoke a greater sense of international solidarity than the long, slow slog of development. The United Nations plays a valuable role in emergency relief, as well as NGOs such as the Red Cross and Médecins Sans Frontières. The issues straddle economics and peacekeeping, since many of the most severe humanitarian problems arise as a result of war or civil strife, which may have economic causes and certainly have economic consequences.

The long agony of the Horn of Africa—Ethiopia, Eritrea, Sudan, Somalia—has military, political, ecological, and economic dimensions, with no clear dividing line between them. Even natural disasters—floods, earthquakes, volcanic eruptions—have wide ramifications since their impacts may be greatly worsened by poverty (poor people are forced to live in dangerous environments) and ecological stress (deforestation and flooding), and since they can affect interstate relations—as between India, Bangladesh, and Nepal over Brahmaputra and Ganges flooding.

There is a compelling need for a holistic approach to disasters and humanitarian assistance that cuts across traditional boundaries. The Economic Security Council could look at problems in the round: trying to identify future flashpoints, mobilizing international support for action on particular problems, and suggesting appropriate interagency co-ordination.

Governments and NGOs are increasingly aware of the ways in which the impacts of disasters can be minimized through systems of disaster planning. But for many developing countries, natural disasters are also an economic disaster. One specific step needs to be taken in this field, in relation to disaster insurance. Many of the costs of disaster in industrial countries are covered by insurance (and reinsurance). This helps victims reconstruct their lives and also provides a spur to better standards of construction and other preventive measures. Developing-country insurers are faced with serious problems in insuring poor people and face a high cost of international reinsurance. Disaster-prone Caribbean islands, for example, have recently lost reinsurance cover entirely.

We would like to see an initiative that would help strengthen the capacity of insurance markets to meet the economic costs of disasters in poor and small countries. Fiercer hurricanes and stronger storm surges are forecast in connection with global warming—natural disasters made worse by human activity, in this case, mainly in industrial countries. Even on more general grounds, however, there is a strong case for special help to these weak economies. The World Bank and regional banks should provide a mechanism and an element of subsidy for pooling insurance risks among these countries.

MIGRATION

Migration is likely to be a subject of growing difficulty.

People from different parts of the world interact most directly through migration. Few multilateral rules exist for migration, but for a good many individuals, the absence of any protection under international law can lead to exploitation and is potentially a source of serious conflict. There is, moreover, an underlying inconsistency—even hypocrisy—in the way many governments treat migration. They claim a belief in free markets (including labour markets), but use draconian and highly bureaucratic regulations to control cross-border labour migration.

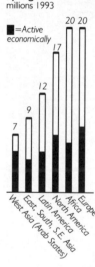

Non-nationals by region
millions 1993

■ =Active economically

20 20
17
12
9
7

West Asia (Arab States)
East, South, S.E. Asia
Latin America
North America
Africa
Europe*

One practical consequence of this restrictiveness is that migration is less important between today's rich and poor countries than it was in the nineteenth century; between 1880 and 1914, some 1 million people a year left Europe for countries of settlement, notably the United States. Roughly comparable absolute numbers have lately been moving, legally or illegally, into the United States, Canada, and Australia, but these are proportionately smaller than a century ago. Western Europe has also received developing-country migrants, who make up small but visible minorities, though new migration has been greatly reduced. At the same time, the well-educated, qualified, and rich in all countries have in general become highly mobile, creating a big disparity in life opportunities between classes as well as between countries.

The fear in rich countries of mass migration from low-income ones is, however, all too real. And given the disparities in living standards and personal freedoms across the Mediterranean and between North and Central America, they are probably well founded, if exaggerated. These fears could be a major factor in reinforcing inward-looking approaches to the world economy.

*Excluding former Soviet Union and Yugoslavia

Distinctions are usually made between those seeking political asylum, refugees, and economic migrants. But in practice the motives are often impossible to disentangle, and fear of mass economic migration is downgrading the status of asylum seekers and refugees, for whom admission criteria are applied more stringently and narrowly. A more farsighted approach to the same problem is taken by NAFTA—trying to assist the labour-exporting country through a widening of trade opportunities.

A measure of multilateral migration management could help to both alleviate fears in receiving countries and protect individual migrants from capricious and inhumane treatment. Migration is likely to be a subject of growing difficulty, and we emphasize the importance of research, analysis, and monitoring of trends in human movements and in policy. The International Organisation for Migration has worked since 1951 with both refugee and labour migration issues. It has been particularly useful in helping alleviate migration crises, together with the UN High Commissioner for Refugees, and in arranging for repatriation. There remains, however, a need to develop more comprehensive institutionalized co-operation regarding migration. More countries should also ratify the UN convention on migrant workers.

Whether regulated or not, labour migration will increase. It is therefore in everybody's interests to develop and strengthen the rules that govern labour migration. During the GATT negotiations, developing countries proposed that the new services regimes being established should provide rules to govern labour services. One way would be to allow developing countries to sell—on a contractual, time-bound basis—labour services to be performed in rich countries. The fundamental rights of unions to negotiate and sign agreements with employers must be safeguarded. Existing ILO conventions may need to be expanded by a code to protect the contract

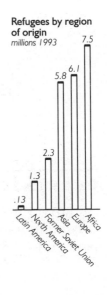

Refugees by region of origin
millions 1993

7.5 Africa
6.1 Europe
5.8 Former Soviet Union
2.3 Asia
1.3 North America
.13 Latin America

worker from discrimination and arbitrary deportation or imprisonment, just as a bank or insurance company establishing business under the financial services code would be protected from discrimination and expropriation.

Immigration is a very sensitive issue, and attempts to put it on a businesslike basis have created as many if not more problems than permanent settlement. First reports of concessions under GATT suggest extreme caution in this area. None the less, one group of countries cannot continue to argue with any credibility that labour mobility must be regarded as off-limits in an increasingly interdependent world economy. We see merit in the idea of a services code for labour, recognizing that it would be of a special character and should not detract from the normal mobility of people, which should also be free of discrimination.

PROTECTING THE ENVIRONMENT

All governments should adopt policies that make maximum use of environmental taxes and the 'polluter pays principle' of charging.

The environment, perhaps more than any other issue, has helped crystallize the notion that humanity has a common future. The concept of sustainable development is now widely used and accepted as a framework within which all countries, rich and poor, should operate. The aspect that particularly concerns us is the global governance implications.

Considerable strides have been made in creating a system of international environmental governance to achieve global sustainable development through the management of cross-border environmental disputes and protection of the global commons. Treaties in effect or awaiting ratification now govern the atmosphere, the oceans, endangered species, Antarctica,

---

Selected International Environmental Agreements

- Whaling Convention (1946; 38 parties to the convention)
- Wetlands (Ramsar) Convention (1971; 17 parties)
- Convention on Marine Waste Dumping (1972; 68 parties)
- Convention on the International Trade in Endangered Species (1973; 17 parties)
- Convention on Ship Pollution (MARPOL) (1973; 74 parties)
- Convention on Long-Range Transboundary Pollution (1979; 35 parties)
- Convention on Migratory Species of Wild Animals (1979; 39 parties)
- UN Law of the Sea (1982; 52 parties)
- International Tropical Timber Agreement (1983; 50 parties)
- Vienna Convention on Ozone Layer (1985), including the Montreal Protocol (1987; 91 parties)
- Convention on Early Notification of Nuclear Accidents (1986; 61 parties)
- Convention on Transboundary Movement of Hazardous Wastes (Basel) (1989; 33 parties)
- Biological Diversity Convention (1992; 4 parties)
- Framework Convention on Climate Change (1992; 5 parties)

---

and trade in toxic waste. The UN Environment Programme has assumed a major role in negotiating and following up on these agreements, together with such groups as the World Meteorological Organization and the International Maritime Organization. Non-governmental organizations, such as the World Conservation Union–IUCN, the World Resources Institute, and the World Wide Fund for Nature, have also made important contributions by creating a climate conducive to official action to improve environmental governance.

One of the outcomes of the 1992 UN Conference on Environment and Development (UNCED) in Rio was the creation of the Commission on Sustainable Development, an intergovernmental body of fifty-two members and now the focal point within the UN system for

SUSTAINABLE DEVELOPMENT AND AGENDA 21

coherence and co-ordination of programmes undertaken by various UN agencies. The CSD should not, however, be seen simply as an administrative co-ordinating body. It exists to give political leadership more generally in the field of sustainable development, in particular in implementing Agenda 21, as agreed at Rio.

Progress in tackling Agenda 21 is very uneven. Although there is a greater appreciation than a few years ago of such global issues as damage to the ozone layer and global warming, much less attention has been paid to the less dramatic but crucial areas of freshwater supply and quality, land degradation, and desertification. The Rio conference failed to agree more than a general declaration of principles on deforestation. These issues are intertwined with poverty and underdevelopment.

The immediate consequences of poverty-related environmental changes are localized and call for strong governance at the national level. But the long-term consequences of neglect are global, and poor countries lack the resources to deal with them adequately.

Agenda 21 suggests a plausible level of commitment by the world community, but it has yet to be confirmed by positive action to put it into effect. The proposed Economic Security Council could bring these issues back to the centre of attention. It is the task of the CSD to prepare the ground. We strongly urge international support for implementation of Agenda 21.

The focus after Rio must be to go beyond the declaratory stage to a proper programme for implementation. The 500 pages of proposals for action contain many and varied suggestions and involve commitments to build capacity at national and international levels. What is clear, however, is that countries facing the most compelling threats to sustainability are generally those with the least capacity—institutional and financial—to deal with them. Implementation of Agenda 21 is therefore inextricably bound up with the issue of additional resources for development.

The Global Environment Facility (GEF) is a small and useful step to increase the instruments and the funding base for Agenda 21. GEF should help developing countries make environmental investments that have global benefits; indeed, it was conceived to finance the incremental costs of projects that have global environmental impacts. One important underlying element in its philosophy is the idea that environmental aid to developing countries helps the donor at least as much as the recipient. But as presently constructed, GEF does have serious limitations. It operates on a small scale: $742-million outlays over the first three years. It is doubtful that much of the funding at present is additional, and it probably represents a diversion of resources from other development aid.

We support the principle of enlargement of the GEF provided it meets the tests of additionality and developmental priority. The potential for meeting these objectives undoubtedly exists, since the rationale and voting structure of the GEF represents a move towards the mutually beneficial 'contractual' approach to aid discussed earlier.

The experience of recent years has proved the importance of instruments that give a firm signal to individuals to change unsustainable life-styles or to firms to change unsustainable production methods but that allow for the working of decentralized, market-based economic systems and do not rely on command-and-control methods.

Examples abound of unsustainable development perpetuated because consumers and producers do not pay the full economic and environmental cost of what they use—the massive waste of water in subsidized irrigation schemes, as in the United States; the low logging and licence charges that encourage over-exploitation of tropical forests; the price support for European farmers that encourages energy-intensive

MARKET INSTRUMENTS AND THE ENVIRONMENT

and chemical-intensive agriculture; the failure to charge adequately for ocean fishing rights, which is currently leading to serious over-fishing; the move to keep energy cheap, which leads to wasteful transport and industrial systems and contributes to excessive carbon emissions.

All governments should adopt policies that make maximum use of environmental taxes and the 'polluter pays principle' of charging. Eliminating the vast sums spent on tax breaks and subsidies for economically wasteful and environmentally unsound activities would be a major fiscal windfall for many governments, although, obviously, scrapping them can lead to political problems. Recent experiences with attempts to remove tax breaks for Brazilian forestry clearance, to introduce Indian farmers to the idea of paying the full cost of their electricity, to curb agricultural subsidies in France, and to close British coal mines all point to the considerable political difficulties. Yet the growing use of market instruments—taxes, user fees, legal liability for emissions—demonstrates that environmental and economic concerns can be efficiently reconciled.

A contribution could be made to alleviating the global warming problem through energy or carbon taxation as envisaged in the EU and the United States. The carbon tax proposal seems the most practical and closest to realization. And individual countries or regions (such as the EU) can introduce it as part of their own domestic tax reform in advance of any global agreement. The aim is to give a general fiscal incentive to energy conservation and a specific incentive to use less carbon-intensive fuels. By contrast, at present most countries tax gasoline quite heavily but not other oil products, and they often subsidize coal. The EU's proposal consists of a pure carbon tax combined with a general tax on energy, partly to avoid the political difficulties (including the incentive to use nuclear power) that just a carbon tax would present.

A carbon tax, even if imposed initially by individual countries, would no doubt be a valuable step forward, signalling that global warming is a serious concern and providing a boost to more sustainable forms of resource use. The EU approach of gradually building up the level of taxation (from $2 a barrel equivalent to $10 by 2000) has the practical merit of avoiding severe adjustment problems. The tax could be used as a step towards a radically different system—one that taxes resource use rather than, as is often the case in industrial countries, employment (through payroll taxes) and savings. This would recognize the need to discourage excessive consumption and would stimulate employment as part of a strategy of sustainable development. And it would provide revenue that could not only fund reductions in other national taxes but also make a contribution to global environmental initiatives.

Inevitably there will be problems of implementation. Industries will complain that their products have become uncompetitive through energy taxes not imposed elsewhere; this has already led to sweeping exemptions from the EU proposal. For this reason, a global approach—or at least a common one among the main industrial countries—is desirable, but its absence should be no excuse for inaction. If tax revenues were used in part to offset other taxes on business (such as those that currently raise the cost of labour), adverse effects on competitiveness could be minimized.

Another approach to the same problem is the use of tradable permits. We would like to see detailed preparatory work under the auspices of the ESC for a system of globally tradable permits to help limit greenhouse gas emissions. Such mechanisms could combine effectiveness, equity, and market efficiency.

Tradable Permits

Tradable permits have been widely used in the United States as a means of pollution control in preference to taxes. The government decides on target pollution levels and issues permits that companies must obtain in proportion to the emissions they generate. Permits can be traded between companies without central direction.

Based on the initial overall success of such schemes, the US government has made them a centrepiece of the recent Clean Air Act controlling sulphur dioxide emissions. They have some clear advantages:

- The government can precisely target emissions if this is necessary for health or environmental reasons in a way that is not possible with environmental taxes.
- There is a market incentive for efficiency. The more a firm cuts back emissions, the more can be earned by selling unused permits.
- Administration is decentralized and through the market. Armies of bureaucrats policing every plant are not needed.
- Because the regulatory objectives are flexible and market-based, they are easier to negotiate and enforce than traditional command-and-control standards.

So far, tradable permits have been successfully used within one country with a well-developed infrastructure for this sort of exchange. Could the same approach be used globally for carbon dioxide emissions? In principle it could, but numerous practical problems must be considered. How would 'rights to carbon emissions' be allocated by country? What would the currency for trading be when countries with excess quotas try to cash in? Which emissions should be included? How would the system be administrated? And how would 'quota hoarding' be avoided?

The problems are immense, and solving them requires a level of trust and quality of global governance beyond current levels. For this reason, voluntary national carbon taxes are more likely to be seen in the short run.

—Michael Grubb
The Greenhouse Effect: Negotiating Targets

THE GLOBAL COMMONS   The most direct challenge to global governance in the environmental field is that presented by 'the tragedy of the commons': the overuse of common environmental assets because of the absence of a sufficiently strong system of co-operative management. The pollution of the global atmosphere and the depletion of ocean fisheries—just like the destruction of local common grazing land—stem from inadequacies of governance when there are neither secure property rights nor collective responsibilities to govern a shared resource. Yet the commons present not only a tragedy but a great opportunity—the unrealized potential, for example, of tapping the energy of deep-sea currents, from aquaculture, and from space research and exploration.

National jurisdiction can hardly be used to protect areas that do not fall within it. International co-operation and legality are the only way in which the global commons can be protected, although the problems obviously differ greatly: space junk and militarization, oceanic sea-beds, forests, Antarctica, pollution in the different layers of atmosphere, and other commons with different degrees of vulnerability to overuse and different users.

The World Commission on Environment and Development sketched an action programme for strengthening global governance in respect of the commons that remains relevant. There are several different kinds of deficiencies at present. In some cases, global governance has been undermined by lack of agreement—such as the opposition (until just recently) of the United States and other industrial countries to aspects of the deep sea-bed regime devised at the Third United Nations Conference on the Law of the Sea.

A different but emerging problem is that as the various global environmental conventions take shape—for species, climate, and forests—governance is fragmented into separate institutions and legal arrangements that do not function in an integrated way. The CSD can play a part in ensuring that there is coherence. The ESC would be a more authoritative body pushing in the same direction. In other cases there are functioning agencies of global governance, but their legitimacy is being questioned. The Antarctic Treaty has a good track record in preventing disputes and ensuring conservation, but it cannot continue to exclude countries, notably those in Africa, that fail to satisfy technological admission criteria.

The pressures of rising population and economic activity on fragile ecological systems are so great that new threats to the global commons may well emerge. It is vital that these be quickly assessed scientifically so as to avoid the dangers of complacency and exaggeration. The CSD has the mandate to convene a panel of internationally respected and independent scientists to provide, through scientific assessment, an early warning system for global hazards. An important task for the proposed Economic Security Council will be to ensure that political impetus is given to early corrective measures when hazards are identified.

What is becoming apparent is the lack of any consistent approach and oversight of the global commons. And it is becoming clear that one body should exercise overall responsibility acting on behalf of all nations, including the administration of environment treaties related to the commons. We believe that the Trusteeship Council should exercise this role, and develop the argument further in Chapter Five.

PRINCIPLES OF GLOBAL ENVIRONMENTAL GOVERNANCE

The Rio conference did much to lay the legal, intellectual, and institutional groundwork for a concerted drive to achieve sustainable development. The concept is now firmly embedded in the debate about policy in economic as well as environmental fields. There remains, however, an overall lack of direction regarding where to go next.

The failure in Rio to agree on an Earth Charter setting out a set of principles to guide future action

216   OUR GLOBAL NEIGHBOURHOOD

or to achieve any agreement on additionality of resource flows for development was a setback. An early contribution of the Economic Security Council could be to ensure global adoption of an Earth Charter.

This task should be made easier by the recent agreement between the Earth Council, Green Cross, and the Netherlands government to collaborate in developing an Earth Charter for world endorsement. This agreement also demonstrates NGO capacity not only to provide leadership in important areas of international effort but also to launch the negotiating process and carry it to a point of maturity that intergovernmental processes would have taken much longer to reach.

FINANCING GLOBAL GOVERNANCE

A start should be made in establishing practical, if initially small-scale, schemes of global financing to support specific UN operations.

At first sight, global financing might seem an unpromising area for action. Governments are having great difficulty in many countries retaining the legitimacy of national tax regimes, and even a tightly knit group such as the European Union has not advanced far in tax-raising powers. Past reports recommending globally redistributive tax principles have received short shrift.

The time could be right, however, for a fresh look and a breakthrough in this area. The idea of safeguarding and managing the global commons—particularly those related to the physical environment—is now widely accepted; this cannot happen with a drip-feed approach to financing. And the notion of expanding the role of the United Nations is now accepted in relation to military security.

Yet there is a widening gap between the financial requirements of programmes widely supported in principle and the money actually made available through traditional channels. The non-financing of agreed peace-keeping operations is one of the more glaring examples. A start should be made in establishing practical, if initially small-scale, schemes of global financing to support specific UN operations.

Several broad principles could be adopted in designing schemes for global financing. First, it would be appropriate to charge for the use of some common global resources on straight economic grounds, using market instruments. Second, it is right that the whole burden should not fall on a small number of industrial countries but should be spread, albeit with an element of progressivity. Third, it would be helpful if new revenue systems did not substitute for domestic taxes or charges but represented additional sources.

Within these broad principles, clearly many difficult technical issues need to be resolved on how any common revenue source would be collected and allocated. One task of the ESC would be to organize technical studies on the aspects of global financing that could get political support.

Taxes are, of course, never politically popular at the best of times—locally, nationally, or at a higher level. Governments have the option of introducing user charges that provide a more direct link between the user and the service than taxation and government expenditure. When something as controversial as global financing is being considered, this seems a sensible place to start.

We specifically do not propose a taxing power located anywhere in the UN system. User chargers, levies, taxes—global revenue-receiving arrangements of whatever kind—have to be agreed globally and implemented by a treaty or convention. Proposals for them can be initiated in the UN system—in the Economic Security Council, when established—and negotiated and approved by the General Assembly before being embodied in an international agreement to be approved and ratified.

Included in any such agreement will be stringent arrangements for allocation of global revenues and accountability for their disbursement and use, so that countries can have confidence in the system and ensure that it works effectively to fulfil its global purposes. Our proposals do not involve major elements of supranationality; they are practical suggestions for sharing the global neighbourhood.

Any system of global taxation requires the identification of a tax base that is politically acceptable to governments but also reflects global processes. One proposal is to tax or charge for foreign currency transactions. Professor James Tobin, an American Nobel-laureate economist, has put forward proposals for such a tax based not just or even primarily on revenue grounds but on the need to improve the efficiency of what is the largest global market. This encompasses a good deal of speculative trading, which is too short-term to reflect fundamental economic factors.

A tax on foreign exchange transactions would dampen this activity (which is of no intrinsic benefit in terms of economic efficiency), raising potentially large revenues. It might also enable governments to pursue more independent monetary policies by allowing a greater disparity of short-term interest rates. Such a tax faces considerable practical problems, however, not the least being the decentralized, unregulated, electronically mediated nature of foreign exchange markets in most industrial countries, with no paper trails to provide a tax base. There would also be an incentive to move markets to tax havens.

The problems may not be insuperable, but they will have to be addressed. We urge the UN and the Bretton Woods institutions to explore the feasibility of such a system in consultation with the regulatory authorities of the leading financial markets. A variant of the Tobin proposal, which also merits study, envisages a computer-based network of foreign currency exchanges to yield a stream of income for the operating agency through user charges. This mechanism, suggested by Professor Reuben Mendez, would avoid the need to track individual transactions.

Another idea would be for corporate taxation of multinational companies to represent a tax base. At present, governments are struggling through bilateral agreements to reconcile different tax regimes. But in a world where more and more companies are truly global it makes little sense to identify tax domains in a narrow, national manner.

Charges for use of the global commons have broad appeal on grounds of conservation and economic efficiency as well as for political and revenue reasons. They would encourage efficient use and conservation, as well as finance institutions of global governance required to police and maintain the commons in good order. We encourage consideration of several possibilities for user charges:

- a surcharge on airline tickets for use of increasingly congested flight lanes, with collection of a small charge—a few dollars—for every international flight;

- a charge on ocean maritime transport, reflecting the need for ocean pollution control and for keeping sea-lanes open to all legitimate users, with special fees (or auctions of licences) for maritime dumping of waste where the level of toxicity does not require outright prohibition;

- user fees for ocean, non-coastal fishing (or auctions of quotas), reflecting the pressures on many stocks and the costs of research and surveillance;

- special user fees for activities in Antarctica, such as fishing, so as to fund conservation on the basis that the continent is part of the common heritage of humanity;

- parking fees (or auction revenues) for geostationary satellites; and
- charges for user rights of the electromagnetic spectrum.

Most of these have rather small, specific revenue implications, and it might be logical to make pledges without actually collecting the funds—to plough the receipts back into the management of the relevant global commons, in other words. Some charges could, however, have enormous implications. A carbon tax introduced across a large number of countries or a system of traded permits for carbon emissions would yield very large revenues indeed, and a detailed exploration is needed of the practical problems of creating global systems of taxes or charges of this kind.

We urge the evolution of a consensus to help realize the long discussed and increasingly relevant concept of global taxation. In this and in other areas, managing economic interdependence will require technically creative and politically courageous innovation.

Summary of Proposals in Chapter Four

Economic Security Council

1   An Economic Security Council should be established within the United Nations to provide political leadership and promote consensus on international economic issues and on balanced and sustainable development, while securing consistency in the policy goals of multilateral economic institutions.

- The ESC should be a representative body, including the world's largest economies, and be not larger than a reformed Security Council.
- The ESC should meet once a year at the level of Heads of Government and otherwise at Finance Minister level.
- The IMF, the World Bank, and the WTO should be invited to report regularly to the ESC. Other institutions such as the Commission on Sustainable Development should report on specific matters.

Trade

2   All governments should quickly enact legislation to implement the Uruguay Round agreement of the General Agreement on Tariffs and Trade and to set up the World Trade Organization.

3   Governments should adopt decision-making structures that require full public examination of the benefits and costs of trade restrictions for the community at large.

4   There is a need for intensified dialogue and better methods of dispute resolution in the WTO and other institutions in order to avoid conflict between the interests of free trade and, in particular, social and environmental concerns.

5   The WTO should set out clear guidelines to define and encourage open regionalism in trade.

6   The WTO should establish new rules to strengthen global competition, and a Global Competition Office should be set up to provide oversight.

7   The WTO and the UN should establish firmer rules on international investment that facilitate direct investment and establish obligations through a code, with a system to accredit and register transnational companies that accept the basic principles of good conduct in that code.

8   The WTO should create global rules for a more liberal and equitable regime in telecommunications and multimedia services.

The IMF and Global Economic Stability

9   The ESC should investigate the adequacy of present supervision of banking and securities markets.

10 The role of the International Monetary Fund should be enhanced by enabling it to:
   - enlarge its capacity to provide balance-of-payments support,
   - oversee policy in major economies as part of a more active policy of seeking policy convergence,
   - release a new issue of Special Drawing Rights, and
   - improve its capacity to support nominal exchange rates.

11 The decision-making structure of the Bretton Woods institutions needs to be reformed and made more democratic, including the use of GDP figures based on purchasing power parity to set the votes that countries have.

DEVELOPMENT ASSISTANCE AND THE FIGHT AGAINST POVERTY

12 Governments should redouble their efforts to meet the target of 0.7 per cent of GDP for official development assistance.

13 The World Bank should be equipped to play a greater role in development financing through an enhanced IDA and by extending its financial intermediation role through greater use of guarantees and cofinancing of big projects.

14 A strategy should be adopted to mobilize aid flows and to demon strate value for money provided. It should include:
   - greater untying of official aid so that recipients can use funds to buy from the cheapest source, and
   - increased cofinancing between governments and non-governmental organizations.

15 A more radical debt reduction is needed for heavily indebted low-income countries, involving at the least 'full Trinidad terms', and for some countries the wiping clean of the slate in the equivalent of bankruptcy proceedings.

16 The capacity of insurance markets to meet the economic costs of disasters in poor and small countries needs to be strengthened.

Migration

17 There should be more comprehensive co-operation on migration, and more countries should ratify the UN convention on migrant workers.

18 Greater access should be given to labour-intensive services in the services regime of the GATT/World Trade Organization.

Environment

19 Strong international support should be mobilized for Agenda 21, and the Global Environment Facility enlarged.

20 Governments should adopt environmental policies that make maximum use of market instruments, including environmental taxes and tradable permits, and commit themselves to use of the 'polluter pays principle'.

21 The EU's proposal for a carbon tax merits support as a first step towards a system that taxes resource use rather than employment and savings.

Financing

22 An international tax on foreign currency transactions should be explored as one of a series of options that also includes creating an international corporate tax base for multinational companies.

23 Charges should be considered for the use of common global resources, such as flight lanes, sea-lanes for ships, ocean fishing areas, and the electromagnetic spectrum, to provide money for global purposes.

REFORMING THE UNITED NATIONS

As noted in Chapter One, global governance is about a varied cast of actors: people acting together in formal and informal ways, in communities and countries, within sectors and across them, in non-governmental bodies and citizens' movements, and both nationally and internationally, as a global civil society. And it is through people that other actors play their roles: states and governments of states, regions and alliances in formal or informal garb. But we also noted that a vital and central role in global governance falls to people coming together in the United Nations, aspiring to fulfil some of their highest goals through its potential for common action.

This chapter deals with the UN and its potential, but always—and sometimes specifically so—within the framework of our wider perspectives of global governance. This issue of the potential for common action has been central to our deliberations.

WE, THE PEOPLES

When governments or people speak of reform of the United Nations, they address a process of change that has to begin in national behaviour.

'*Quot homines, tot sententiae*': As many persons, so many opinions. This would not be an inappropriate aphorism to describe how the UN is viewed nearly fifty years after its creation. But there is one thread common to these many opinions; none looks to the UN with any sense of ownership. The Charter was proclaimed in the name of the people of the world: 'WE THE PEOPLES OF THE UNITED NATIONS....' The assertion that it was the people of the world who were creating a world body was little more than a rhetorical flourish. But the proclamation was symbolic of the hopes of the founders of the UN for what they were creating.

As it turned out, the hopes were not to be fulfilled. Save for rare glimpses of what might be—as during Dag Hammarskjöld's Secretary-Generalship—the people of the world never developed a sense that the UN was theirs. It did not belong to them. It belonged, if to anyone, to governments—and then only to a few of those. It was the domain of high politics. It touched the lives of people in ultimate, not proximate, ways. A sense of ownership did emerge for a time as the many millions who were only notionally part of 'WE THE PEOPLES' in 1945 ceased to be subjects of European empires and became citizens of new states who saw a seat in the United Nations as a seal on their independence. Yet even for them, as for most of the people of the founder nations, the UN remained a thing apart.

It was only slightly different for governments. The United Nations was there to be used, and not infrequently abused; to be an instrument of national interest where it could be; and to be bypassed where it could not be made to serve that interest. During the cold war, it became the instrument of collective enforcement action only rarely.

The newer countries tried to place the UN centre-stage, but the majorities they mustered in the General Assembly could only recommend, not determine. Too often the 'new majority' mistook voting power for decision-making power, with inevitable frustration. They simply could not prevail over the minority that exercised power in the Security Council or in the world economy. In time, even they lost hope. And the UN bureaucracy, once fired with imagination and zeal, became frustrated and disillusioned.

Fifty years after San Francisco, the United Nations is viewed predominantly, by both people and governments, as a global third party—belonging to itself, owned by no one except its own officials, and even, to an extent, dispensable. In many capitals, the United Nations is seen—particularly during international crises involving those countries—as 'them', not 'us'. And that is how it is often treated.

Yet the UN is 'us'. Although the membership consists of states represented by governments, these governments are increasingly accountable to people for their international actions; and governments, like the UN, are gradually becoming more open to international civil society organizations and other non-governmental voices. The UN is a complex collectivity, but in essence it is made and maintained by its members. The UN is 'us' because its systems, its policies, its practices are those that member-states have ordained. Its decisions are decisions taken or declined by its members. Some aspects of management are in the Secretary-General's keeping; but, save for that, the UN is its members. When they disown it, they repudiate themselves.

More to the point in relation to this report, when governments or people speak of reform of the United Nations, they address a process of change that has to begin in national behaviour, not on the banks of the East River in New York. National behaviour is a product of national decision-making and national policies: it is here that strengthening of the UN must begin. Worthwhile reforms of UN structures ought to be pursued, and we propose several in this report, but the greatest failings of the UN have not been structural: they have been collective failings of the member-states. This is true of the failure of the UN's Economic and Social Council (ECOSOC) to fulfil the aims of the

THE UN
IS 'US'

Charter, and of the failure of the Security Council to implement an effective global security system based on the Charter scheme. When we deplore how far the world body has fallen short of the Charter's promise of economic and social advancement for all peoples, it is not the failures of some monolithic supranational entity that we lament, but the lapses of members of the United Nations—of governments and, to some degree at least, people. The point cannot be made too emphatically.

As the UN's fiftieth anniversary approaches, there are unquestionably many achievements of the United Nations that ought to be acknowledged. For these, the member-states deserve credit, as do the other relevant UN actors. Among the successes must be counted the containment of conflict, particularly of some regional conflicts during the cold war. Decolonization, the advancement of human rights, the Law of the Sea, and the contributions made by the great global conferences on issues ranging from the position of women to the environment also rank among the successes. And high on the list are some of the action-oriented UN programmes—ones that translate a substantial global consensus for action into the reality of 'doing'. The United Nations Children's Fund (UNICEF) and the Office of the United Nations High Commissioner for Refugees (UNHCR) are good examples of these practical, universally acclaimed elements of the UN system. They represent what is best in international co-operation. They must not be taken for granted, for although they work well, they need enhanced support if their work is to be sustained, let alone enlarged.

The same is true of other UN activity in, for example, the fields of agriculture, health, meteorology, and labour. In all cases, organizational effectiveness depends on leadership: both from the international community, in terms of commitment to the programmes and financial support, and from the institution itself, particularly the person heading it—the Director-General or Secretary-General.

International leadership is discussed further later. Here we stress that while good institutional leadership makes a great difference to the quality of international effort, it cannot make up for the absence or decline of support for that effort from the world community. Neighbourhood action is in the end only as effective as neighbourhood commitment and resources allow it to be.

In addition to these successes, however, there are many— all too many—failures. They are to a large extent matters for reproach of the UN's membership. The founding states in San Francisco did not endow the United Nations with powers and capacities beyond the control of its membership. They were right not to do so, and those powers and capacities remain with member-states. To improve the United Nations system, the world must essentially look to the exercise of those powers and capacities residing in member-states. It is an exercise that depends on the will of member-states. 'WE THE PEOPLES', through our governments and through our own new empowerments, must be the principal agents of change of the United Nations and of international institutions generally.

In that process of reform, it will be important to reflect the realities of change discussed in Chapter One. The period ahead will not be like the immediate post–San Francisco period, during which the United Nations was almost the exclusive international actor beyond governments. Already that exclusivity has gone, and internationalism will be the stronger for the new roles that fall to global civil society. The UN system will still be at the centre of international action, as nation-states will remain the main international actors, but two kinds of accommodation must now be made for global civil society. The first is facilitation of practical contributions by elements of civil society within a reformed UN system—not just the allocation of space within its reconstructed structures. The second is acknowledgement of the relevance of the roles that will be played by civil society outside the UN system. This Chapter's discussion of UN reform includes the need to offer new opportunities for civil society to contribute to global governance.

Many factors have contributed to the failures of the United Nations. But there are two important respects in which the Charter and the system of internationalism it ushered in were severely disabled virtually from the outset. The first disjuncture came with nuclear weapons; the second, with the cold war.

Even as the Charter was being negotiated and signed at San Francisco, the atomic bomb was being developed in Los Alamos, New Mexico, a thousand miles away. Few in San Francisco, including most of those who would play the role of founders, knew of this development. The Charter they were negotiating was for a world from which the scourge of war would be removed by 'collective action'—a world in which 'armed force shall not be used, save in the common interest'. The first atomic bomb was exploded over Hiroshima on 6 August 1945, just forty-one days after the Charter was signed. By the time the United Nations was established, on 24 October 1945, the world that it was to serve had changed in fundamental ways.

An effort was soon made to return to the premises of San Francisco. The very first resolution of the General Assembly requested specific proposals 'for the elimination from national armaments of atomic weapons and of all other major weapons adaptable to mass destruction', and also to ensure the use of nuclear energy for peaceful purposes only. Moved by the United Kingdom and co-sponsored by the United States, the Soviet Union, and France, it was passed unanimously.

In the Atomic Energy Commission established by that resolution, the United States suggested a set of wide-ranging measures (known as the Baruch Plan) for bringing all nuclear activity, from uranium mining to power generation, under international control and for destroying its still minuscule stockpile of atomic bombs. The Soviet Union saw this as a ploy to prevent it from developing its own nuclear capability. It delayed the proceedings in the Commission for three years—until in 1949 it had tested its own weapons. Within the first five years of the founding of the United Nations, the nuclear arms race was under way. It was to last for most of the UN's first fifty years, transforming the world for which the Charter was designed in San Francisco.

The ramifications of the cold war cracked and weakened the very foundations of the Charter. To appreciate how far this state of affairs departed from the goals marked out in San Francisco, recall the aims to which the founding nations pledged themselves in the Preamble to the Charter:

- to practise tolerance and live together in peace with one another as good neighbours;
- to unite our strength to maintain international peace and security;
- to ensure, by the acceptance of principles and the institution of methods, that armed force shall not be used, save in the common interest; and
- to employ international machinery for the promotion of the economic and social advancement of all peoples.

In large measure, this report is a composite proposal for fulfilling those goals, but they were hardly the aims that dominated the post-war era.

Given that the United Nations system was so hobbled from the outset, it is remarkable that it accomplished so much in so many areas of international co-operation. That achievement is in large measure a tribute to the ability and dedication of UN staff—particularly the early generation of UN officials, who brought to their work a rare measure of zeal and a belief in the United Nations not yet overlaid by cynicism.

The international public service—the staff of the United Nations system—has not been fairly judged. Many of its members have been selfless servants of all the member-states of the United Nations and have devoted their lives to furthering the aims of the Charter. As in all bureaucracies or corporations, some individuals have been less efficient, less committed, less effective than others. Some of these have been foisted on the United Nations by their governments. Overall, however, the international community has reason to be grateful to the men and women who have worked at UN headquarters and in the specialized agencies and programmes. These traditions of dedicated international service are now endangered, and there has been concern that the system is functioning at less than its optimum level. The UN needs to set the highest standards of efficiency at all levels of its operations. Later in this chapter we suggest some measures to remedy the situation.

Credit is also due to the diplomatic foot-soldiers of member-governments—the staff of Permanent Missions to the UN and in capitals, through whom governments participate in the United Nations system. These officials deserve more appreciation than is generally given for their role in making the UN system work. Sometimes theirs is a very difficult task (it took more than twenty years to agree on the definition of 'aggression', for example), and even the smallest achievements contribute to the progress of the organization and the advancement of its aims. Many of these officials have, as a result of their work with the UN, become its champions. They are part of a world-wide constituency that speaks up for the United Nations, placing the responsibility for its failures where it mainly belongs—with the member-states.

| THE OPTION OF RENEWAL | The UN Charter bears the stamp of its time, and a half-century later it needs adjustment. We address the 'constitutional' issues, such as the reform of the |

Security Council, that we believe are crucial to better global governance. And we do so frankly. But we have believed from the outset, and our work in the Commission has further convinced us, that these changes apart, a primary need is for the world community to make greater, more imaginative, more creative use of existing provisions of the Charter.

Certainly, we do not subscribe to the notion that the UN should be dismantled to make way for a new architecture of global governance. Since it is not the Charter that has failed but the policies and practices of its members, much of the necessary reform of the system can be effected without amending the Charter—provided that governments have the will to inaugurate real change. The few amendments we propose will themselves help create an environment favourable to a return to the spirit of the Charter. As member-states celebrate the UN's fiftieth anniversary, they should be animated by the spirit of the Charter in seeking change.

The world now has a real opportunity to improve on the record of the past and to respond effectively to the current challenges of global governance. The Commission believes that this can be done through a process of reform—more remodelling and refurbishment than tearing down and rebuilding. But the renovation must be more than cosmetic, and it must be accompanied by new ways of living in our global neighbourhood.

THE SECURITY COUNCIL

A new class of 'standing' members should be established until a full review of the membership in the first decade of the new century.

If any feature of the United Nations system established at San Francisco should now be regarded as 'provisional', it is the composition of the Security Council and the veto powers of its five permanent members. But the 'great powers' that had won World War II did not intend these arrangements to be temporary. As leaders in the fight against Fascism and aggression, their position was understandable. It led to the conviction that they themselves should have special powers in the world of the future—notwithstanding formal acceptance of the principles of universality and the equality of member-states. These privileges, as enshrined in the Charter, were to dominate the system of internationalism developed and ordained by the 'great powers'.

The Security Council was the key institutional arm of the system, specifically charged with ensuring peace and security in the world. It was the only organ of the UN with power to take decisions that bound all member-states and to authorize enforcement action under the collective security provisions of Chapter VII of the Charter.

In San Francisco, it was decided that China, France, the United Kingdom, the United States, and the Soviet Union should be 'permanent' members of the Security Council, and that each should have a veto over Council decisions. The Council would be a small body, originally with only eleven members: the permanent five plus six rotating members who would each serve for only two years.

The elements of privilege—permanent seats and the power of veto—were vigorously contested in San Francisco, both as a matter of principle and by countries whose people had also fought and died in the war against Fascism. But the victorious 'great powers' prevailed. A few months earlier, Churchill, Roosevelt, and Stalin had already made up their minds on this issue. The vision of a new world order informed by the lofty principles of the Charter was combined with the narrow presumption that only the victors could guarantee the realization of those principles.

As a practical matter, it should also be recalled that neither the Soviet Union nor the United States would have ratified the Charter without the veto provision. And that the veto acts as a sort of safety fuse in the UN system by making it impossible for the organization, by a simple majority vote in the Security Council, to go to war with one of the great powers under Chapter VII of the Charter. Whether this is wisdom or weakness is a matter of judgement.

The implied lack of faith was as much in each other as in the non-permanent members of the Council and the many other countries that remained outside it. Each permanent member would have the power to thwart any other. They would have the power to prevent the Security Council from taking any action they did not want. This provision, though virtually a contradiction of the other terms of the Charter, became its cornerstone. In 1945, the realities of power were such that unless other countries accepted the permanent membership of the five with their right of veto, there would have been no Charter. 'THE PEOPLES' of the world would not have had a United Nations established in their name. The judgement in favour of having an imperfect international body rather than none at all was, we believe, as right at that time as it was inevitable.

But righteousness in victory was not the only factor driving the victors to insist that they should be members of the Security Council in perpetuity, and should forever have a veto. Perhaps it was partly because they foresaw the possibility of changes in the relative power of states that the victors reserved the veto power to themselves; they may, on the other hand, have been less mean-spirited than this, simply failing to anticipate current developments, in which UN membership has grown while the economic and even the military distinctions between veto powers and non-veto

UNFORESEEABLE CHANGE

powers have diminished markedly. Certainly the notion of 'enemy states' should have no place in the Charter now.

In any case, it is later events, not the founders' intent, that require the 1945 arrangements for the Security Council to be treated as provisional. Nor have those arrangements proved sacrosanct. In 1963, acknowledgement of new circumstances led to a modest amendment of the Charter: the number of non-permanent members was increased from six to ten, with the Council's total strength going up from eleven to fifteen and the number of votes required for a decision from seven to nine. This occurred when UN membership had more than doubled from the original 51 to 113. Today it stands at 184.

Compared with 1963, there are now many compulsions for change besides the enlargement of the membership. The Security Council has become more active and effective, raising the challenge of making its membership structure more equitable, while preserving the capability and political support necessary for it to play a major role. From 1946 until the end of 1989, the cold war seriously sapped the vigour of the Council. Only rarely was its true potential used. The Council held 2,903 meetings and passed 646 resolutions in that period. But from the beginning of 1990 through mid-1994, it had almost daily informal consultations and 495 formal meetings, and passed 288 resolutions—26 on the Gulf War and 53 in relation to the situation in the Balkans. Between January 1993 and June 1994 alone, there were 134 resolutions. There were 98 resolutions and presidential statements just on the conflict in the former Yugoslavia through the end of June 1994, illustrating the complexity of many recent conflicts.

Peacekeeping has registered a similar increase. At the end of 1990, the United Nations was involved in eight operations with a total of 10,000 troops. At the

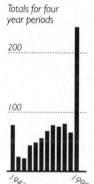

Security Council resolutions

Totals for four year periods

200

100

1946–49

1990–93

OUR GLOBAL NEIGHBOURHOOD

end of June 1994, seventeen operations were being conducted, with more than 70,000 troops, costing about $3 billion on a yearly basis.

Between 1945 and 1991, the Security Council authorized the use of force only twice for any purpose other than self-defence (in the American-led defence of South Korea and in the UN mission in the Congo). Between 1991 and mid-1994, in contrast, the use of force under Chapter VII of the Charter has been authorized in five cases—in the Gulf, Somalia, the former Yugoslavia, Rwanda, and Haiti.

On present trends, it is prudent to assume that in the years ahead the UN should continue to be able to play a major role in maintaining peace and security around the world. We have discussed these probabilities and the consequent need to strengthen the UN's capacity in Chapter Three, and we do so further in this chapter with special reference to the need for commensurate resources—financial or otherwise.

With a larger role, however, comes an insistent need for more than formal legitimacy. If the Security Council is at last going to play the role envisaged for it in the Charter, it must be perceived as fully legitimate in a broad sense by nation-states and people. Its current unrepresentative character is the cause of great disquiet, leading to a crisis of legitimacy. Without reform, it will not overcome that crisis; without legitimacy in the eyes of the world's people, it cannot be truly effective in its necessary role as a custodian of peace and security. Equally, reform must be managed in such a way as not to diminish the effectiveness and political vitality of this central institution.

We believe that the Security Council today is too closed a shop. Permanent membership limited to five countries that derive their primacy from events fifty years ago is unacceptable enough. Matters are made worse when working practices reduce the transparency

A 'CLOSED SHOP'

of Council proceedings and widen the gap between the permanent members and the other members of the Council, or between the Council and the wider UN membership.

There has been concern at frequent resort to private consultations among the five permanent members—and occasionally among just some of the five—who then come to the Council having reached an agreement among themselves. This devalues the role of the non-permanent members, who have little opportunity to influence the Council's decision. Another practice is to hold informal sessions of the Council. Like the private consultations among permanent members, these are closed meetings, with no record kept of the discussions. Furthermore, unlike formal sessions of the Council, they do not allow non-Council members to be present and contribute to the discussion. Increasing unease with these trends has led recently to some effort to move away from the closed shop atmosphere. Although the role of private consultations and of informal Council meetings in advancing the work of the Council is accepted, resorting to these too frequently is clearly unhealthy.

The general position has been so unsatisfactory that there is a strong demand among member-states of the UN for reform. The matter was specifically raised in a resolution in the General Assembly put forward by India in 1992. The Secretary-General, at the request of the Assembly, invited all governments to communicate their views. Almost all that responded have endorsed the call for change.

The General Assembly decided in December 1993 to set up an open-ended Working Group to further consider all aspects of the issue of an increase in membership and other matters related to the Council. The need for reform is widely acknowledged.

In developing our own proposals, we have been mindful not to make the best the enemy of the good. We believe that the international community wants to see changes in the permanent membership and in relation to the veto. The commitment to systems of fair representation in decision-making, which has received increasing emphasis within national politics, has not been sufficiently respected in the composition and procedures of the Security Council. The problem is, of course, that with the permanent members shielded by the ironclad armour of the veto, the world can move towards reform of the Security Council only with their support or at least their acquiescence. We do not believe that the case for reform is lost on them, or that they will place the perpetuation of their privileges above all other considerations. Even so, there are realities of power that we have to acknowledge.

These lead us to believe that reform of the Security Council may have to be undertaken in two stages—one stage being the process of reform set in train in the year of the fiftieth anniversary; the other in a decade or so as the international community and members of the Security Council themselves develop confidence in the reform process.

Ultimately, the world must find a better basis for constituting its highest organ of governance than permanent membership for a few countries. But that point has not been reached yet. The category of permanent membership will have to continue for the time being. On the other hand, we believe so strongly that the veto is an unacceptable feature in global governance that clearly the number of veto-wielding members should not be increased in any new arrangements. To add more permanent members and give them a veto would be regression, not reform.

Similarly, confining any enlargement of the permanent membership to a group of countries already well represented in the Council—such as the industrial countries—would make the Council even more unrepresentative. It should be enlarged to make it more representative of the UN's members. The

Commission recognizes, of course, that the Council must not become so big that it is ineffective. But we believe that with a UN membership of nearly 200, an increase in the size of the Council from fifteen to, say, twenty-three would not be unreasonable or result in an unwieldy body.

NEW
'STANDING'
MEMBERS

We recommend that a new class of 'standing' members be established, and that the first group should serve until a full review of the membership of the Security Council in the first decade of the new century—when the position of the original permanent members should also be reviewed and account taken of the new realities of regionalism. Of these new members, two should be drawn from industrial countries and three from among the larger developing countries. Of the two from industrial countries, presumably one will be from Asia and one from Europe. Of the three from developing countries, we would expect one each to be drawn from Asia, Africa, and Latin America.

In many respects, the new standing members suggest themselves; but we recommend that the General Assembly propose them, and in doing so be guided by the consideration that standing members of the Security Council should be able to contribute in more than a token way to the maintenance of international peace and security and to the other purposes of the United Nations.

We also recommend that the number of rotating members be raised from ten to thirteen. The number of concurring votes required for a decision of the Council should likewise be increased from nine to fourteen, preserving existing proportionality.

In Chapter Four, we proposed the establishment of an Economic Security Council as an apex body to give political leadership and promote consensus on international economic issues that pose threats to security in its widest sense. We will not repeat here those arguments about the composition of the Economic Security Council—save to underline the fact that the Security Council reforms suggested are complementary in nature and will allow the international community to take a major step towards fulfilling the potential of the Charter in the peace and security area of global governance.

PHASING OUT THE VETO

The new standing members will not possess a veto, and we believe the aim should be for the power of the veto to be phased out. To begin with, the reform package should involve a concordat among the five permanent members by which they agree that while retaining the veto, they would in practice forgo its use save in circumstances they consider exceptional and overriding in the context of their national security. The veto in this period would be available only in extreme cases.

The permanent members have been moving in this direction in recent years. The veto has been used only once since 1990, and then only on a relatively minor issue—the blocking by the Russian Federation of a resolution on the financing of the peacekeeping force in Cyprus. By the time of the review in, say, 2005, today's permanent members will have become accustomed to participating in global governance without the veto but without, in the meantime, being deprived of it entirely in cases of extraordinary importance to them.

THE GENERAL ASSEMBLY

High among the changes that should mark the fiftieth anniversary of the UN is the revitalization of the General Assembly as a universal forum of the world's states.

The UN Charter does not set out the principal organs of the United Nations in a hierarchical order, but the General Assembly is listed first in Article 7. It is the only 'principal organ' under the Charter that consists of all the members on a 'one member, one vote' basis. It is the symbol of the UN as a universal organization in the democratic tradition.

The establishment of the General Assembly may even have implied that a first step was being taken towards a parliament of the world. It was hardly that. It was not a parliament to which the Security Council was a cabinet in need of continuous support. Nor was the relationship structured to provide the separation of powers that is a feature of some democratic systems. The General Assembly was, from the outset, only a deliberative forum; it had power to discuss and recommend, to debate and pass resolutions, but no real authority, certainly no power to take decisions binding on member-states.

The special value of the General Assembly is its universality, its capacity to be a forum in which the voice of every member-state can be heard. The opportunity for countries to ventilate issues, bring complaints to the floor in the General Debate, and suggest new ideas in Committees of the Assembly is of vital importance to the health of global society. The world's leaders recognize this; that is why they go to the General Assembly each year. From the President of the United States to the President of the Maldives, they take to the Assembly their views on matters of international moment, their policies and their problems, their commitments and their constraints, their hopes for the UN and their criticisms of it.

When the leaders of the member-states speak in the Assembly's General Debate each September, the world is really coming together at the level of its political leadership in a most salutary way. To someone having to listen to all these speeches, the experience may be one of tedium, only occasionally intellectually stimulating. We emphasize, however, how important to many countries are the two weeks of the General Debate when governments—usually through Foreign Ministers, but sometimes Heads of Government—have an opportunity to bring their concerns and perceptions to the forefront of international attention.

What goes on beyond the speeches, however, when the leaders are in New York for the General Debate is of equal, if not greater, importance as the speeches in the Assembly. The innumerable meetings between Heads of Government or ministers on bilateral and sometimes on regional matters are at least as important as anything said or done within the Assembly itself. This political interaction is also a part of the Assembly's deliberative function. Its value should be more widely appreciated, particularly by the media. And, as we urge later, there is need for more of it.

FAILURES, BUT SUCCESSES TOO

This is not to say that all is well with the General Assembly. In one sense it has fallen short of its potential. Whatever the founders may have thought in San Francisco, the Assembly ought over the years to have become more significant in the UN system. In fact, it has become less of a 'principal organ' than at least some of its founder-nations might have hoped.

This outcome is only partly caused by its own failures. Marginalization resulting from a focus on the role of the Security Council, particularly in recent years, has been a contributory factor. The Security Council could hardly be blamed for an ineffectual General Assembly during the years when its own role was curbed by cold war constraints. Yet even then, with the veto restraining the Security Council, the five permanent members—at different times, according to the voting balance in the General Assembly—were not about to be overwhelmed by a General Assembly majority.

In 1950, when the absence of the Soviet Union from the Security Council over the issue of who should represent China allowed the Council to mount the action to protect South Korea, the United States, with a large and reliable Western majority in the General

Assembly, put through the Uniting for Peace Resolution or 'Acheson Plan'. This resolution, which the Soviet Union denounced as a breach of the Charter, transferred to the General Assembly the powers of the Security Council should the latter be blocked by the veto. Later on, when the West no longer had an automatic majority in the Assembly, the United States and the other Western permanent members once again became strong defenders of the exclusive powers of the Security Council in matters of peace and security.

Criticism of the General Assembly should not go too far. It has been a useful sounding board on many issues of world concern. It has also been a launchpad for some valuable new ideas in the UN's first fifty years. A good example was the initiative taken by Dr Arvid Pardo, Malta's Ambassador at the UN, in 1967 in the First Committee of the General Assembly to advance the concept of the sea and sea-bed beyond national jurisdiction as a common heritage of humankind. This led to fifteen years of intellectual effort and global negotiation under UN auspices, and ultimately the 1982 Convention on the Law of the Sea. The entry into force of this Convention, on 16 November 1994, has taken an agonizingly long time, principally because of concerns in major industrial countries about its deep sea-bed provisions.

Another good example of the General Assembly using its deliberative process to move the world towards better global governance is in the broad area of human rights. Here the Assembly's role has been of vital importance, starting with the Universal Declaration in 1948. The Assembly also played a key part in keeping such long-standing issues as apartheid, Namibia, and Palestine on the world agenda.

Where the General Assembly has notably failed to achieve results, or even to influence events significantly, has been on North/South issues. The long debate in the 1970s on a New International Economic

Order and the two-year process centred on the Conference on International Economic Co-operation in Paris were ambitious efforts to spur progress in the field of development. For the failure of the North-South dialogue, both parties must share the blame. Developing countries were over-ambitious and too rigid in their strategy, persisting for too long with an unrealistically wide agenda, and later overrating the importance of negotiations for the Common Fund to stabilize commodity prices. And they placed their faith in resolutions built on the shifting sands of illusory consensus. Industrial countries, for their part, showed an obdurate resistance to change and refused to use the UN as a forum for negotiation.

We discussed in Chapter Four the consequences of this failure to move forward in the economic area. Greater progress should have been made in the General Assembly and its subsidiary bodies. That it was not is essentially the fault of member-states. But in the process, the General Assembly was made to give hostages to fortune and is only now recovering from the damage it suffered. Recently there has been some evidence of the Assembly asserting its role in promoting international co-operation in the economic, social, and related fields with its call for the Assembly's President to engage in broad-based consultations on 'An Agenda for Development'. We welcome this practical activity on the part of the Assembly.

Article 17 of the Charter requires the General **BUDGETARY** Assembly to consider and approve the budget of the **CONTROL** organization and imposes an obligation on member-states to meet the expenses of the organization as apportioned by the Assembly. This approval authority could have been used to strengthen the Assembly's role in global governance. It could have been the basis for the Assembly exercising real influence on the policies and programmes of the UN when the budget is discussed in its Fifth Committee. But even without any special privileges in the Assembly under the Charter, the industrial countries—the largest contributors to the UN budget in absolute terms—have severely constrained the exercise of the Assembly's collective authority.

While this Commission has been working, one of the members, Brian Urquhart, has been conducting with Erskine Childers—both international civil servants with extensive knowledge of the UN system and its strengths and weaknesses—a study of the UN. They were examining what changes might be made within the system to overcome some of its weaknesses (short of what could be called 'constitutional change' requiring amendment of the Charter, and excluding peace and security issues). In *Renewing the United Nations System,* they have refuted the claim that those who make the largest financial contributions are entitled to special prerogatives in budgetary matters. The point is that countries pay according to their capacity. For the smallest and poorest countries, the burden of their assessed or mandatory contribution to the UN's regular budget is likely to be heavier and in per capita terms sometimes higher than for the wealthiest, because of the rule that each member-state has to pay at least 0.01 per cent of the regular budget and no member has to pay more than 25 per cent. (See Table 5–1.)

It is wholly appropriate for the General Assembly to exercise the budgetary authority envisaged by the Charter. Certainly it would be salutary for the process of revitalizing the General Assembly if the authority to approve the budget of the organization and apportion contributions were exercised more genuinely by the collective membership. Industrial countries have persuaded the Assembly that these decisions must be taken by consensus. That would be a sound procedure, but it is unbalanced because of the de facto

TABLE 5–1

**Contributions to the UN Regular Budget
by Some Member-States**

Member-state	Assessed Percentage of UN Regular Budget	UN Contribution as a Percentage of National Income
Sao Tome and Principe	0.01	0.2511
Maldives	0.01	0.1626
Saint Kitts and Nevis	0.01	0.1566
Netherlands	1.50	0.0104
Austria	0.75	0.0103
Sweden	1.11	0.0103
Poland	0.47	0.0077
United States	25.00	0.0076
Bangladesh	0.01	0.0007

Source: Compiled from background material prepared for the UN Committee on Contributions.

threat of a rich-country veto. The General Assembly's membership must protect its rightful authority to approve the budget and allocate contributions to it.

STREAMLINING PROCEDURES

The efforts to revitalize the work of the General Assembly go back a long way. In recent years, the Assembly has begun to come to grips with a wide range of procedural and administrative matters that bear on its effectiveness. In 1990, it approved the conclusions of the Special Committee on the Charter of the UN and on the Strengthening of the Role of the Organization concerning the rationalization of UN procedures. The following year, the Assembly adopted a resolution on the functions and responsibilities of the President of the Assembly. These are encouraging signs of revitalization.

We believe that more use can be made of the President of the General Assembly in the UN system. It is a post of high status that rotates among all regions and that can be made more functional. What is required is a willingness to enhance the place of the General Assembly as a 'principal organ'. The President can be the link through which one element of enhancement takes place—a link to the Security Council through briefings and consultation, to the Secretary-General on the basis of a more fully developed liaison, and to member-states through visits that help bring the UN to the peoples of the world. In the overburdened UN system, the office of President of the Assembly should be creatively enlisted in the cause of global governance.

Much work is under way to advance the process of streamlining and modernizing the procedures of the Assembly itself and of its committees. There is room for reducing and rationalizing the General Assembly's agenda, which in recent years has grown too big to be dealt with adequately; for limiting the number and frequency of reports requested of the Secretary-General; and for merging and restructuring the main committees of the General Assembly. A start was made in 1993 at the forty-seventh session with a resolution to reduce the number of committees from seven to six. We suggest a further step in this direction. Other revitalization proposals, which focus on arrangements for in-depth Assembly discussion of reports from the Security Council and on guidelines for rationalizing the agendas of the Assembly and its main committees, have been taken up in the Working Group set up by the Assembly's President in November 1993.

A NEW CULTURE OF DIALOGUE	The world needs to take more advantage of the presence of its political leaders in New York at the time of the General Debate or on other special occasions. The UN needs to cultivate intellectual interaction among leaders. At present, they limit themselves to talking at each other through formal speeches or with each other mainly on a one-to-one basis. The opportunity for collective thinking does not exist.

An Assembly of 184 is not the most suitable for such activity, but the answer is not to avoid it altogether. At the forty-eighth session, plenary meetings were set aside to consider the specific question of narcotic drugs. A conscious effort should be made to move further in this direction. One approach could be a meeting of the General Assembly in the first half of the year structured to promote collective interaction. An experiment could be made with a selective forum, including representatives from relevant regional groups and set up as a subsidiary organ of the General Assembly, to consider key policy questions on the Assembly's agenda. Issues such as refugees, food security, water scarcity, or drug abuse would all benefit from such dialogue without waiting for an international conference staged on a grandiose scale.

The General Assembly should not allow the Security Council to altogether pre-empt the discussion of peace and security matters. The Assembly itself can make important contributions in the area of conflict resolution. The General Assembly Special Committee on Peacekeeping Operations already exists, and has gained in stature in recent times. It could be used to put forward specific proposals on peace operations.

The Assembly can suggest peace operations that do not require a military component. One example is the UNTEA Operation in West Guinea (West Irian), on temporary administration and the transfer of power from the Netherlands to Indonesia (decided in 1962). Humanitarian action has assumed a critical importance in recent UN peace operations, as in Rwanda, Somalia, Croatia, and Bosnia. Such action falls within the jurisdiction of the General Assembly, and there is no reason why it should not make proposals in this field. A more controversial but also available device is the Uniting for Peace Resolution of 1950 mentioned earlier, under which the General Assembly can decide on a peace operation when the Security Council is deadlocked. This was invoked in November 1956 in setting up the United Nations Emergency Force for deployment in Egypt.

We are pleased that these and related matters have been discussed by the informal Working Group of the General Assembly on the Secretary-General's report *An Agenda for Peace*. In the global neighbourhood, the world has to develop the capacity and habit of dialogue at all levels—and not merely among those with kindred political or economic philosophies or those from the same region, but across the board.

REVITALIZING THE ASSEMBLY

High among the changes that should mark the fiftieth anniversary of the UN is the revitalization of the General Assembly as a universal forum of the world's states. Even with a reformed Security Council and a new Economic Security Council, many member-states with a capacity to contribute significantly to the policies and programmes of the UN and to global governance will have to stay on the sidelines.

A General Assembly that occupies more of the stage and reorders its work to make it more focused and result-oriented will allow these countries a meaningful role in world governance through their work in the Assembly. What is needed at every level in the UN—the Secretary-General's Office, the Security Council, the specialized agencies, and all the organs of the system—is a recognition that it is in the interest of the system as a whole to have a more vigorous and effective General Assembly. It can and should play a vital legitimating role in the UN consonant with the universality of its membership. In the years ahead, the General Assembly must be seen to be a 'principal organ' of the United Nations system, fulfilling the promise of the Charter.

Trusteeship of the Global Commons

The global commons should be subject to trusteeship
exercised by a body acting on behalf of all nations.

The Trusteeship Council, one of the UN's six principal organs, played an important role in the post-war
process of decolonization, overseeing the progress of
trust territories to self-government or independence.
It has now completed its work; Palau in the South Pacific—the last such territory—had its trust status ter-
minated in 1994 when it became a self-governing
territory in free association with the United States.

Meanwhile, a new need has emerged for trusteeship to be exercised over the global commons in the
collective interest of humanity, including future generations. The global commons include the atmosphere,
outer space, the oceans beyond national jurisdiction,
and the related environment and life-support systems
that contribute to the support of human life. The new
global trusteeship also needs to encompass the responsibilities that each generation must accept towards
future generations.

These are areas of vital interest to all nations. Prudent and equitable management of the global commons, including prevention of overuse of such
resources as fish, is crucial to the future well-being and
progress, perhaps even the survival, of humanity. The
management of the commons, including development
and use of their resources, as well as the articulation of
the rights and responsibilities of states and other entities in respect of the commons, needs to be pursued
through international co-operation.

The global commons should be subject to trusteeship exercised by a body acting on behalf of all nations.
The nature of the responsibilities involved makes it appropriate that this body be a principal organ of the United

Nations. We propose, therefore, that the Trusteeship Council, now free of its original responsibilities, be given the mandate of exercising trusteeship over the global commons.

We envisage the Trusteeship Council becoming the chief forum on global environmental and related matters. Its functions would include the administration of environmental treaties in such fields as climate change, biodiversity, outer space, and the Law of the Sea. It would refer, as appropriate, any economic or security issues arising from these matters to the Economic Security Council or the Security Council. Later in this chapter we suggest that the Commission on Sustainable Development (CSD), which now reports to ECOSOC, report to the proposed Economic Security Council. We would expect this new group to refer matters related to the global commons or other appropriate issues to the new Trusteeship Council.

The new role proposed for the Trusteeship Council would be fully in keeping with the important responsibilities assigned to it when it was established as a principal organ of the United Nations, with its own chamber at the UN in New York. The change in its role will require Chapters XII and XIII of the UN Charter to be revised. The new Council could be composed, as the Trusteeship Council was, of representatives of a number of member-states. Previously, the number was related to the number of territories in trusteeship and was therefore not fixed. The new Council should have a fixed number. We suggest that the General Assembly determine the number and the criteria for selection.

The functions of the Council in this new role are such that it would benefit from contributions from civil society organizations. Governments, in considering the reconstitution of the Trusteeship Council, should examine how best this could be secured. The Charter provided that 'each member of the Trusteeship Council shall designate one specially qualified person to represent it'. A similar provision would leave it open to governments to nominate a public official or someone with the required qualifications from civil society. Additionally, the procedures of the new Council could be drawn up to facilitate contributions by civil society organizations.

Many administrative and other matters will need to be considered if this proposal is to be implemented, but we believe they can all be satisfactorily handled. The most important step to be taken is the conceptual one that the time has come to acknowledge that the security of the planet is a universal need to which the UN system must cater.

GLOBAL CIVIL SOCIETY

There must be a place within the UN system for individuals and organizations to petition for action to redress wrongs that could imperil people's security.

To be an effective instrument of global governance in the modern world, the United Nations must also take greater account of the emergence of global civil society. The crucial role that the new actors play in the management of global affairs requires a reassessment of the relationship between the UN and its family of organizations and the growing world-wide array of organized non-state activity.

The desire of people to be involved in the management of their affairs, the need to be active in areas where government is unable or unwilling to act, and the development of new communication technologies that convey information broadly and help people interact across national borders are encouraging what some have called a global associational revolution. This is fuelled by the realization that so many of the issues requiring attention are global in scope.

The idea that people have common interests irrespective of their national or other identities and that they are coming together in an organized way across borders to address these is of increasing relevance to global governance.

NON-
GOVERNMENTAL
ORGANIZATIONS

Global civil society is best expressed in the global non-governmental movement. As a group, non-governmental organizations (NGOs) are diverse and multi-faceted. Their perspectives and operations may be local, national, regional, or global. Some are issue-oriented or task-oriented; others are driven by ideology. Some have a broad public-interest perspective; others have a more private, narrow focus. They range from small, poorly funded, grassroots entities to large, well-supported, professionally staffed bodies. Some operate individually; others have formed networks to share information and tasks and to enhance their impact.

The Commission met representatives of many parts of the NGO community. We believe their wider involvement can benefit global governance. NGOs, national or international, are not without imperfections. None the less, in their wide variety they bring expertise, commitment, and grassroots perceptions that should be mobilized in the interests of better governance.

Over the years, NGOs have provided vital assistance to the UN in the conduct of its work, particularly in social, economic, and humanitarian areas. They often provide independent monitoring, early-warning, and information-gathering services that can be especially useful in preventive diplomacy. They can serve as unofficial or alternative channels of communication, and can help establish relationships that create the trust necessary to bridge political gaps. More and more, NGOs are helping to set public policy agendas—identifying and defining critical issues, and providing policy makers with advice and assistance. It is this movement beyond advocacy and the provision of services towards broader participation in the public policy realm that has such significance for governance.

A major challenge for the international community is to create the public-private partnerships that enable and encourage non-state actors to offer their contributions to effective global governance. Incorporating a multitude of diverse partners into the management of common affairs will be an exceedingly complex affair. Existing institutional variety suggests that a mix of processes and procedures will be required. Systems for collecting information and sharing intelligence, for debating options, for performing specific tasks, and for making and implementing decisions will have to be customized according to the issue as well as the interests and skills of the people and institutions concerned.

Another, even more clearly identifiable sector with a role in global governance is global business. In Chapter One, we noted the enlarged scale and much more international scope of private enterprise, with some of the larger transnational firms dwarfing the majority of national economies. There is today much wider acceptance of private enterprise and of the benefits of a competitive market system. There remains a need, none the less, to avoid excessive concentration of economic power in private hands, and to have the state protect the public through antitrust or competition policies.

THE GLOBAL BUSINESS SECTOR

Business must be encouraged to act responsibly in the global neighbourhood and contribute to its governance. There are signs that this community is beginning to respond to the opportunities to exercise such responsibility. Some of the largest transnational corporations are in the forefront of 'futures' research, mapping out long-range global scenarios and assessing their implications for corporate responsibility. The work carried out in preparation for the 1992 Earth Summit by the Business Council on Sustainable Development—including *Changing Course,* which it produced as the business community's contribution to the Summit—is illustrative of this new role. More routinely, many firms have long worked with governments, international organizations, and NGOs in the management of trading regimes based on primary commodities such as coffee, rubber, or sugar.

The international community needs to enlist the support of transnational business in global governance and to encourage best practices, acknowledging the role the private sector can play in meeting the needs of the global neighbourhood. Wider acceptance of these responsibilities is likely if the business sector is drawn in to participate in the processes of governance.

PROVIDING SPACE

Some way needs to be found, therefore, to provide more space in global governance for people and their organizations—for civil society as distinct from governments. Several measures have been taken in recent decades in recognition of this. Many government delegations to the General Assembly, for example, include back-bench members of the legislature, some from opposition parties. Some include NGO representatives. The latter was particularly true of delegations to the Earth Summit in Rio de Janeiro and the Population Conference in Cairo.

A welcome feature of the Rio Summit was the provision made for the involvement of the NGO community in the preparatory meetings to the Summit itself. There was a conscious opening up of the process so that the consultations were not restricted to governments.

In the interlinked global conferences that have followed the Rio meeting, NGOs continued to have a strong impact on both the preparatory processes and the conferences. The influence of NGOs, particularly women's groups, in shaping the final text of the conference was a noteworthy feature of the International Conference on Population and Development in Cairo.

That both governments and the UN increasingly recognize the contribution that NGOs can make in developing policies is a positive step. It would be logical to look for opportunities to extend collaboration so that NGOs able to help put policies into effect are enlisted as partners in the implementation stage as well.

There is still some resistance in the UN to the non-governmental sector. This is hardly surprising given the nature of the Charter and of the United Nations as an intergovernmental organization. The more this attitudinal barrier is crossed, however, the easier it will be to discern how non-governmental participation can be promoted to the greater good of the world community. A start has been made. The role of NGOs in the work of the Commission on Human Rights and in other fora, especially with issues concerning the environment, the rights of women, and population, has grown significantly in recent years. We have explored institutional arrangements that could further serve this purpose.

One suggestion widely canvassed is to establish 'an assembly of the people' as a deliberative body to complement the General Assembly, which is representative of governments. What is generally proposed is the initial setting up of an assembly of parliamentarians, consisting of representatives elected by existing national legislatures from among their members, and the subsequent establishment of a world assembly through direct election by the people. It has also been suggested that the assembly of parliamentarians could function as a constituent assembly for the development of a directly elected assembly of people. We encourage further debate about these proposals.

A PEOPLE'S ASSEMBLY?

When the time comes, we believe that starting with an assembly of parliamentarians as a constituent assembly for a more popular body is the right approach. But care would need to be taken to ensure that the assembly of parliamentarians is the starting point of a journey and does not become the terminal station.

An assembly of parliamentarians is not the answer to the need for involving new actors in global governance. What it will provide alongside the General Assembly is an opportunity for global dialogue among parliamentarians. Such organizations as the Inter-Parliamentary Union and Parliamentarians for Global Action already serve that purpose well, and they are among the organizations whose closer association in the processes of governance is desirable.

Whatever the merits of these ideas, the world should not move in this direction before the General Assembly has developed a revitalized role for itself. An assembly of parliamentarians or people should not become a substitute for such revitalization. But deferring action on a parliament of people requires, we believe, that action be taken to add to the area within the UN system where voices other than those of governments can be heard.

| A FORUM OF CIVIL SOCIETY | Our first proposal is that, pending the evolution of a forum in the nature of a parliamentary or people's assembly within the UN system, a start should be made by convening an annual Forum of Civil Society. This should consist of representatives of organizations accredited to the General Assembly as Civil Society Organizations—a new and expanded category of accredited organizations recommended later in this chapter when ECOSOC is discussed. |

We attach much importance to this proposal, and we believe civil society itself must be involved in consultations to develop it further. Consideration should be given in these consultations to the value of organizing regional forums to enable a wider number of organizations to provide an input to the global forum at the UN. A forum of 300–600 organs of global civil society would be desirable and practicable. How they are identified is a matter that civil society itself should canvass. How the Forum functions within the UN system is a matter for agreement with the UN, particularly the General Assembly.

Our consultations with representatives of international civil society brought home the need both for a Forum of Civil Society and for civil society itself to have a substantive role in determining the character and functions of the Forum. Regional consultations will be a necessary feature of that process.

It would be both functionally and symbolically desirable for the Forum to meet in the Plenary Hall of the General Assembly in the run-up to the Assembly's annual session. Although the Forum must have the right to construct its own agenda, it might wish to consider items on the forthcoming session's agenda. These arrangements would need to be agreed with the Assembly, and we suggest that the President of the Assembly convene a Working Group of organizations of international civil society and members of the Assembly to develop the proposal. We see no need to amend the Charter to bring this Forum into being.

The Forum would offer international civil society direct access to the UN system and provide an entry point for its views into the deliberations of the UN. It could not take decisions for the Assembly, but it can help the Assembly to decide—by informing its discussions and influencing its conclusions. For the Assembly to begin its annual session each September with the benefit of the considered views of the Forum would be a qualitative change in the underpinnings of global governance. The Forum process will also strengthen the capacity of civil society to influence the governments of member-states of the UN on issues on the Assembly's agenda—and those off it.

As such, the Forum represents a major step forward. We see its role as quite different from that of the present annual conference of NGOs organized by the UN Department of Public Information, as it is intended to provide civil society across a wide spectrum an opportunity to influence the intergovernmental debate in the General Assembly. And, of course, it is not a substitute for existing partnerships between international institutions and civil society or for enlarging interaction between them.

A RIGHT
OF PETITION

In one critical area there is a clear need to enlarge the capacity of civil society to secure UN action: threats to the security of people. In Chapter Three, we recommended Charter recognition of the right of the international community to respond to grave threats to the security of people, notwithstanding their essentially internal character. The Security Council will be able to exercise its power in the specific condition of threats to the security of people, but we are less than confident of the consistency with which governments will be prepared to move against other governments in these domestic situations—certainly in advance of a catastrophe dramatized by the media on the proportions of Somalia or Rwanda.

The time has come to provide some direct means for civil society to get the international community to consider the need to act in such cases, and to do so at an earlier stage. We propose that this be made possible through a new 'Right of Petition' available to international civil society.

We recall the productive role played by the Special Committee on the Implementation of the Declaration on Decolonization—known as the Committee of 24—established by the General Assembly in 1961.

Although its mandate was narrow, the Committee, along with its Subcommittee on Small Territories, Petitions, Information and Assistance, provided an opportunity for causes to be aired and grievances voiced, and ultimately for action to be taken to advance decolonization.

Although the process of decolonization is virtually over, there are still causes that need to be aired, grievances to be addressed, and action to be taken by the international community to redress wrongs. These are often in areas that engage the attention of non-governmental actors—not just NGOs in the strict sense, although they are a major part of the constituency needing to be heard.

The Commission believes that there must be a place within the UN system for individuals and organizations to petition for action to redress wrongs that could imperil people's security if they remain unaddressed. The Right of Petition and the arrangements by which it can be exercised would have to be strictly circumscribed in scope for the facility to be manageable and effective. This could be achieved through the careful delineation of its parameters and the development of a screening process, with clear criteria to bring forward the most pressing representations.

The UN Commission on Human Rights has begun to meet some of the need for machinery of this nature. The appointment of the High Commissioner for Human Rights will strengthen the Commission's role. But the Right of Petition needs to have both a narrower focus and longer reach. We propose that it deal with complaints about threats to the security of people—the enlarged concept of security discussed in Chapter Three. We have set out there how recourse to the Right of Petition can bring such issues on to the agenda of the Security Council and provide authority for international response, particularly in terms of Chapter VI action devoted to the resolution of conflict—but ultimately, in extreme cases, by enforcement action under Chapter VII.

Our purpose is to enable civil society to activate the UN's potential for preventive diplomacy and the settlement of disputes where the security of people is or could be endangered by conflict situations within states no less than between them.

The Committee of 24 was a committee of government officials. But such individuals are less appropriate for a body to which petitions are addressed. We favour the formation of a Council for Petitions—a high-level panel of five to seven persons, independent of governments and selected in their personal capacity, to entertain petitions and make recommendations on them. It would be appointed by the Secretary-General with the approval of the General Assembly. It should be a Council that holds in trust 'the security of people' and makes recommendations to the Secretary-General, the Security Council, and the General Assembly.

It would be a Council without any power of enforcement. But the eminence of its members and the quality of its proceedings can foster a measure of respect that will give its conclusions considerable moral authority. This new Council could be established either through the creation of a subsidiary organ or through a Charter amendment; we propose the latter, and that the Council be given the specific mandate indicated here. But these are matters for discussion and negotiation. To start, the General Assembly should establish a task force (not limited to representatives of governments) to examine this proposal and recommend how it might be implemented.

More than anything else, we believe that the link we have proposed with the Security Council itself and the Charter amendment to allow UN action following an initial finding by the Council for Petitions would represent a substantial evolution of global governance responsive to the needs of people and the concerns of global civil society.

This proposal, in its newness, is bound to invite scepticism. And some will view it with concern. We believe, however, that global governance must incorporate new voices and provide a practical opportunity to right the massive wrongs that imperil people. If not, the world faces dangers that have severe implications for peace and security, and for the quality of life in the global neighbourhood.

THE ECONOMIC AND SOCIAL SECTORS
The time has come to retire ECOSOC.

Chapter IX of the UN Charter deals with 'International Economic and Social Co-operation'. Member-states pledged themselves to act in co-operation with the organization to promote the specific objectives in the economic and social fields set out in Article 55, namely:

- higher standards of living, full employment, and conditions of economic and social progress and development;
- solutions of international economic, social, health, and related problems, and international cultural and educational co-operation; and
- universal respect for, and observance of, human rights and fundamental freedoms for all without distinction as to race, sex, language, or religion.

Article 55 opens with an acknowledgement of the relevance of 'conditions of stability and well-being' to 'peaceful and friendly relations between nations'. It is clear from this article, as well as from the Preamble to the Charter and the principles and purposes set out in Article 1, that the founders intended the United

> **Mutual Interests**
>
> The extent to which the international system will be made more equitable is essentially a matter for political decision. We are looking for a world based less on power and status, more on justice and contract; less discretionary, more governed by fair and open rules. A start must be made in that direction, and the obvious places to start are those where positive mutual interests in change can be identified. We believe there are numerous such interests. But greater efforts are required to place them at the centre of debate.
>
> *—North-South: A Programme for Survival*
> Report of the Independent Commission
> on International Development Issues

Nations to be the world community's principal instrument in promoting global economic and social progress and achieving 'better standards of life in larger freedom' for all the world's people. The Charter envisaged that the UN, in playing this role, would coordinate the work of intergovernmental organizations in the economic, social, and related fields.

During the 1960s and 1970s, attempts were made to see how far the notions of mutual interests and interdependence could be accommodated by incremental changes to the structure that, while not interfering with the basic design, gave developing countries more opportunities for influencing global decision-making in certain specific areas.

From very early in the 1980s, it became clear that these efforts would not bear fruit. The Cancun Summit of 1981 signalled the beginning of an era in which the major industrial countries became more unyielding in their opposition to notions of broader participation in the management of the world economy. And developing countries that had played a leading role in pressing the Third World's case through the Group of 77 (G77) during the 1970s retreated increasingly during the 1980s into a stance of weary acquiescence.

This was in part because their bargaining power had been weakened by the debt crisis and other negative trends in the world economy. But their attitudes were also influenced by ideological shifts that assigned the primary role in development to market forces rather than to action by the state. An associated change was to move the emphasis away from the negotiation of intergovernmental arrangements and towards policy and institutional reform at home. The tide of international opinion has moved away from the agreements and codes proposed as the nucleus of a New International Economic Order.

The constituency for multilateral technical co-operation through the United Nations also become weaker. For a variety of reasons, larger industrial countries have always hesitated to assign a significant role to the United Nations in technical co-operation— hence the insistence from the very beginning on the financing of the UN Development Programme (UNDP) and other technical assistance programmes through voluntary rather than assessed contributions.

As pointed out in Chapter Four, it is paradoxical that a decline in co-operation for development should be taking place just when the world is becoming increasingly interdependent, a number of multisectoral issues are coming to the fore, new players are emerging in the world economy, and the economic future of some leading countries is uncertain. For these and other reasons more fully set out in Chapter Four, we propose an Economic Security Council (ESC) be established at the apex of the UN system in the economic and social sectors. This does not eliminate, however, the need for other institutional changes in the economic and social fields. Indeed, our proposal for an ESC is premised on the expectation of the process of procedural and administrative reform going forward, including the winding down of some bodies whose rationale has disappeared.

The world should not wait for a crisis or a bout of confrontation before tackling this supplementary task of institutional adaptation and reform. Indeed, had governments implemented fully the provisions of the Charter dealing with economic and social matters, at least some of the present global deficiencies might not have been present.

<table>
<tr><td>REFORMING
UN ECONOMIC
AND SOCIAL
OPERATIONS</td><td>

The operational activities of the United Nations are carried out both by specialized agencies and by programmes and funds. In addition to the four major specialized agencies—the International Labour Organisation (ILO), the World Health Organization (WHO), the Food and Agriculture Organization (FAO), and the United Nations Educational, Scientific and Cultural Organization (UNESCO)—there are a number of more specialised, technical agencies, such as the International Civil Aviation Organisation, the World Meteorological Organization, and the Universal Postal Union (UPU). These were set up separately by governments; each has its own constitution and governing body to determine its policies and programmes. Some preceded the UN; the ILO, for example, was set up in 1919, and the UPU, more than a century ago. The specialized agencies are to a large extent independent of the UN General Assembly and the UN Secretariat.

</td></tr>
</table>

The programmes and funds, however, have been set up by decisions of the General Assembly and form part of the central UN. They include the United Nations Development Programme, the United Nations Children's Fund, the World Food Programme (WFP), and the United Nations Population Fund. The United Nations Environment Programme, the UN Conference on Trade and Development (UNCTAD), and the Office of the UN High Commissioner for Refugees are also in this category.

The UNHCR, which expected to have a three-year life span when it was set up in 1951 to deal with the remaining World War II refugees, has seen the demands on it expand inexorably over the last two decades. It has had to cope with larger and more complex problems of refugees and also of persons displaced within their own country by civil conflicts. Its actual activities often relate to what is done through, for example, WFP and UNICEF, both with strong field operational capacity. The special mandate of the UNHCR is one of its most important assets, providing an identity that may often give it special access. In any humanitarian operation, however, effective co-ordination, in particular in the field, is needed. As pointed out in Chapters Three and Four, this is an area in need of much attention.

The world community can certainly take pride in what the UN has achieved through these various agencies and programmes. Some can lay claim to dramatic or monumental successes, such as the WHO-led eradication of smallpox and UNICEF's programme of mass vaccination to save children's lives. Some UN staff, notably of the UNHCR, UNICEF, and WFP, risk their lives working in the midst of the world's worst conflicts. The technical agencies perform low-profile but absolutely vital functions—for example, in weather forecasting and aviation safety.

There can be no doubt about the crucial value of the activities of the range of UN organizations. Much criticism of the UN often reflects ignorance about the nature, extent, and utility of their services. Nevertheless, there is scope for improvement in terms of both responding to new needs and making present operations more effective and efficient. There have been many proposals for institutional reform, some more carefully thought out than others. We believe that reform today should go beyond institutional tinkering and start at the top of the system. That is where we have focused our attention and why we have proposed an Economic Security Council that would, by offering leadership on economic and social matters, provide guidance for the whole UN system on policy in these fields.

The ESC will not, however, provide operational governance for UN agencies and programmes. That has to be done through the governance mechanisms already in place within the system. Responsibility rests principally with governments, which have decision-making power in the different governing bodies.

To achieve maximum benefits from the UN system as a whole, including the International Monetary Fund, the World Bank, and the World Trade Organization, there is clearly a need for better co-ordination of the work of the various parts. As governments set out the policy of the various agencies through their separate governing bodies, it is governments that are best placed to secure co-ordination. But they are represented through different ministries in the different agencies, and there are few signs that they follow co-ordinated national approaches. While these factors limit what the UN itself can achieve, there is a need for further efforts within the UN system to develop more efficient methods of working in tandem. There have been proposals for enhancing the role of the Secretary-General and for strengthening the Administrative Committee on Co-ordination, perhaps transforming it into an Executive Committee of the UN system. Such proposals need to be further explored.

As a Commission, we have chosen not to give specific advice on interagency co-ordination. We have given our attention to other aspects of reform that we feel are of greater importance, such as the creation of an ESC and the revitalization of the General Assembly. These reforms should be complemented by changes in the programmes and agencies themselves. The specialized agencies should consolidate and enhance their position as recognized centres of authority in their respective fields.

WHO, for example, should develop its position as the global centre of authority for health and social affairs ministers of all countries. Though some of its work is oriented largely towards developing countries, the AIDS pandemic reveals how crucial issues can be of direct concern to all countries. As globalization proceeds, WHO's importance as a reference point for national health administrations on health standards, legislation, statistics, and much else can be expected to grow.

FAO's developmental work has tended to overshadow its role as a centre of authority. The world over, agricultural ministers face such key issues as the revolution in genetic engineering, growing concern about food security and food safety, and the inequitable aspects of international pricing and subsidy systems for food products. FAO has a role to play in promoting international consensus on the best way forward in such matters.

The reforms of UNESCO need to buttress its capacity for high-quality work. The continuing revolution in communications and computer technology, for example, provides an array of issues to be faced, some of which fall within UNESCO's area of responsibility. It should clearly be much further ahead than it is today on these issues. Given the importance of knowledge in the information-based world of today and the potential of UNESCO in this field, it deserves universal support.

ILO is unique in being a tripartite organization, bringing two important sectors of civil society—trade unions and employers' federations—together with governments to address basic labour market issues. With the increasing openness of global markets and greater labour mobility, this organization will only grow in relevance. By providing a forum for discussion and standard-setting, ILO can help reduce social and labour market conflicts.

If the specialized agencies do not develop their character as centres of authority, those roles will increasingly have to be taken over by such institutions as the World Bank, research networks (such as the Consultative Group for International Agricultural Research), and regional organizations. Their contributions are highly desirable. Institutional competition and division of labour may well work for the better. We believe, however, that the specialized agencies have a unique character as global organizations and a part to play in a system of global governance that should be safeguarded.

PROGRAMMES AND FUNDS

Within the UN system, the governance and financing of the cluster of programmes and funds need to be radically improved. Though these were set up by the General Assembly under the Charter, that document provides little guidance on the distribution of powers and responsibilities or on governance and funding arrangements. In fact, the governing bodies of the funds and programmes originally adopted working procedures based on the normative 'parliamentary' function of the UN. As a result, long Council meetings with speeches and resolutions became the annual pattern. In between these gatherings there were few opportunities to address issues of organization or work except in informal, sometimes arbitrary, ways.

Members of the UN have a strong interest in transparent rules. Yet what emerged was a system in which the influence of member-states increasingly became an illusion. More committees and other formal structures with broader representation did not enable them to exercise more influence over operational activities. A more modern and efficient mode of governance is clearly required.

Initiating Reform by the General Assembly: The Nordic UN Project

The most recent and comprehensive study of the economic and social operations of the United Nations is the so-called Nordic UN Project. In 1991, after years of preparation, the four Nordic governments presented the project's proposals for reforming the governance and financing of the UN's activities in development.

The December 1993 decision by the General Assembly to introduce major reforms was a sign that the world community had at last recognized the need to strengthen the UN's economic and social activities. In 1995, the General Assembly will decide how these reforms are to be carried out.

One major reform is to improve the governance of UN programmes and funds. In place of the large, time-consuming, and often ineffectual governing boards, thirty-six-member executive boards that will meet more frequently will be introduced.

All countries need to be involved in giving policy guidance to the executive boards. The Nordic UN Project proposed that an International Development Council should be created to fulfil that parliamentary role.

On financing, the Nordic UN Project proposed that the present voluntary contributions should be complemented by assessed contributions from all countries and negotiated contributions from aid-giving countries. The aim was to achieve greater consistency and fairer burden-sharing. Negotiations on a financing system are now under way, on the basis of a new report by the Secretary-General.

The General Assembly took a first step towards creating improved governance structures in 1993 when it adopted a resolution on the 'restructuring and revitalisation of the UN in the economic, social and related fields'. A process is now under way to institute smaller executive bodies to give continuous guidance and direction to management. These bodies would translate general policy guidance into specific activities in each fund and programme. The new governing bodies would be more oriented to dialogue and decisions than to statements and resolutions. They are expected to make the governance of these programmes and funds more accountable, transparent, and efficient.

Policy-making and operations are two distinct activities. All UN members should share in policy-making but not all need to be constantly present in overseeing implementation. The UN must be able to combine the principles of universality and representativeness in policy-making with accountable, transparent, effective governance at the operational level. To do this, a constituency system for grouping countries should be more widely adopted, so that all countries would have a voice on the executive board through a constituency representative.

In addition to more efficient governance structures, UN operational activities need improved funding systems. The benefits of a reformed UN development system can be fully realized only if financing becomes more orderly and predictable, and if increases in contributions are more equitably shared.

The pattern of financing of various parts of the United Nations does not follow any clear principle. A

GEF: An Emerging Constituency System

The Global Environment Facility (GEF) was set up in 1991 to help finance the incremental costs for developing countries of new environmental investments with global benefits. A joint undertaking of the UN Environment Programme, UNDP, and the World Bank, it is an innovative arrangement that has provided an opportunity to develop new forms of governance. Especially interesting is its constituency system, by which GEF has attempted to combine representativeness with efficiency.

GEF has more than 100 member-states, but the Governing Board has only thirty-two, each representing a constituency. There are sixteen constituencies for developing countries, fourteen for industrial countries, and two for Eastern Europe. The countries in each constituency choose a board member and an alternate. New members join an existing constituency. Documentation is sent to all member-countries. Each constituency determines its own process of consultation and decision-making.

OUR GLOBAL NEIGHBOURHOOD

bewildering variety of special-purpose contributions, trust funds, and other extra-budgetary arrangements have made it difficult for both donors and recipients to identify where priorities are set and decisions made, and thus to guide and control activities.

Funding mechanisms have proliferated, with hundreds of trust funds in the UN and its agencies. There has been a corresponding erosion of accountability and transparency, as these funds are mostly outside the control of the governing bodies. This problem is not limited to the UN: the World Bank has had hundreds of trust funds.

The general trend in the provision of finance for UN programmes and funds has been sturdy growth in the 1970s, decline in the 1980s, and modest growth over the past few years. This description covers important differences between different parts of the system. At present the trend is also for humanitarian and emergency assistance to eat into the funds that might otherwise be available for long-term development.

Many factors have helped shape the present funding arrangements, which have led to unpredictability and instability besides providing inadequate resources. The arrangements have an ad hoc and short-term character. It was not until the mid-1970s that attempts were made to bring a minimum measure of order and commitment into what could only be described as a rudimentary set of financing mechanisms. There has been a lack of consistency between the programme objectives as adopted by governments and their attitude to the provision of resources.

The funding of most UN development programmes also depends on a small group of countries. Ten countries provide around 80 per cent of the contributions to UNDP, for instance. The trend in the 1970s and 1980s towards an increasingly uneven sharing of the burden among donors is untenable in the long run.

A serious drawback of voluntary funding is that it leads to uncertainties about how much resources will be available. Contributions are pledged on a short-term basis; this impedes meaningful planning and administration of technical co-operation programmes that require a more long-term approach.

A new funding system should be designed so as to combine voluntary, short-term funding with negotiated, long-term, burden-shared contributions, linked to the funding needs of approved operational programmes.

The total funding needs, as well as the sharing among donors of funding responsibilities, should be considered in the process of negotiating the content of programmes. The traditional UN way of deciding on programmes without any assurance of funding has led to the situation today in which UNDP is able to carry out only 75 per cent of approved country programmes. The practice of deciding on operational plans without agreeing on how they are financed has to be changed.

Another disruptive effect of the present financing system is that the management of each programme has to spend an inordinate amount of time trying to obtain funds from capitals around the world. Donor countries are continually being pressed for contributions from various parts of the UN system. This has adverse consequences for priority-setting both within programmes and in these capitals.

Furthermore, earmarking of funds has become a common practice. Some see this as a pragmatic way of dealing with deficiencies in the present system. But when earmarking becomes frequent, the whole idea of a common programme whose benefits are equitably apportioned is undermined.

In the United Nations, as in other organizations, members have to strike a balance between their rights and their obligations. In the Commission's view, many members fail to do that in the UN. It has been too easy to ignore the obligations of responsible membership. Such membership requires an integration of programme decisions and funding commitments, fair burden-sharing among a wider range of rich nations, and a longer-term approach in order to make operational activities more stable and secure through assured financing.

Beyond improvements in governance and financing, the need to have today's wide variety of separate programmes and funds, and their high administrative costs, must also be faced. Ways of pooling administrative functions or otherwise making savings on them must be considered. The identities of individual programmes, for example of UNICEF, have undoubted value, but this need not be an obstacle to a more efficient operation. For UNDP, it will be particularly important to enhance its role as the lead development agency within the UN system.

The economic and social activities of the United Nations can be made considerably more efficient and effective. For that to be achieved, there must be clear, comprehensive, and consistent policy guidance from the member-states.

THE ECONOMIC AND SOCIAL COUNCIL: ECOSOC

The Economic and Social Council, established as one of the principal organs of the United Nations, was intended to promote the economic and social purposes set out in Article 55. It was to do so under the authority of the General Assembly and with the aid of the specialized agencies. A great deal of work has been done by these agencies and by the UN programmes and funds. But the UN, and in particular ECOSOC, has fallen far short of its envisaged role of co-ordination and overall direction in the economic and social fields. That is partly because this role is still being contested nearly fifty years after San Francisco—despite the clear intent of the Charter.

ECOSOC, and the Second and Third Committees of the General Assembly, are currently the principal headquarter bodies where deliberations take place on economic and social issues and housekeeping matters. Many countries have expressed concern about the effectiveness of these bodies. Overlapping mandates leading to repetitive debates, lengthy agendas, and voluminous documentation are among the major complaints.

Recent efforts to reform ECOSOC have resulted in some improvements. The introduction of a 'high-level' segment has created a more practical forum for dialogue and co-ordination on economic and social issues. In particular, ECOSOC's 'parliamentary' role of giving policy guidance to the UN's operational work has become more effective. Its theme debates provide a new opportunity to address specific issues at a political level.

The efforts to date have been, however, more like a salvage operation. What is needed is a new vessel better designed and equipped to carry economic and social issues towards practical goals. The time has come to retire ECOSOC. With a revitalized General Assembly, a reformed Security Council, and a new Economic Security Council, the case for a fifty-four-member residual forum for economic and social issues becomes questionable. The reforms being attempted should improve ECOSOC's performance; but the Economic Security Council is altogether more promising machinery for addressing major economic and social issues.

With the Economic Security Council in place, a retained ECOSOC would need to make its membership universal and therefore co-incident with the Committees of the General Assembly. But what is needed, we believe, is to wind up ECOSOC, to merge the Second and Third Committees (which deal, respectively, with economic and financial issues and with social, humanitarian, and cultural questions), and to programme the dialogue and negotiation schedules of all three within the newly merged Committee. This will involve a Charter amendment of Chapters IX and X.

Selected United Nations Agencies and Programmes

UN Specialized Agencies

FAO	Food and Agriculture Organization
ICAO	International Civil Aviation Organization
ILO	International Labour Organization
IMO	International Maritime Organization
ITU	International Telecommunications Union
UNESCO	United Nations Educational, Scientific, and Cultural Organization
UNIDO	United Nations Industrial Development Organization
UPU	Universal Postal Union
WIPO	World Intellectual Property Organization
WHO	World Health Organization
WMO	World Meteorological Organization

UN Programmes and Organs

IAEA	International Atomic Energy Authority
INSTRAW	International Research and Training Institute for the Advancement of Women
UNCHS	United Nations Centre for Human Settlements (HABITAT)
UNCTAD	United Nations Conference on Trade and Development
UNDP	United Nations Development Programme
UNEP	United Nations Environment Programme
UNFPA	United Nations Population Fund
UNHCR	Office of the United Nations High Commissioner for Refugees
UNICEF	United Nations Children's Fund

Bretton Woods Institutions

IBRD	International Bank for Reconstruction and Development (World Bank, which includes IDA, the International Development Association, and the IFC, the International Finance Corporation)
IMF	International Monetary Fund

Fifty years is long enough to know what works and what does not work within any system. ECOSOC has not worked. Whatever the justification for it in 1945, that experience of non-performance must weigh with the world community. For us, the establishment of the ESC tips the scale decisively in favour of the restructuring we have proposed.

The winding up of ECOSOC will raise a number of ancillary questions. One is the relationship with other bodies that now report to ECOSOC—all too often to little or no effect. The Committee for Development Planning, for example, has long been a victim of ECOSOC's habit of receiving reports but ignoring the issues they raise. More significant now is the require-ment for the Commission on Sustainable Development to report to the General Assembly through ECOSOC. We believe that the CSD should report to the Eco-nomic Security Council—a procedure that will move its reports to an appreciably higher level of consider-ation. Major recommendations of other bodies now reporting to ECOSOC should also go to the ESC. Recommendations below that level of importance or immediacy can go to the merged Second and Third Committee of the General Assembly.

Other matters related to winding up ECOSOC need to be addressed. ECOSOC is the body to which NGOs are currently accredited—some 980 in mid-1994. Such accreditation should instead be to the Gen-eral Assembly itself. We suggest that all existing accreditations be transferred—along with an improved process for continuing review of accreditations—and new ones processed in a General Assembly context.

For this purpose we propose a stronger emphasis on 'civil society' organizations—including, of course, today's NGOs but looking to an even wider field, such as private-sector organizations and citizens' move-ments. As noted earlier, such accredited organizations should be involved in a Forum of Civil Society in advance of each annual General Assembly session.

To a larger degree than was the case with ECOSOC, the Economic Security Council can become both a long-term policy forum and an early warning instrument. If discussions on pressing global economic and social issues were carefully prepared for the Economic Security Council, the international community would have a unique opportunity to address major questions of socio-economic policy, and to strive to achieve a meeting of minds on them. The follow-up of the debate could then be entrusted to the relevant agencies.

By such means, governments can try once again to arrange for a genuine dialogue on development that avoids the mere recital of prepared positions, and that tries to reach conclusions of practical value to all parties. Among other things, this will require exceptional effort and leadership by the Secretariat. Still, a subsidiary body of the Economic Security Council would need to deal more frequently with other specific concerns of member-states, and to monitor the implementation of decisions taken in other UN forums concerned with economic and social questions.

UNCTAD AND UNIDO: CHANGED REALITIES

In the roughly thirty years of its existence, the UN Conference on Trade and Development has served the developing countries in many ways. It has been, first of all, a deliberative forum where special attention was given to their trade and development problems, and where issues were highlighted that would later claim the attention of the international community (such as the special problems of the least developed countries, technology transfer, and international trade in services).

It was also an organ within which issues could be moved from the deliberative to the prenegotiating and negotiating stages. Even where the debate on particular issues did not lead to negotiations within UNCTAD itself, discussions there gave visibility to them, and built up pressure for action elsewhere.

UNCTAD provided significant support to efforts by developing countries to expand trade and economic co-operation among themselves at the subregional, regional, and interregional levels. Among the most recent efforts in that regard were the East and Southern African Preferential Trading Area and the General System of Preferences among Developing Countries. It was also a useful source of technical assistance; particularly well known are its activities in shipping and trade documentation. And, finally, through its group system of work, UNCTAD has supported the development of the Group of 77, which has served as a mechanism for uniting developing countries in their effort to secure greater benefits from the international economic and financial system.

Today, it is no longer necessary for all these functions to be performed in a single specialized institution. None of these functions has the significance it had in the 1960s. As far as deliberation on major development issues is concerned, the UN as a whole can be more effective if its deliberative work is centred in a single forum rather than fragmented among several organs. An Economic Security Council supported by an appropriate Secretariat has a clear advantage over UNCTAD, since it can deal more conveniently with multifaceted issues without fighting with other bodies about questions of competence.

In the field of trade itself, all member-governments have agreed to the creation of the WTO, which will have much wider and more explicit deliberative functions than GATT. Except for the least developed and the very smallest countries, many of which found membership and participation in GATT to be a somewhat expensive undertaking, it would be difficult for developing countries to claim convincingly that they need to retain UNCTAD as a supplementary forum for engaging industrial countries in dialogue on trade issues.

With respect to support for economic co-operation and integration efforts among developing countries, the world-wide trend among them now is to focus on general trade liberalization rather than exclusive trade among themselves. Perhaps more attention will be paid to co-operation and integration on a sectoral or functional basis, where agencies other than UNCTAD have a strong advantage.

In relation to technical assistance, all but the least developed and the smallest are now better able to provide technical services for themselves. In the particular case of shipping, the International Maritime Organisation has accumulated expertise and experience in practically all the areas covered by UNCTAD. Individual developing countries are also able to assist others on a bilateral basis; in shipping and ports, for example, South Korea, Singapore, and Hong Kong are very well equipped to train nationals from other developing countries. In a sense, UNCTAD has, by its very success in some countries, 'worked itself out of a job' in others.

Events have also affected UNCTAD's role in the efforts of developing countries to improve their international economic position. Their varied experiences in achieving economic progress and the general change in the approach to development have altered perceptions of their relations with the rest of the world. Furthermore, while developing countries now have the Group of 15, in addition to the Group of 77, to advance their interests, their representative bodies have less need for UNCTAD's technical support than in the G77's fledgeling days.

Somewhat similar considerations apply in the case of the UN Industrial Development Organization (UNIDO), which was set up when industrialization was just beginning in most developing countries.

Governments were expected to be the prime movers in accelerating industrial development at a time when most of them lacked the technical and managerial capacities to perform that task. An honest broker was therefore needed to mediate between transnational corporations and developing-country governments, to help the latter get the best possible deal from foreign investors in the industrial sector.

By now, however, all but the least developed and smallest have established a wide range of industries, accumulating considerable experience both in industrial promotion and negotiation with TNCs. A number of other agencies have also emerged as sources of technical assistance in those fields. Overall, industrial development is no longer viewed as a unique solution to the economic development of developing countries.

If a case can be made for the retention of UNCTAD and UNIDO in some form, it will have to rest on the need to provide substantial support to the least developed and smallest countries in trade and industrial production. Such support would involve technical assistance in analytical work and the development of information systems for trade negotiations and their follow-up; trade efficiency; development and trade of tradable services; and industrial promotion. Provision of this does not, however, need such substantial institutions as UNCTAD and UNIDO. Arrangements could be made to provide it through UNDP, with contributions from the World Bank group and the International Trade Centre as appropriate.

The winding up of these two organizations will not be without anguish, for all organizations develop constituencies that support them even after their reason for existing has disappeared. It is important, however, for the UN system to demonstrate a capacity not merely to change its way of doing things within ever-widening institutional structures, but from time to time to shut down institutions that can no longer be justified. We believe that this is the case with UNCTAD and UNIDO now. We favour their closure, but recommend that as a first step an in-depth review be undertaken of the proposal so that all opinions can be canvassed and a decision made in the interests of the countries concerned and the credibility of the UN system.

Our views on the future of UNCTAD and UNIDO have been developed in the broader context of our ideas on the improvement of global economic governance to make it more effective and more equitable. Our suggestions on the composition of the Economic Security Council are designed to make the ESC more responsive to the interests of developing countries than existing arrangements for global economic governance are. We have also suggested changes in the distribution of votes within the Bretton Woods institutions to give developing countries a bigger voice in their decision-making bodies. The Commission believes that global interests will be well served by the package of reforms proposed here, within which those relating to UNCTAD and UNIDO—and to ECOSOC—are only one element.

We emphasize, therefore, that these proposals for the winding up of institutions in the context of the new world that is emerging are linked to our overall proposals for reform of the world economic system and, specifically, to the establishment of the Economic Security Council. There needs to be balance in the world system, and this will not be achieved by preserving economic decision-making in the hands of a small directorate while dismantling institutions established initially to redress that imbalance. The time has come for a much more even-handed process of reform along the lines of our integrated proposals. In this matter, it will not be possible, either politically or in practical terms, to make progress in an unbalanced way.

Since 1975—the International Year of Women—the international community, under the initiative of the UN, has done extraordinary work to put women on the political agenda at the global level. The UN Conferences on Women in Mexico in 1975, in Copenhagen in 1980, and in Nairobi in 1985 helped build consensus on a number of measures: operational strategies in favour of women; international conventions to protect women's rights and improve their status; international, regional, and national institutions and mechanisms to sensitize public opinion and to undertake the execution, follow-up, and evaluation of women's programmes.

These efforts have enlarged recognition of the need for women to participate more fully and meaningfully in decisions that affect the life of the global community. This has facilitated a greater participation by women's organizations in the debates on such matters as the environment, population, peace, and human rights.

The UN Conference on Women in Beijing in 1995, on the twentieth anniversary of the Mexico conference, provides an opportunity to assess progress and to improve the mechanisms for advancing the interests of women. The aim must be to make these interests an integral part of the totality of the concerns of the international community, and to give them institutional and political legitimacy.

In the field of employment, the United Nations system must, through its own staffing policies, set high standards rather than simply match what is achieved in member-countries. The Secretary-General has expressed his commitment to the goals set by the General Assembly, and we call for intensified efforts to achieve further increases in the proportion of women in both professional and senior positions. We also suggest that the functions of the United Nations Ombudsman should include monitoring of recruitment and promotion within the UN system to ensure gender equity.

We propose the appointment of a Senior Adviser on Women's Issues in the office of the Secretary-General to be responsible for proposing ways to integrate gender into General Assembly debates, monitoring the application of General Assembly decisions, stimulating political and diplomatic thinking towards advancing the cause of women, representing the Secretary-General on women's issues, and, above all, being the principal advocate of the interests of women within the UN system.

We also propose the creation of similar positions within the executive cabinet of each of the specialized agencies and institutions of the United Nations. These senior advisers would co-ordinate all policies and activities for women in their agencies, using a network of staff to monitor gender issues in each division of the organization. They would oversee programmes for women to ensure that women are involved at all stages of their conceptualization, planning, and operation in every agency.

We cannot emphasize too strongly, however, that the potential of efforts to improve the quality of life for all people depends on political will at the national level. If that will is absent or only lip-service is paid to the need for change, if women are not more prominent politically in all countries, if a new generation of men and women do not together insist within their communities on an end to gender discrimination, these attempts to put women at the centre of global governance will elude human society and thus impoverish it.

REGIONALISM

The UN must prepare for a time when regionalism becomes more ascendant world-wide, and even help the process along.

Between the world of nation-states and the global community of people lie the various manifestations of regionalism. Organizations for regional co-operation of varying capacity and effectiveness now cover most parts of the world, and regional collaboration remains a strong aspiration world-wide.

The spectacular success of regionalism in Europe and more recently in North and South America is inspiration to all who strive towards a world beyond frontiers. Progressing from a customs union through a single market towards monetary and political union, the European Union (EU) has continuously extended its areas of integration, developing ever stronger supranational institutions. It has not only fostered co-operation between states, but has also contributed to stability within states, thus being a force for conflict prevention. The EU continues to be a strong pole of attraction to countries outside it and has become a decisive factor in the unification of the European continent, though it may not be the appropriate model for all regions.

The spread of open regional economic groupings is a comparatively recent trend. It is, however, increasingly recognized that they could help overcome historic rivalries and tensions, foster democratic processes, enhance the collective value of small and fragmented markets in the creation of trade and the expansion of exports, help develop shared infrastructure, and tackle common environmental and social problems. They can also facilitate the often difficult integration of countries in the world economy.

The potential of regional co-operation has in many ways been insufficiently exploited in most parts of the world. Some areas have several overlapping regional initiatives, while political tensions and incompatibilities have blocked the formation or extension of these groups in others. Many existing regional organizations have been inefficient even in terms of the limited purposes for which they were set up.

Experience has borne out that strengthening regional integration takes time and demands strong political commitment and an adequate legal and institutional framework. It relies heavily on favourable political circumstances, which, however, are often spurred by interacting internal and external pressures. There is no single model. The diversity of arrangements—such as the EU, the Association of South-East Asian Nations, the North American Free Trade Agreement, MERCOSUR, and other Latin American agreements—shows that these mechanisms can be attuned to the specific needs and features of regions, reflecting their political sensitivities, cultural traditions, and models of society.

New opportunities for regional co-operation should now, for instance, emerge in Southern Africa and in the Middle East, where joint management of such scarce resources as water seems particularly suitable as an initial step in building a framework of co-operation.

REGIONALISM AND GLOBAL GOVERNANCE

The development of regionalism cannot be isolated from global institutions. Affecting each other in many ways, these groups should be linked in a dynamic process of interaction. Regional arrangements have the potential to complement and contribute to global governance, but may not produce a positive outcome automatically. On the one hand, the organizations are spread unevenly and in different gradations across the world. This may raise fears of exclusion, and lead to imbalances between and within regions. On the other hand, as they grow stronger, regional organizations could turn into conflicting blocs obstructing global governance. It is our view, however, that regionalism has the capacity to contribute to building a more harmonious and prosperous world.

To make better use of the actual and potential force of regionalism while avoiding the possible dangers, a system of global governance must encourage, as well as accommodate in its institutional structure, expressions of regionalism that are compatible with the purpose and principles of the UN Charter. The challenge is to use both global and regional arrangements in a mutually supportive way. Decentralization, delegation, and co-operation with regional bodies can lighten the burden of global organizations, while generating a deeper sense of participation in a common effort.

Although regional groupings are now too uneven in their capacities to form balanced pillars of global governance, associating them with the work of global institutions would help prepare them for such roles. This is a long-term process, but certain institutional changes can help it. In Chapter Three, we noted how the Secretary-General could enlarge the involvement of regional bodies in security-related activities under Chapter VIII of the UN Charter. There is also a need to encourage and support autonomous efforts to build regional co-operation efforts in areas where regionalism has made little headway, and to facilitate participation by regional organizations in global institutions.

These organizations should be drawn into multilateral frameworks of co-operation. Global institutions, in particular the UN, should review their procedures to offer increasing participation to regional bodies. This would create an incentive for them to strengthen their internal cohesion, and also commit them to global frameworks. A dynamic process would thus be set in motion that could help make governance more efficient and representative. The voice of countries with little influence would be heard through organizations speaking with the aggregate weight of a group representing common regional interests. Eventually, this could lead to the representation of the countries of a region, through a single regional seat, in restricted bodies such as the Security Council or the proposed Economic Security Council.

The UN must therefore prepare itself for a time when regionalism becomes more ascendant world-wide, and even help the process along. It is committed to doing so; the Secretary-General has called repeatedly for a strengthening of regionalism in global governance, in development no less than in peace and security.

Some recent developments, while having no immediate impact on regionalism, may have a bearing on efforts to promote regional collaboration in future. A proposal has been made to have only one UN system office in any developing country, headed by a UN Co-ordinator appointed by the Secretary-General, without personal responsibility for the management of any one programme.

Along these lines, an interesting experiment is under way in the newly independent states of Eastern Europe where 'UN interim offices' have been established to better organize various activities in these countries. They conduct normal development and public information functions and also provide resources for preventive diplomacy and the peaceful settlement of disputes. This development holds much potential, and we encourage sympathetic consideration of it when the Secretary-General reports on the experiment in due course. A movement in this direction is bound to have an impact on the future of UN regional activities.

We wish to make a special point about the UN Regional Commissions: the Economic Commission for Europe (ECE), the Economic Commission for Latin America and the Caribbean (ECLAC), the Economic and Social Commission for Asia and the Pacific (ESCAP), the Economic Commission for West Asia (ECWA), and the Economic Commission for Africa (ECA). These were meant to decentralize the work of the UN so as to bring it closer to the diversity of development experience and prospects in different parts of the world. Their programmes and activities, sometimes in conjunction with UN specialized agencies, have varied greatly, but have for the most part focused on providing authoritative analyses of the economic and social problems of countries and regions, especially where member-countries lacked the capacity to do so themselves.

The Commissions, notably ECE and ECLAC, have played a valuable pioneering role in these respects, producing analytical documentation of high quality that has been of value to governments. But they have also faced constraints, such as the large and disparate nature of a region (ESCAP), intraregional political problems (ECWA), and shortages of human and financial resources (ECA). Meanwhile, many governments have now strengthened their capacities for economic analysis, planning, and policy design, and the World Bank and regional development banks also provide elaborate analytical services. Furthermore, partly because of the Commissions' influence on governmental thinking, many regional and subregional organizations have been set up by the countries themselves to further cooperation and integration.

These autonomous instruments of regional collaboration and integration, some of which have been weakened both by internal and external developments, should be strengthened and expanded. That objective could be helped if resources now expended on the UN Regional Commissions were diverted to the support of these organizations and their activities. The continuing utility of the Commissions now needs to be closely examined and their future determined in consultation with governments in their regions.

Supplementing 'Constitutional' Change

There would probably be no serious financial problem for the United Nations if all governments paid their assessed contributions in full and on time.

From the beginning, our work as a Commission has had a wider scope than reform of the United Nations system, and we have sought in this report to deal with the UN system in that wider context. We believe, however, that the UN remains the essential centre for harmonizing the actions of nations. That is why reform of the UN system is a central part of the responses we suggest to the challenge of global governance. We agree with the External Affairs Committee of the Canadian House of Commons that 'the world needs a centre, and some confidence that the centre is holding; the United Nations is the only credible candidate'. We believe our proposals for change will contribute significantly to the effectiveness and credibility of the United Nations.

Our report has concentrated on the larger issues that cannot be avoided and that the fiftieth anniversary of the UN provides a chance to tackle. Some of these are what might be called 'constitutional issues' involving Charter amendment. The challenges of global governance cannot be met in a truly adequate way unless member-states are ready to commit themselves to at least a modicum of constitutional change. We have said from the outset, however, that there is great unused potential in the Charter, and much effort must be devoted to what might be described as 'micro' reforms of the system, drawing on the evolution of the UN and the accumulated experience of its first fifty years.

The study of the UN system by Erskine Childers and Brian Urquhart referred to earlier pays detailed attention to just such reforms and recommends a series of changes to improve the system. On two matters, we specifically reinforce their recommendations—improving the quality and image of the UN bureaucracy, and financing the UN system.

THE SECRETARY-GENERAL AND THE SECRETARIAT

The Secretary-General of the United Nations is the head of the UN Secretariat and the world's foremost international civil servant. While the original primary role of the Secretary-General was as Chief Administrative Officer of the United Nations, the political functions of the office have long since dominated the work.

Peace and security matters, conflict resolution, and peacekeeping are—and will remain—essential concerns. Other aspects of the job, less conspicuous until now, have also been of major importance, however, and are becoming more so. The Secretary-General has to promote the development of international law and be a monitor and protector of human rights. The need to come to grips with a range of complex global problems adds to the already challenging task. A successful approach to global problems needs a leader to shape the global agenda, provide intellectual leadership, and encourage collective action.

To succeed in these infinitely demanding tasks, the Secretary-General needs to co-ordinate the work of what is at present a rambling UN system of specialized agencies and programmes, and to strengthen the structure of the Secretariat, allowing for the orderly delegation of some of the many tasks of the office.

Most of all, the world needs to give itself the chance of securing the best possible individual to do the job. The present procedure for appointing the world's leading international civil servant is, to say the least, haphazard and disorganized. Furthermore, the veto power of the permanent members of the Security Council dominates and inhibits the process. Over the years, this process has become an increasingly parochial way to secure a nomination that can obtain the support of all five permanent members and the required vote in the General Assembly. There is no organized search for suitable candidates, no interview, no systematic assessment of the qualifications required or presented by candidates. No company in the business sector would dream of appointing its chief executive officer in this manner.

A radical improvement should contain the following elements:

- the veto would not apply to the nomination of the Secretary-General, but candidates from the five permanent members could be considered (to date, they have been excluded);
- individuals should not campaign for the office;
- the appointment should be for a single term of seven years;
- governments should consider seriously the qualifications required of the Secretary-General;
- the Security Council should organize a world-wide search for the best-qualified candidates; and
- the qualifications and suitability of candidates should be systematically checked.

The procedure for selecting the heads of UN programmes, funds, and specialized agencies should similarly be improved to secure the best possible candidates. More attention should also be given to the recruitment, development, and future of the international civil service as a whole. Each Secretary-General brings unique qualities and skills to this high office. But each needs an organizational environment that complements his or her attributes. Managing the UN system to ensure that it provides this vital support is critical to the success of the UN. Management is not therefore a peripheral function of the Secretary-General, who needs practical support from member-governments in carrying it out.

One important step is to rebuild the quality and morale of the international public service. This will require a less rigid adherence to the quota system, with the Secretary-General having greater latitude to select the best candidates. The practice of securing clearance from governments before appointing their nationals is not healthy, nor is the practice followed by some countries of topping up the salaries or other compensation of their nationals.

In general, there is a need to professionalize the appointment of senior officials. Each post should carry a job description; candidates should be interviewed by independent panels, and performance appraised at regular intervals. On far too many recent occasions, concern has been expressed about the suitability of individuals appointed to senior posts.

The apparent preoccupation with geography, and the related tradition of inherited posts (though there has recently been some improvement here), does not contribute to sound management. Any organization would wish to ensure appropriate geographical representation in its staffing, if it is to serve the peculiar needs of its individual member-states. But slavish adherence to a national quota system weakens an organization. It would be fitting for the fiftieth anniversary if the General Assembly were to set its face against the continuance of this practice in its present form throughout the UN system.

If the Secretariat of the United Nations is to regain authority among agencies, governments, and the public at large, an emphasis on professionalism must pervade all levels of the organization. The recruitment process must be insulated from governmental lobbying for or blackballing of candidates. Personnel offices in the system devote much time fending off staff of permanent missions trying to promote candidates, often themselves. The General Assembly should decide that save in very exceptional circumstances, no member of a permanent mission should be recruited to the Secretariat before a stated interval has elapsed after service in the mission.

In the Secretariat itself, the Secretary-General's recent reorganization of headquarters positions should be given sufficient opportunity to operate before further changes are contemplated. One missing element, however, is a Deputy Secretary-General for International Economic Co-operation and Development.

Given the current and foreseeable situation in the world, the Secretary-General simply cannot find the time to give the required leadership in the economic and social sectors. It is of the utmost importance that a single chain of command should be established under that individual to give coherence and direction to the work of the various Secretariat entities, and to bring a new presence to bear with respect to interagency co-operation. Such an official should be appointed by the General Assembly on the recommendation of the Secretary-General. The latter should be advised by an independent panel of specialists in the economic and development field appointed in the same way, which should carry out a careful evaluation of candidates, including interviewing them.

Part of the problem with the professional staff at the Secretariat is said to be the less attractive terms and conditions of employment compared with the Bretton Woods institutions. At the same time, some governments have been somewhat disingenuous in complaining about the high level of Secretariat salaries, while subsidizing their nationals in order to get them to accept certain posts or to remain in them. This unacceptable practice should be stopped immediately. And efforts should be made to achieve greater comparability with the salaries paid at the International Monetary Fund and the World Bank.

Salaries are not the only factor accounting for the relative unattractiveness of UN posts. Opportunities for professional development, such as contacts with outside professionals and attendance at professional meetings, are more limited than elsewhere. It is consistent with strengthening professionalism that staff should be given adequate opportunities to interact with their peers.

FINANCING THE UNITED NATIONS

To a greater extent than ever before, governments and peoples are turning to the UN as they seek solutions to global problems. They want the world organization to take on a vast number of urgent tasks: to solve political crises, to keep the peace, to undertake humanitarian relief, to lead the fight against poverty and disease, to spearhead action against environmental degradation—and much more.

In *An Agenda for Peace: One Year Later,* issued in mid-1993, Secretary-General Boutros-Ghali urged the Security Council to:

brace itself to expect the unexpected. In the years just ahead, major developments will affect the role and functions of the Security Council:

- *Competing entities—States, groups and individuals— will request UN intervention to protect their security;*
- *Threats to international peace and security will emanate from situations essentially of a non-military nature, including social disarray created by movement toward democracy, and economic tension created by the costs of both development and non-development;*

- *Increasing political pressure will shape the evolving mechanisms of consensus-building on security decisions.*

The UN must be a central and vital part of any system of global governance. However much is rightly handed on to non-governmental actors and regional arrangements, the agenda of the UN will be a heavy one. The organization is not equipped today to handle all the demands being placed on it. There is a limit to what it can do and these limits must be acknowledged. Yet what remains is a great deal in areas critical to human progress. To discharge these responsibilities, the UN must be restructured and we have made many recommendations to that end—most of them cost-saving in nature. None of these changes will suffice, however, unless the UN's finances are placed on a sounder basis than at present.

There are two problems: the income of the United Nations is not sufficient to cover its costs, and many member-states do not pay what they are expected to pay. To fulfil its responsibilities, the United Nations must be assured of its resources. In 1993, the independent advisory group co-chaired by Shijuro Ogata and Paul Volcker presented a number of constructive recommendations for a more effective financing of the United Nations. In 1994 the Secretary-General presented his analysis of the financing issue for discussion by the General Assembly. Chapter Four includes our own proposals for international revenues as a source of finance for UN activities.

The resources given to the United Nations for its peacekeeping operations in 1992 were less than the combined cost of operating the Fire and Police Departments of New York City. The international community should face up to the need for timely payment of these relatively modest amounts for an effective UN system. Paying in full and on time has become of critical importance.

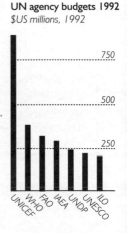

Shares of the main UN budget by use, *1992*

—100%

Peacekeeping 34%

Refugees and humanitarian relief 24%

Administration 17%

Economic development 14%

Other 11%

UN agency budgets 1992
$US millions, 1992

750

500

250

UNICEF WHO FAO IAEA UNDP UNESCO ILO

The Facts About UN Budget Growth

The facts about UN budget growth have often been mythologized.

In 1946 the UN Regular Budget was $21.5 million. In 1992 it was $1,181.2 million. This represents an increase by 55 times during 46 years, which would not in itself be a horrendous growth for an institution that started from scratch.

The UN's regular budget has always been raised from members and expressed in US Dollars, the value of which has greatly declined since 1946. Thus, in real terms the UN regular budget has grown only 10 times since 1946. The same real-terms growth pattern has applied to the regular budgets of the assessment-financed specialized agencies (ILO, FAO, UNESCO, WHO).

Since 1946 the UN's membership has increased from 51 to 184, bringing onto its agenda the condition of virtually the whole of humankind, the numbers of which have more than doubled. Governments have commendably launched dozens of major global programmes in response to these increased commitments. Against this background the UN's budgetary increase has, if anything, been extraordinarily modest. Eight years ago demands to reduce the budget forced a 13 per cent UN staff cut and a hiring freeze; today there are complaints from the same sources about the Secretariat's difficulties in handling the peacekeeping and other emergencies now being heaped upon the organization.

The estimated total world-wide expenditure through the UN system in 1992 was $10.5 billion. Some idea of what this sum means in reality may be gauged from the fact that the expenditure of the citizens of the United Kingdom on alcoholic beverages for a year is three-and-a-half times the actual UN-system expenditure.

The UN system's expenditure was only [0.05] per cent of the world's gross domestic product, and only [0.07] per cent of the GDP of 24 industrial countries. It represented an expenditure of $1.90 per human being alive in 1992. This would not seem to be exorbitant in a world whose governments spent about $150 per human being on military expenditures.

Significantly, 39 per cent of this amount ($4.09 billion, $0.74 per capita) was for emergency work in peacekeeping and humanitarian assistance. This underscores the failure to use the UN system to tackle the root causes of what usually become extremely costly problems.

> 'Seldom have so many important people
> argued so tenaciously about so little money.'
> John G. Stoessinger
> —Excerpts from Erskine Childers with Brian Urquhart,
> *Renewing the United Nations System*

Actually, there would probably be no serious financial problem for the United Nations, at least not at its present level of operations, if all governments paid their assessed contributions in full and on time.

In 1993, for example, only eighteen countries (accounting for 16 per cent of the budget of the UN) paid in full by the January 31 deadline. And by 31 October 1994, governments owed the UN a total of $2,100,000,000. One third of this amount was for the UN regular budget, and the rest for its peacekeeping operations. The United States owed the most ($687,000,000), followed by Russia ($597,000,000).

The financial default of many member-states has debilitated the organization. Withholding contributions has even become a destructive way of exercising influence. It is essential that it must not pay not to pay. Those who choose not to adhere to the financial rules should be deprived of the right to vote, in accordance with Article 19 of the UN Charter. That rule, on depriving a member of its vote in the General Assembly, has not been used consistently. From now on, it should be applied in all relevant cases in order to promote financial discipline.

'The expenses of the Organisation shall be borne by the Members as apportioned by the General Assembly', according to Article 17 of the Charter. The General Assembly regularly decides on a scale of assessments, showing how much each member is required to contribute to the budget of the UN. The formula is grounded in the principle of relative capacity to pay. The assessments are calculated on a ten-year average of each state's gross domestic product, with adjustments for low per capita income and high foreign debt. Separate assessments are made for the peacekeeping operations. In addition, member-states make voluntary contributions to cover the costs of many UN programmes of development assistance.

The richest country in the world, the United States, is today assessed to pay 25 per cent of the regular UN budget. That means that the UN is forced to rely on a single country for as much as a quarter of its regular income. The United Nations would be well served not to depend so much on large contributions from any country.

In 1985 Olof Palme, as Prime Minister of Sweden, presented a proposal to the General Assembly that secured significant support among the members. It was to place a ceiling on the contribution of any member-state, with consequential adjustments in the assessments of other member countries with a capacity to pay.

We believe this was an eminently sound suggestion. The high US share, though justified by that county's wealth, has been exploited by elements hostile to the UN. Perhaps not surprisingly, the Palme proposal was opposed by the Reagan administration, anxious to maintain the leverage that its level of contribution seemed to buy. The Clinton administration has, however, signalled a move in the direction of the Palme proposal in one respect: it has indicated it wishes to reduce its contribution (now 30 per cent) to the peacekeeping budget.

The UN should revive the concept of the Palme proposal and the General Assembly should initiate a process to adjust assessments to the regular budget so that no member-country pays more than an agreed percentage—a ceiling that can be adjusted over time to allow a realistic transition. This will open up a new era in which the UN's finances are not so constantly threatened by arrears and default. And an era in which the UN system, and its reform, are not held hostage to shifting national priorities.

Summary of Proposals in Chapter Five

The Security Council

1　The Security Council should be enlarged to make it more representative of the members of the United Nations.

- A new class of five 'standing' members should be created to serve until a further review around 2005.
- The number of non-permanent (rotating) members should be raised from ten to thirteen.
- The five permanent members should agree to forgo using the veto except in circumstances they consider to be of an exceptional and overriding nature.
- The arrangements should be the subject of a further full review around 2005, which should decide on the phasing out of the veto, the future basis of membership, and arrangements for regular future reviews.

The General Assembly

2　The General Assembly should protect its members' authority to approve the UN budget and to allocate contributions.

3　The General Assembly should be revitalized as a universal forum of the world's nations, and its agenda reduced and rationalized.

4　The General Assembly should meet in a theme session in the first half of each year to discuss a selected issue of major importance.

Trusteeship Council and Civil Society

5　The Trusteeship Council should be given a new mandate: to exercise trusteeship over the global commons.

6　A Forum of Civil Society should be convened in the period leading up to the annual session of the General Assembly, with an expanded category of accredited organizations.

7　A new 'Right of Petition' should be made available to international civil society to bring to the UN's attention situations in which the security of people could be endangered; a Council for Petitions should be formed to receive petitions and make recommendations on them.

Economic and Social Sectors

8 The UN's economic and social activities need to be more effective and efficient, the specialized agencies need to develop as centres of authority in their fields, and programmes and funds need better systems of management and financing.

9 ECOSOC should be wound up, the Second and Third Committees of the General Assembly merged, and the dialogue and negotiation schedules of all three programmed within the new merged Committee.

10 UNCTAD and UNIDO should be closed down, subject to a review of the impact of such action on the countries concerned and on the credibility of the UN.

11 The UN's capacity to advance the rights of women should be enhanced; senior advisers on women's issues should be appointed to the office of the Secretary-General and in other parts of the UN system.

Regionalism

12 The UN should examine, in consultation with the respective governments, the continuing usefulness of its Regional Economic Commissions, and should strengthen organizations formed by countries to pursue regional collaboration.

Secretariat and Financing

13 The procedure for appointing the Secretary-General needs to be radically improved, and the appointment restricted to a single term of seven years.

14 The provision in the UN Charter for depriving countries that do not fulfil their financial obligations of the right to vote needs to be applied consistently.

15 UN budget assessments should be adjusted so that the organization is not dependent on too large a contribution from any one country.

Strengthening the Rule of Law World-Wide

The rule of law has been a critical civilizing influence in every free society. It distinguishes a democratic from a tyrannical society; it secures liberty and justice against repression; it elevates equality above dominion; it empowers the weak against the unjust claims of the strong. Its restraints, no less than the moral precepts it asserts, are essential to the well-being of a society, both collectively and to individuals within it. Respect for the rule of law is thus a basic neighbourhood value. And one that is certainly needed in the emerging global neighbourhood.

Unfulfilled Potential

The rule of law was asserted and, at the same time, undermined; from the outset the World Court was marginalized.

When the founders of the United Nations drew up the Charter, the rule of law world-wide loomed as one of its central components. They established the International Court of Justice at The Hague—commonly known as the World Court—as the 'cathedral of law' in the global system. But states were free to take it or leave it, in whole or in part. The rule of law was asserted and, at the same time, undermined. Each state could decide whether it was going to accept the compulsory jurisdiction of the World Court. And a great many did not. Thus, from the outset, the World Court was marginalized.

Most of the time, international law works well without a need to resort to adjudication. International treaties have been an important basis for achieving co-operation on matters ranging from aviation and shipping to environmental protection and trade. Compliance with legal standards has generally been good even when the short-term interests of a state might have favoured a breach. The great majority of disputes are resolved peacefully.

Nevertheless, in the post-war era the development of international law on some issues, and its use to resolve disputes, has fallen short of what many hoped for. The period was characterized by the rule of military power and economic strength—and these were exercised often in denial, or even defiance, of international legal norms. The world must change course as it works to build the global neighbourhood.

INTERNATIONAL LAW

Comparatively recent in origin, international law includes the body of legal rules and principles that apply among states and also between them and other actors, including those of global civil society and other international organizations. Scholars once argued that international law was not law in the true sense, as there was no international police force to enforce it, no sanctions if it were disobeyed, and no international legislature. But with the growth in use of international law, these arguments are heard less often today.

The standing of international law is now unquestioned. The challenge today—as at the national level—is to sustain the respect for law that has developed. Not surprisingly, some argue that there has been more progress in developing the rules of war than the rules of peace.

Although states are sovereign, they are not free individually to do whatever they want. Just as local norms and customs (often embedded in national constitutions) mean that a state cannot do whatever it wishes within its own borders, so global rules of custom constrain the freedoms of sovereign states. There may be no police force, although the Security Council sometimes compels compliance with international law, but a commonality of self-interest dictates that general conformity is to the advantage of all.

International standards are usually self-enforced, with states, international institutions, and civil society organizations applying a general social pressure for compliance. Many international regimes include reporting requirements and systems of oversight and control. States and individual officials value a reputation for respecting legal commitments. In many states, national law and national courts help promote compliance with international standards.

The rules of international law, like the precepts of international morality, are normative, prescribing standards of conduct. They often embody ethical standards, just as national laws do.

THE LAW-MAKING PROCESS

These rules derive from state practice, from what states actually do, just like the customary or common law found within many legal systems. But unlike moral rules, they lend themselves to adjudication and, at least potentially, enforcement.

In the multilateral area, the United Nations has played a leading and dynamic role. It also serves as the official repository for any treaty or international agreement between member-states. The post-war decades have witnessed a veritable explosion in treaties, most of which are registered with the Secretariat of the United Nations. This volume of activity confirms that modern states desire to order at least some of their international relations within a properly developed legal framework.

This was not always the case. Until the post-war period, international law suffered as a global concept by being centred on Europe. Developing countries, in particular, felt—not without justification—that international law was both based on Christian values and designed to advance Western expansion. It was made in Europe, by European jurists, to serve European ends.

Now, however, particularly given the independence of former colonies, many nation-states can and do take an active part in the process of international law-making. Even when they choose not to, their own conduct of international affairs—their own state practice—is in itself a source of international customary law.

No longer is it credible for a state to turn its back on international law, alleging a bias towards European values and influence. Indeed, European states now sometimes argue that the process that once upheld their own values and morality has lost its cutting edge through the impact of other states on customary international law and compromises to achieve the wide endorsement essential to international conventions. But the need for compromise is true of all law. A binding compact needs the strongest consensus.

Many international organizations, such as the International Labour Organization and the International Maritime Organization, play significant roles in multilateral convention-making. Global civil society organizations, such as trade unions and industry associations,

---

The Principal Sources of International Law

Article 38(1) of the Statute of the World Court, which is the most frequently cited text for sources of international law, provides that the Court shall apply:

a. international conventions, whether general or particular, establishing rules expressly recognized by the contesting states;

b. international custom, as evidence of a general practice accepted as law;

c. the general principles of law recognized by civilized nations; and

d. judicial decisions and the teachings of the most highly qualified publicists of the various nations, as subsidiary means for the determination of rules of law.

Other sources of international law include general principles of equity, and certain widely supported and generally accepted resolutions or declarations of the UN General Assembly and other international organizations.

---

make significant contributions to the process. The UN International Law Commission (ILC) also has an important role. This thirty-four-member subsidiary organ of the UN General Assembly was established in 1947 to make recommendations for the progressive development and codification of international law. After the ILC has completed work on a draft convention, it sends it to the General Assembly, which may convene an international conference to draw up a formal convention. The ILC's role is to draft and recommend. This function needs to be highlighted and expanded.

Through this multilateral treaty-making process, international law can be codified, with customary international law expressed in written statements. In this way it can be modernized much more quickly than by waiting for state practice to develop to the point where it coheres into law. Just as national parliaments have tended to resort to legislation to modernize domestic legal systems, so too has the international community depended on law-making.

This has occasionally happened with commendable speed, especially where commonly shared values were threatened, proving that international law-making need not always be a long, drawn-out process. One landmark achievement was the 1988 Convention against Illicit Traffic in Narcotic Drugs and Psychotropic Substances. The UN quickly obtained agreement on new features of the international framework for combating international drug trafficking, including measures on mutual legal assistance to seize, freeze, and arrange forfeiture of the proceeds of drug trafficking.

A second notable example is the Montreal Protocol on Substances that Deplete the Ozone Layer, signed in 1987 by many of the world's nations when the scientific evidence of the connection between chlorofluorocarbon use and the decay of the earth's protective ozone layer became clearer. Yet the sense of urgency that drove law-making in these two cases is absent all too often.

Ratification and scrutiny are important to the legitimacy and acceptability of international legal instruments. Nevertheless, internal political processes within nation-states themselves may also become obstacles to adoption of international standards. Perhaps the most startling example of a government failing to secure domestic support for new treaty obligations occurred when isolationists in the US Senate blocked that nation's ratification of the decisions taken at the Paris Peace Conference of 1919. As a result, not only did the United States have to conclude its own bilateral peace treaty with Germany, it also failed ever to become a member of the League of Nations.

In the contemporary world, populist action has the potential to strike down the carefully crafted products of international deliberation, usually on the grounds of nationalism. Yielding to internal political pressures can in a moment destroy the results of a decade of toil. One of the challenges for governments in an era of democracy is to ensure that the public understands the nature of international law-making processes and supports them. Only then can long-term considerations prevail over short-term expediency.

STRENGTHENING INTERNATIONAL LAW

In an ideal world, acceptance of the compulsory jurisdiction of the World Court would be a prerequisite for UN membership.

Most international disputes are settled by negotiation. Third parties, including other states and individuals, may provide 'good offices' or may take on more proactive roles as mediators or conciliators. In international as in domestic politics, not all disputes are suitable for binding third-party settlement.

Nevertheless, for international law and the ethical values it protects to be enforced, there must be a credible forum staffed by individuals of the highest standing, independence, and integrity, who are willing and able to adjudicate on the grave matters that come before them. In its absence, freedom of political manœuvring is maximized, and self-serving interpretations of international law can be asserted unilaterally in the Security Council and elsewhere. Only when the interests of both parties are served by binding third-party settlement are disputes referred to forms of adjudication.

The Statute of the World Court provides for the Court to entertain contentious cases only between states. The Court is needed because of the long-established practice that in sovereign (as distinct from state trading) matters, states enjoy immunity from the jurisdiction of each others' courts unless immunity is expressly waived to settle a specific dispute.

The World Court is but the latest in a series of tribunals and procedural arrangements dating back to the Conventions for the Pacific Settlement of Disputes concluded at the first and second Peace Conferences at The Hague, in 1899 and 1907. The goal was to establish a court in which all had confidence. Elihu Root, then US Secretary of State, observed in his instructions to his delegation that the objection to arbitration rested not on an unwillingness of states to submit disputes to impartial arbitration, but to an apprehension that the arbitrators would not be impartial.

What Elihu Root wanted then—and what the world still needs today—is a tribunal that states have confidence in, composed of 'judicial officers, and nothing else, who are paid adequate salaries, who have no other occupation, and who will devote their entire time to the trial and decision of international causes by judicial methods and under a sense of judicial responsibility'. The UN Charter sought to provide such a tribunal. The judges of the World Court are adequately remunerated, have no

ABIDING BY THE RULES

conflicting interests, and devote their entire time to the trial and decision of international cases and to academic writings on the development of international jurisprudence.

The Court has jurisdiction only where the states that are parties to a dispute have agreed to abide by its decision. This can happen in any of three ways. States in dispute that have accepted the 'compulsory jurisdiction' of the Court as laid out in Article 36, paragraph 2, of its statute may agree to submit a case to it. In May 1989, the Republic of Nauru commenced proceedings against the Commonwealth of Australia under this optional clause. Nauru was seeking a declaration from the Court that Australia was bound to make restitution or reparation for the damage and prejudice Nauru had suffered, primarily as a result of Australia's failure to remedy the environmental

---

The Compulsory Jurisdiction of the World Court

1. The jurisdiction of the Court comprises all cases which the parties refer to it and all matters specially provided for in the Charter of the United Nations or in treaties and conventions in force.

2. The states parties to the present Statute may at any time declare that they recognise as compulsory *ipso facto* and without special agreement, in relation to any other state accepting the same obligation, the jurisdiction of the Court in all legal disputes concerning:

    a. the interpretation of a treaty;

    b. any question of international law;

    c. the existence of any fact which, if established, would constitute a breach of an international obligation;

    d. the nature or extent of the reparation to be made for the breach of an international obligation.

3. The declarations referred to above may be made unconditionally or on condition of reciprocity on the part of several or certain states, or for a certain time.

           —Article 36 of the Statute of the International Court of Justice

---

damage it had caused there. Australia accepted the Court's decision on jurisdiction by participating in the merits phase. However, the case was subsequently settled by the parties out of court.

A second ground for jurisdiction is where the disputing parties have previously agreed in a treaty to submit to the Court any disputes that may arise under it. Cases under this category are started by a unilateral filing of an application. A notable example of this was the case brought by the United States in 1979 against Iran over the seizure of the US Embassy in Tehran and the detention of US diplomatic staff. In a more recent case, Bosnia-Hercegovina instituted proceedings against the truncated Yugoslav state (Serbia and Montenegro) in March 1993, alleging genocidal behaviour.

In the third category, states may refer a dispute to the Court by a special agreement. This involves the submission of a dispute, or of particular questions relating to a dispute, to a Court whose membership is more or less known at the time of submission. An example of this was the reference to the Court of the dispute between Libya and Malta on the delimitation of the continental shelf between the two countries, on which the Court made a decision in 1985.

Of the UN's 184 member-states, 57 have accepted the Court's jurisdiction under the optional clause, and ad hoc consent is not forthcoming in nearly enough cases. We view these statistics as alarming. Treaties are the principal source of jurisdiction in contentious cases before the World Court. At present, some countries accept the Court's jurisdiction without qualification in all cases that may arise. Many others do so only when the state wishing to proceed against them has also done so. A number of states, however, are willing to use the World Court only when it suits their short-term interests. This last situation is wholly unsatisfactory.

The standing of the Court was challenged by the actions of both France and the United States in the 1970s and 1980s. In the *Nicaragua* case, the United States responded to a suit brought by Nicaragua by appearing and strenuously contesting the right of the Court to hear the case. But when the Court ruled in favour of having competence to do so, the United States refused to participate further in the case. After condemning the Court for deciding that it had jurisdiction, the United States in October 1985 withdrew its consent to the compulsory jurisdiction of the Court under Article 36(2) of the Court's Statute.

A decade earlier, the *Nuclear Tests* cases had been brought by Australia and New Zealand against France under the Court's compulsory jurisdiction clause. France refused to appear or to abide by the Court's interim order to avoid nuclear tests causing the deposit of radioactive fall-out on Australian or New Zealand territory. From two countries that claim leadership in international affairs, these were both serious blows to the rule of law world-wide.

These cases do not represent a general attitude of defiance of the Court. Indeed, the Court has gradually increased in stature and is now used more frequently. However, misgivings as to judicial methods and judicial responsibility linger—fed in some instances by inferences, rightly or wrongly drawn, that a particular judge has stretched international jurisprudence beyond its limits. Similar criticisms are often heard about national courts of the highest repute. Nevertheless, even a semblance of justification for such criticism needs to be removed. That is why transparent and justifiable structures and processes for judicial appointment are needed.

The criteria and methods for the selection of judges for the World Court must be addressed; without confidence-building mechanisms, the ability of the international community to assert and protect its core values through a truly effective Court will remain elusive.

In an ideal world, acceptance of the compulsory jurisdiction of the World Court would be a prerequisite for UN membership. Those who wish to belong to the community of nations should be willing to abide by its rules and demonstrate their willingness by accepting the competence of its highest legal body. This opportunity has been missed, however. The United Nations and its membership are now facts of life, and some states—including, at present, four of the five permanent members of the Security Council—have denied the Court compulsory jurisdiction under the optional clause. In the interest of maintaining the rule of law in the global neighbourhood, we urge these states to reconsider their position.

Each member of the community of nations that has not already done so should accept the compulsory jurisdiction of the Court. At the same time, we propose a number of measures to respond to the concerns of those who have expressed a lack of confidence in this body.

THE CHAMBER PROCEDURE

Certain states are uneasy about the World Court as an arbitrator of disputes. Yet some have none the less on occasion used the Court's so-called chamber procedure. Under this method, a small group of Court judges, as few as three or five, is agreed to by the states that are party to a dispute; these judges then sit, in effect, as arbitrators.

Some still see this procedure as a diminution of the standing and function of the Court. We understand that reaction, but prefer to see resort to the chamber procedure as evidence of states' willingness to submit to independent decisions. On this the international community must build.

The Chamber Procedure

Under the existing chamber procedure, the World Court may call together a smaller group of judges than would hear a case at a sitting of the Court as a whole. This chamber then deals with a particular case. As the judges to serve on the chamber are chosen by the court after consultation with the parties, in practice they are selected with the positive approval of the parties.

The chamber procedure has been used several times in the last decade. It was used for the first time in 1981 by the United States and Canada in the Gulf of Maine case. In that case, a special agreement of 29 March 1979 provided for the submission to a special chamber of the Court a question as to the course of the single maritime boundary that divides the continental shelf and fisheries zones of the two countries in the Gulf of Maine area. The chamber held that the delimitation line was to be effected in accordance with equitable criteria so as to arrive at an equitable result.

The chamber procedure is not without dangers. Chambers of judges selected by the parties to a dispute are arbitral in character rather than genuinely adjudicatory. Decisions by chambers consisting of a minority of judges or judges from the same region may not be recognized as binding precedents by the full Court in later cases. In litigation involving states from one particular region, a party-selected chamber could end up consisting of judges only from that region or legal culture. The use of chambers also could threaten the unity of the Court. These dangers must be avoided.

Clearly, states may be more willing to accept the Court's jurisdiction if they can participate in determining the judges who constitute the ad hoc chamber. However, the chamber procedure should be modified in ways that address these dangers. One way to do this would be to require the President of the Court to appoint a member to serve on a chamber with the members of the Court selected by the parties to the dispute.

Some states opt to remain outside the compulsory jurisdiction of the World Court because of the process for the selection and re-election of judges to the Court. Judges are elected by the General Assembly and the Security Council. Successful candidates must command the support of a majority in both fora. They are elected for nine years.

We would like to see introduced a system of screening of potential members of the Court for both jurisprudential skills and proven objectivity. This practice is already followed in many countries, which have processes for consultation with or even approval by independent national bodies before a person is elevated to high judicial office.

Such a system would not affect the involvement of all states through the General Assembly or displace the role of the Security Council in the political act of selection. It would mean judges were chosen from a slate of candidates who all have the required experience, skills, and independence of mind. Both the General Assembly and the Security Council would be free to ask for a further set of candidates.

We believe that this procedure would lead to a panel of judges that commanded the confidence all nations seek. Further consultations are needed on how precisely the screening process should be framed. Clearly it should involve eminent jurists of independent mind from all the regional groups of the United Nations, and consist of people who have no ambitions themselves to sit on or practise before the Court. National law societies of member-states could play a role in the process.

To remove any residual misgivings about the independence of the Court, judges should be appointed for only one term of ten years, and then retire on full pension. This should be coupled with a compulsory retirement age of 75. It is contrary to the traditions of many legal systems for judges to submit themselves for re-election or reselection. It is also contrary to UN guidelines and basic principles on the independence of the judiciary. By limiting appointments to one term, it should be possible to avoid the demeaning spectacle of judges canvassing personally or through diplomats in New York for their reappointment—and seeking support, in some instances, from the representatives of states with cases outstanding on the Court list. More important, any suspicion that a judge's conclusions had been tempered by thoughts of re-election would be excluded. The choice of judges for the World Court has assumed too high a level of politicization. Unchecked, this can only further erode confidence in the Court.

We repeat, however, that the final decision would and should be a political one. It is altogether right that those who have to submit themselves to the Court's jurisdiction should have confidence in those appointed to sit in judgement. But the parameters of those processes should be contained within bounds. The proposed changes in the way judges are appointed and in their terms could be implemented by a procedural resolution of the General Assembly without any formal amendment to the statute of the Court. Doing so would ensure that the whole process of selection and tenure yields a bench of judges in whom, collectively and individually, the world community can have complete confidence.

STEPS TO
COMPULSORY
JURISDICTION

If the compulsory jurisdiction of the World Court in all cases will not be accepted immediately by every member of the United Nations, there are some areas of the law in which all states might be persuaded to accept it. A start might be made with disputes between states over continental shelf and exclusive economic zone boundaries, and possibly other land and maritime boundaries. The World Court possesses considerable experience in this area.

The Court's proven expertise and the existence of a mature body of case law deserve to be recognized. The fact that such disputes can threaten peace and security is further good reason why states should be ready to accept the Court's universal competence in this area.

A development in this direction would also be consistent with moves in other fora. It is now a near-universal practice for states in trading agreements to concur in advance to submit disputes to arbitration under one of the well-established international arbitration centres around the world. There is also a practice of providing in advance for dispute resolution procedures in major treaties, the most recent example being the Understanding on Rules and Procedures Governing the Settlement of Disputes signed in Marrakesh in April 1994. Under the new system, members of the World Trade Organization commit themselves not to take unilateral action against perceived violations of the trade rules. They have pledged instead to use the new dispute settlement system, and to abide by its rules and procedures.

Some Disputes About Land or Maritime Boundaries

Pursuant to a special agreement, Burkina Faso and Mali submitted a dispute concerning a part of their common frontier to a special chamber of the World Court. The Court held in December 1986 that in accordance with the traditional principle of Spanish-American law, *uti possidetis*, the boundary in the disputed area was to coincide with the delimitation of the former French colonies as of the end of the colonial period. Both parties welcomed the decision of the Court and indicated their willingness to accept it as final and binding.

Denmark filed an application with the full Court (pursuant to the optional clause of the Court's Statute) to delimit the maritime boundary between Greenland (Denmark) and the island of Jan Mayen (Norway). This was the first maritime case in which jurisdiction was predicated on the Court's compulsory jurisdiction. The boundary finally established by the Court in June 1993 fell somewhere between the Norwegian and Danish claims.

The world community needs to minimize the occasions in which states in dispute have first to agree on a settlement mechanism before the merits of the case can be examined. This would speed up possible resort to third-party settlement, based on international legal norms, while providing an incentive for rapid agreement on the substance of a dispute ahead of any hearing. States should be encouraged to include in future agreements and treaties provisions that spell out the mechanism for the settlement of any disputes that may arise.

If progress can be made in this way, international confidence may build to the point where doubters are won over to the concept of compulsory jurisdiction in all matters. To aid this process, areas of jurisdiction should be identified in which acceptance of the compulsory jurisdiction of the World Court could be achieved on a piecemeal basis.

EMPOWERING THE SECRETARY-GENERAL

At present, the Security Council, the General Assembly, and other organs and agencies of the United Nations have the power to request advisory opinions from the World Court. In view of the emphasis now rightly placed on preventive diplomacy, the UN Secretary-General also should be able to refer the legal dimensions of emerging disputes to the World Court at an early stage for an advisory opinion. Such action may well—in at least some instances—assist in the peaceful determination of a dispute that otherwise might threaten international peace and security. States generally have a strong wish to be seen as having international law on their own side, and the prospect of a decision that this was not the case could be a salutary one. Having the Secretary-General take this step could also provide a political cooling-off period while the Court came to a decision.

There will be instances, of course, where resort to the Court may be inappropriate or ineffectual. Yet no one suggests that a domestic court has no deterrent effect just because it is not omnipotent. Limitations on effectiveness are no excuse for failing to reinforce the Secretary-General's position in this practical way.

It follows that the World Court would itself need to develop fast-track procedures for handling such matters, which should have higher priority than other cases before the Court. There should be time-saving reforms, including streamlining of procedures. Such techniques are increasingly being used in the highest courts of individual states, and could also be used at the World Court. The availability of fast-track procedures might well encourage governments to turn to the Court if they thought they could get a quick pronouncement on their side, as a way to influence public opinion.

THE SECURITY COUNCIL AND THE WORLD COURT

The Security Council should make greater use of the World Court as a source of advisory opinions.

The Security Council is, of course, the supreme organ of the United Nations. It can even second-guess the World Court by refusing requests to implement the Court's decisions. Some of its resolutions are themselves a source of international law, and propositions of international law are frequently asserted in the Council.

We considered at length whether the Security Council should subject its own decisions to review by the World Court, at least on procedural matters. If it did so, the Council would be in the same position as several member-states in their own jurisdictions, where courts can adjudicate on the legality of state action. No explicit power is given to the World Court to review the legality at international law of Security Council actions. Yet in many states, including the United States, this power of review by the highest national courts has arisen even in the absence of explicit constitutional or statutory language. In addition, the UN

Charter refers to the International Court of Justice as the organization's 'principal judicial organ'. It can be argued that this implies a power of judicial review.

An example of the confusion that can result from the Security Council acting as it does is provided by the present dispute stemming from the crash of Pan Am flight 103 over Lockerbie in Scotland. Libya has been required by the Security Council to extradite suspects who are its citizens. Yet under the 1971 Montreal Convention for the Suppression of Unlawful Acts Against the Safety of Civilian Aircraft, Libya is entitled to have these individuals tried in a Libyan court. Furthermore, as a general principle of international law, states are not required to surrender their own citizens (to whom they owe a duty of protection); they should instead prosecute them in their own countries. If an international criminal court existed (as advocated later in this chapter), it could have heard the case against the Libyan suspects for this act of international terrorism.

Notwithstanding that some states have often used precepts of international law as a shield to justify their failure to act responsibly within the protection of their own borders (for example, Libya has failed to prosecute the Lockerbie suspects even in its own courts), questions have arisen about whether the Security Council should have respected Libya's rights at international law, rather than endeavouring to override them. And some have questioned whether, in a legal sense, the placing of the bomb that caused the aircraft to crash—despicable though it was—really did constitute a threat against international peace and security, and whether the Security Council had a firm basis for the action it has taken.

The World Court would probably seek to avoid confrontation with the Security Council by regarding it as enjoying exclusive competence to judge whether particular actions constituted a threat to international peace and security. But just where the line might be drawn is difficult to say. Certainly, recurring disputes between the Council and the Court as to competence would be wholly undesirable, and in the best interests of neither.

It is also true to say that an overly legalistic approach might cut off developments that, if allowed to progress, might be of benefit to all. The present degree of humanitarian concern in the international protection of human rights is a good example of a development that most around the world would applaud. Yet at an earlier stage, this might have been hampered had the World Court come down firmly on the side of a state not being exposed to interference in its internal affairs, as guaranteed by the UN Charter.

Although we see the value of the Security Council not being completely free from legal oversight, we do not recommend at this stage a right of review of all Security Council decisions in the World Court. In any event, if eventually there is a form of judicial review, it would probably need to be confined to certain issues relating to the 'constitutionality' of Security Council actions, to the defence of the Charter itself, and to certain related rule of law issues. The Court would intervene only when there was a clear conflict between a decision of the Council and its constitution.

We also considered whether a state or group of states should be able to petition the World Court to provide advice on proposed action by the Security Council. While the Council cannot be challenged once it has reached a decision, should its decision-making process be the subject of advice and counsel by the World Court? For reasons discussed already, we concluded that such a mechanism would expose both the Security Council and the Court to the real risk of friction.

Still, we looked for ways in which instances of potential illegality by the Security Council could be minimized. The mechanism we suggest is having a distinguished legal person available to provide to the

Security Council at an early stage independent advice on international legal propositions. Such an individual—perhaps a retired member of the World Court—would be appointed (or reappointed) by the Security Council on the advice of the ILC or some other expert legal body. This person would act vis-à-vis the Security Council in much the same way that an Attorney-General does vis-à-vis the Cabinet in most parliamentary democracies. As the Attorney-General, the Council's legal adviser would not in any way usurp the ultimate responsibility of the Council to take the definitive political decision on any matter in respect of which his or her advice is sought.

A legal expert who provided advice that commanded respect could play a key role in clarifying issues and contributing to a speedier—and more assuredly lawful—conduct of the Council's business. Most important, this would not simply be an additional function for existing UN staff members. The legal expert would need to enjoy independence from the Secretary-General's own advisers. The expert would be the Council's own lawyer, serving the international community with a mandate to warn the Council privately, during informal consultations, if it is in danger of transgressing legal norms. Respect for the rule of international law must start with the highest organ of the UN system.

The Security Council should also turn to the World Court more often in the dispatch of its own business. Provision for this already exists, but is too little used. Obviously, much of the Council's business is of compelling urgency and time constraints have contributed to its opting, in effect, to act as its own arbiter on the applicability of international law in particular circumstances. But this has happened more frequently than many would have wished. We would prefer to see the Council taking this course as a last resort, after having carefully considered the feasibility of asking the Court for an advisory opinion.

This further emphasizes the need for the World Court to have procedures that would expedite the resolution of urgent cases. We certainly feel the Security Council should make greater use of the World Court as a source of advisory opinions and, wherever possible, avoid being the judge in disputes on what international law may or may not be in particular cases.

AN INTERNATIONAL CRIMINAL COURT

The absence of an international criminal court discredits the rule of law. It must be established soon.

The concept of an international criminal court is an old one. Efforts to establish such a court date back to 1945. Since then, the feasibility has been studied by several reputable institutions, including the International Law Commission. We believe that the absence of such an international court discredits the rule of law. It must be established soon. A major step was taken towards establishing an international criminal court in July 1994, when the ILC adopted statutes for a proposed court. This is a welcome development.

Some have argued that such a court would infringe on national sovereignty, because national courts have exclusive jurisdiction over crimes committed on their territories. Yet sovereign states have already recognized international jurisdiction over crimes by ratifying or acceding to treaties prohibiting genocide, torture, and other crimes against humanity. The 1948 Genocide Convention actually envisages the possibility of an international criminal court.

Also, certain crimes, such as acts of terrorism, are international precisely because they occur across national borders. As noted earlier, the bombing of Pan Am flight 103 over Lockerbie, Scotland, is a tragic example of an international crime that transcended many borders and that could have been tried before an international criminal court had one existed.

Some argue, too, that an international criminal court should only be established on an ad hoc, case-by-case basis. The time it has taken to agree upon and establish a court to deal with crimes committed during the conflict in the former Yugoslavia, however, supports the argument for a permanent court.

Some question why the Yugoslav conflict has become the focus of an ad hoc court when other crimes against international law are being, or have been, perpetrated elsewhere. A similar tribunal has been proposed to try perpetrators of genocide in Rwanda. It is precisely such apparent selectivity that would be avoided by having a standing court. Its existence might also serve as a source of deterrence. And a standing court would overcome the problems of delays and selection that an ad hoc court could face. As in a domestic setting, justice delayed can be justice denied.

An international criminal court should have an independent prosecutor or a panel of prosecutors of the highest moral character, as well as the highest level of competence and experience in investigating and prosecuting criminal cases. Upon receipt of a complaint or at his or her own initiative, the prosecutor's primary responsibility would be to investigate an alleged crime and prosecute suspected offenders for any crimes that are within the court's jurisdiction. The prosecutor would, of course, have to act independently and not seek or receive instructions from any government or other source. The Security Council could also refer cases to the court when it determined that the crime in question constituted a threat to international peace and security.

The matter is a complex one, giving rise to questions of legal systems, investigations, procedures, and punishments, to name but a few. If it must be established by treaty, it will clearly take many years, even decades, before it is in place. We urge swift examination of various possibilities, and early action on the most promising. We would like to see such a court instituted as a matter of the highest priority.

ENFORCING INTERNATIONAL LAW

The very essence of global governance is the capacity of the international community to ensure compliance with the rules of society.

In a world in which the rule of international law was respected, enforcement procedures would not be needed. In a world in which it is not, universal enforcement may not be achievable.

Of course, international law can be, and is, enforced through a number of avenues. Domestic courts in the legal systems of many member-states take account of international rights and obligations in deciding on cases that come before them. And in an increasing number of legal systems, there is a growing awareness of the universality of international law and the norms it embodies, and a readiness to consider these when judging individual cases. The norms of international law—particularly on human rights—are already guiding judges in cases in individual countries as they rightly seek to ensure, to the extent allowed by their legal system, that universally recognized norms and values are protected domestically.

We applaud this development, recognizing as it does the commonality of global identity. This process should be encouraged by courts being more ready than in the past to admit cases in which individuals and non-governmental organizations (NGOs) seek to enforce compliance with international norms in domestic courts, or wish to ensure that their government's foreign policy is in conformity with them.

Numerous regional and supranational mechanisms also exist: the Inter-American Court of Human Rights, the European Court of Human Rights, and the European Court of Justice, to name but three. And as noted earlier, dispute-settlement mechanisms are increasingly being provided in international treaties. States, corporations, and individuals should also consider resorting to such institutions as the International Center for the Settlement of Investment Disputes, a tribunal set up by the World Bank.

A necessary condition for strengthening the rule of law world-wide is an efficient monitoring and compliance regime. Without this, states are tempted to embrace international norms and agreements and then not follow through on their obligations. The very essence of global governance is the capacity of the international community to ensure compliance with the rules of society.

The International Center for the Settlement of Investment Disputes

The International Center for the Settlement of Investment Disputes (ICSID) was created by the Convention on the Settlement of Investment Disputes in 1965 to provide a forum for conflict resolution in a framework that carefully balances the interests and requirements of all the parties involved. Its main objective is to promote a climate of mutual confidence between investors and states favourable to increasing the flow of resources to developing countries under reasonable conditions.

ICSID's jurisdiction is limited to investment disputes between parties, one of which must be a Contracting State or governmental entity, and the other a non-governmental entity that is a national of another Contracting State. ICSID awards are binding and not subject to any appeal or other remedy except those provided by the ICSID Convention. Each Contracting State, whether or not it or any of its nationals have been parties to the proceedings, must recognize an ICSID award as binding and enforce the pecuniary obligations imposed by the award as if it were a final judgement of a court of the state.

International law is routinely observed by states because they believe it is in their best and long-term interest to do so. But it is breached whenever the violators believe that such action will fetch them handsome rewards, and that they can get away with it. Incentives and disincentives are needed to encourage compliance and deter non-compliance.

We recognize that questions of compliance can often be contested. The acceptable level of compliance will also depend on the issues, the context, and the type of obligation involved. In the environmental field, for example, technical and financial assistance will help reduce the inability of certain states to comply with new and emerging standards. Thus the 1990 amendments to the Montreal Protocol on Substances that Deplete the Ozone Layer made this the first major treaty under which the parties actually put up some funds to help developing countries defray the incremental costs of compliance. We recommend the inclusion of such provisions in treaties where that is an effective way of achieving compliance by states that might otherwise find it difficult to do so.

Similarly, in the security field, there are areas in which arrangements for compliance are clearly insufficient. Examples are crimes against humanity, terrorism, and kidnapping. The international criminal court just recommended could enhance compliance in the security and human rights area. The best way to secure compliance with other security-related rules is to stop violations before they take place. This is the essence of preventive diplomacy, as discussed in Chapter Three.

Beyond the court system, the technical, organizational, and lobbying skills of some NGOs are an efficient means of achieving enhanced compliance. We encourage these groups to continue lobbying and pressuring governments, multilateral institutions,

Helping States Comply with International Treaties

Treaty signatories may have the will to carry out the provisions of the document they have just agreed to, but they do not always have the means to do so. In recognition of this problem, at the London meeting when the Montreal Protocol on Substances that Deplete the Ozone Layer was first amended, forty-three countries set up a multilateral fund to help developing countries produce substitutes for chlorofluorocarbons (CFCs) and to purchase CFC recycling equipment.

A total of $240 million was pledged for 1991–93. However, by the end of 1993, only $135 million of the total pledged had been put into the fund.

transnational corporations, and other subjects of international law to comply with their international legal obligations. Although these groups are essential in bringing about desired policy goals under domestic as well as international legal systems, few international agreements or implementing bodies explicitly acknowledge this role or include NGOs in their compliance mechanisms.

Greater transparency will also increase the likelihood that national policy decisions comply with agreed international standards. Above all, increased resort to as well as improvement of dispute-settlement procedures will help clear some of the ambiguity that frequently serves as justification for non-compliance.

Membership of the United Nations confers considerable advantages, rights, and privileges. Enjoyment of these benefits creates a responsibility to comply with the rules of the UN Charter. The easiest and most efficient way to encourage or secure compliance with international norms is through voluntary, not coercive, means. Methods to encourage compliance include direct contact, publicity and the mobilization of shame, deterrence, peaceful settlement procedures, sanctions, and, as a last resort, expulsion from intergovernmental organizations or the UN itself.

In most cases, a judgement of the World Court is enough to settle a dispute, and states generally comply. In exceptional cases of non-compliance, however, the only effective enforcement may be through a Security Council resolution. We do not emphasize formal enforcement measures; but failing voluntary compliance, we recommend Security Council enforcement of World Court decisions and other international legal obligations.

Article 94 of the Charter gives the Security Council the power to 'make recommendations or decide upon measures to be taken to give effect to the judgement' of the World Court. This provision has been dormant. Because of the veto, the Security Council has been powerless against a permanent member, even in legal matters. In the *Nicaragua* case referred to earlier, the Security Council was not in a position to enforce a judgement against a country that had the power of veto. We believe a reformed Security Council, as proposed in Chapter Five, will be less constrained in promoting compliance with World Court decisions.

PROMOTING INTERNATIONAL LAW

The global neighbourhood of the future must be characterized by law, not lawlessness.

The traditional ways that international law is formed and developed are time-consuming and generally lack any sense of urgency. Even allowing for the delay inevitable in negotiating a text that achieves the consensus support of the global community, these processes fail to provide the international law-making service that today's modern, fast-paced global community requires.

International law has evolved techniques to respond to this challenge. Standards may be set by instruments (such as resolutions of some international organizations) that are technically non-binding but in fact have considerable influence on behaviour. If applied in practice, these standards may begin to assume some legal status. This is the hardening of so-called soft law.

Treaties may establish procedures for rapid amendment when new data become available, as in the Montreal Protocol. Or they may be applied provisionally while awaiting formal ratification. Differential obligations may be established for states facing different conditions, in order to reach agreement on higher and more effective standards. Institutions may have special rule-making powers, binding even states that do not formally agree to a particular rule. Influential standards may be proposed by civil society organizations. Customary international law may be established more quickly now than in the past. Rules not binding on all states may nevertheless influence behaviour: for example, regulations adopted by a few states may be copied in others and eventually applied in most national systems.

Law-making has evolved, but the gradualism at the core of the present system remains an inheritance from the past. It was suitable for a world community with far fewer states and where technology, population, and the environment were not matters of concern. It was a leisurely, club-like approach to international law-making that simply cannot serve today's global society.

Accordingly, some appropriate body should be mandated to explore ways in which international law-making can be expedited—without, of course, calling into question the consensual nature of international law itself. There is clearly no profit in embarking on international law-making for its own sake and without realistic chances of attracting sufficient support for new proposals.

Efforts are made by international law-making fora within the UN system to liaise with outside counterparts, such as The Hague Conference on Private International Law, to eliminate overlap and assign responsibilities. This is all well and good. But a single organization should formally co-ordinate international law-making, setting timetables and establishing lines of authority. We see such an organization—which could be a revamped International Law Commission—as being proactive. Its immediate tasks should be to energize states and give international law-making the prominence it requires, both in terms of priorities and of resources allocated to it by member-states.

To reach all these goals, we look for the emergence of a group of 'good global citizen' states and representatives of civil society organizations. This group should be prepared to work together and provide leadership. They should lead by example and moral suasion, and work towards the ends we have outlined in all international fora where they are active. In particular, there is work to be done in reforming aspects of the UN system, whether by Charter amendment or otherwise. Without a mechanism to carry this programme forward, the full potential of the international rule of law as a means for peaceful resolution of disputes will remain unrealized.

The emerging global neighbourhood needs to live by a new ethic that is underpinned by a culture of law. The world community has at least the beginnings of a potentially effective legal system to support global governance arrangements. Myriad contemporary multilateral and bilateral treaties and arrangements exist, along with established customary law. In addition, several judicial and non-judicial mechanisms exist that, with the necessary political will, can effectively encourage compliance or enforce the law.

The weaknesses in the international legal system today are largely a reflection of weaknesses in the overall international system. Although there is urgent need for new laws, for better compliance mechanisms, and for more effective enforcement machinery, political will on the part of states is an indispensable requirement for progress in this direction.

The world must strive to ensure that the global neighbourhood of the future is characterized by law, not by lawlessness; by rules that all must respect; by the reality that all, including the weakest, are equal under the law and that none, including the most powerful, is above the law. This, in turn, requires a will to lead by those who can, and a willingness by the rest to join and help in the common effort.

Summary of Proposals in Chapter Six

Strengthening International Law

1 All members of the United Nations should accept the compulsory jurisdiction of the World Court.

2 The chamber procedure of the World Court should be modified to address its dangers and to increase its appeal to states.

3 World Court judges should be appointed for one ten-year term only, and a system introduced to screen potential members for jurisprudential skills and objectivity.

4 States should be encouraged to include in future agreements and treaties provisions for the settlement of any interstate disputes.

5 The UN Secretary-General should have the right to refer the legal aspects of emerging disputes to a full bench of the World Court for advice at an early stage.

The Security Council

6 A distinguished legal person should be appointed by the Security Council to provide independent advice on international legal propositions to the Council.

7 The Security Council should make greater use of the World Court as a source of advisory opinions and, wherever possible, avoid being the judge of what international law may or may not be in particular cases.

Enforcing International Law

8 An international criminal court should be established with an independent prosecutor or panel of prosecutors of the highest moral character as well as the highest level of competence and experience.

9 International treaties should include provision to help countries that may otherwise face financial hardship in complying with them.

10 Failing voluntary compliance, Security Council enforcement of World Court decisions and of other international legal obligations should be pursued.

11 An appropriate body should be asked to explore ways in which international law-making can be expedited without calling into question the consensual nature of international law.

CHAPTER SEVEN

A CALL TO ACTION

In this final chapter, we set out our main conclusions and proposals, and then look at how the world community might consider these and other proposals on the fiftieth anniversary of the United Nations.

SUMMARY OF COMMISSION PROPOSALS

A global civic ethic to guide action within the global neighbourhood, and leadership infused with that ethic, is vital to the quality of global governance.

This section recapitulates the principal conclusions and recommendations thus far. A more complete list is found at the end of earlier chapters and we do not repeat them all. In recalling our major proposals, however, we emphasize the degree to which we see them as a coherent body of reform proposals—not inseparable, of course, but mutually reinforcing. We encourage their consideration as such.

Global governance, once viewed primarily as concerned with intergovernmental relationships, now involves not only governments and intergovernmental institutions but also non-governmental organizations (NGOs), citizens' movements, transnational corporations, academia, and the mass media. The emergence of a global civil society, with many movements reinforcing a sense of human solidarity, reflects a large increase in the capacity and will of people to take control of their own lives.

GOVERNANCE, CHANGE, AND VALUES

States remain primary actors but have to work with others. The United Nations must play a vital role, but it cannot do all the work. Global governance does not imply world government or world federalism. Effective global governance calls for a new vision, challenging people as well as governments to realize that there is no alternative to working together to create the kind of world they want for themselves and their children. It requires a strong commitment to democracy grounded in civil society.

The changes of the last half-century have brought the global neighbourhood nearer to reality—a world in which citizens are increasingly dependent on one another and need to cooperate. Matters calling for global neighbourhood action keep multiplying. What happens far away matters much more now.

We believe that a global civic ethic to guide action within the global neighbourhood and leadership infused with that ethic are vital to the quality of global governance. We call for a common commitment to core values that all humanity could uphold: respect for life, liberty, justice and equity, mutual respect, caring, and integrity. We further believe humanity as a whole will be best served by recognition of a set of common rights and responsibilities.

It should encompass the right of all people to:

- a secure life,
- equitable treatment,
- an opportunity to earn a fair living and provide for their own welfare,
- the definition and preservation of their differences through peaceful means,
- participation in governance at all levels,
- free and fair petition for redress of gross injustices,
- equal access to information, and
- equal access to the global commons.

At the same time, all people share a responsibility to:

- contribute to the common good;
- consider the impact of their actions on the security and welfare of others;
- promote equity, including gender equity;
- protect the interests of future generations by pursuing sustainable development and safeguarding the global commons;
- preserve humanity's cultural and intellectual heritage;
- be active participants in governance; and
- work to eliminate corruption.

Democracy provides the environment within which the fundamental rights of citizens are best safeguarded and offers the most favourable foundation for peace and stability. The world needs, however, to ensure the rights of minorities, and to guard against the ascendence of the military and corruption. Democracy is more than just the right to vote in regular elections. And as within nations, so globally, the democratic principle must be ascendant.

Sovereignty has been the cornerstone of the interstate system. In an increasingly interdependent world, however, the notions of territoriality, independence, and non-intervention have lost some of their meaning. In certain areas, sovereignty must be exercised collectively, particularly in relation to the global commons. Moreover, the most serious threats to national sovereignty and territorial integrity now often have internal roots.

The principles of sovereignty and non-intervention must be adapted in ways that recognize the need to balance the rights of states with the rights of people, and the interests of nations with the interests of the global neighbourhood. It is time also to think about self-determination in the emerging context of a global neighbourhood rather than the traditional context of a world of separate states.

Against this backdrop of an emerging global neighbourhood and the values that should guide its governance, we explored four specific areas of governance central to the challenges of the new era the world has entered: security, economic interdependence, the United Nations, and the rule of law. In each case we have sought to focus on governance aspects, but these are often inseparable from substantive issues that we have had to address.

PROMOTING SECURITY	The concept of global security must be broadened from the traditional focus on the security of states to include the security of people and the security of the planet. The following six concepts should be embedded in international agreements and used as norms for security policies in the new era:

- All people, no less than all states, have a right to a secure existence, and all states have an obligation to protect those rights.
- The primary goals of global security policy should be to prevent conflict and war and to maintain the integrity of the environment and life-support systems of the planet by eliminating the economic, social, environmental, political, and military conditions that generate threats to the security of people and the planet, and by anticipating and managing crises before they escalate into armed conflicts.
- Military force is not a legitimate political instrument, except in self-defence or under UN auspices.
- The development of military capabilities beyond that required for national defence and support of UN action is a potential threat to the security of people.
- Weapons of mass destruction are not legitimate instruments of national defence.
- The production and trade in arms should be controlled by the international community.

Unprecedented increases in human activity and human numbers have reached the point where their impacts are impinging on the basic conditions on which life depends. It is imperative that action should be taken now to control these activities and keep population growth within acceptable limits so that planetary security is not endangered.

The principle of non-intervention in domestic affairs should not be taken lightly. But it is necessary to assert as well the rights and interests of the international community in situations within individual states in which the security of people is extensively endangered. A global consensus exists today for a UN response on humanitarian grounds in such cases. We propose a UN Charter amendment to permit such intervention but restricting it to cases that in the judgement of a reformed Security Council constitute a violation of the security of people so gross and extreme that it requires an international response on humanitarian grounds.

There should be a new 'Right of Petition' for non-state actors to bring situations massively endangering the security of people within states to the attention of the Security Council. The Charter amendment establishing the Right of Petition should also authorize the Security Council to call on parties to an intrastate dispute to settle it through the mechanisms listed in Article 33 of the UN Charter for the pacific settlement of disputes between states. The Council should be authorized to take enforcement action under Chapter VII if such action fails, but only if it determines that intervention is justified under the Charter amendment referred to in the previous paragraph on the grounds of the violation of security of people. Even then, the use of force would be the last resort.

We suggest two measures to improve UN peace-keeping. First, the integrity of the UN command should be respected; for each operation a consultative committee should be set up, as was originally the case, with representatives of the countries that contribute troops. Second, although the principle that countries with special interests in relation to a conflict should not contribute troops should be upheld, the earlier view that the permanent members of the Security Council should not play an active part in peacekeeping should be discarded.

New possibilities arise for the involvement of regional organizations in conjunction with the UN in resolving conflicts. We support the Secretary-General's plea for making more active use of regional organizations under Chapter VIII of the Charter.

The UN needs to be able to deploy credible and effective peace enforcement units at an early stage in a crisis and at short notice. It is high time that a UN Volunteer Force was established. We envisage a force with a maximum of 10,000 personnel. It would not take the place of preventive action, of traditional peace-keeping forces, or of large-scale enforcement action under Chapter VII of the Charter. Rather, it would fill a gap by giving the Security Council the ability to back up preventive diplomacy with a measure of immediate and convincing deployment on the ground. Its very existence would be a deterrent; it would give support for negotiation and peaceful settlement of disputes.

The international community must provide increased funds for peacekeeping, using some of the resources released by reductions of defence expenditures. The cost of peacekeeping should be integrated into a single annual budget and financed by assessments on all UN member countries—with an increase of the peace-keeping reserve fund to facilitate rapid deployment.

The international community should reaffirm its commitment to eliminate nuclear and other weapons of mass destruction progressively from all nations, and should initiate a ten-to-fifteen year programme to achieve this goal.

Work towards nuclear disarmament should involve action on four fronts:

- the earliest possible ratification and implementation of existing agreements on nuclear and other weapons of mass destruction;
- the indefinite extension of the Non-Proliferation Treaty;
- the conclusion of a treaty to end all nuclear testing; and
- the initiation of talks among all declared nuclear powers to establish a process to reduce and eventually eliminate all nuclear arsenals.

All nations should sign and ratify the conventions on chemical and biological weapons, enabling the world to enter the twenty-first century free of these weapons.

For the first time in history, the world's dominant military powers have both an interest in reducing world-wide military capabilities and the ability to do so. The international community should make the demilitarization of global politics an overriding priority.

Donor institutions and countries should evaluate a country's military spending when considering assistance to it. And a Demilitarization Fund should be set up to help developing countries reduce their military commitments, and collective military spending should be reduced to $500 billion by the end of the decade.

States should undertake immediate negotiation and eventual introduction of a Convention on the curtailment of the arms trade—including provision for a mandatory Arms Register and the prohibition of the financing or subsidy of arms exports by governments.

MANAGING ECONOMIC INTER-DEPENDENCE

The globalization process is in danger of widening the gap between rich and poor. A sophisticated, globalized, increasingly affluent world currently coexists with a marginalized global underclass.

The pace of globalization of financial and other markets is outstripping the capacity of governments to provide the necessary framework of rules and co-operative arrangements. There are severe limits to national solutions to such failures within a globalized economy, yet the structures of global governance for pursuing international public policy objectives are underdeveloped.

The time is now ripe—indeed overdue—to build a global forum that can provide leadership in economic, social, and environmental fields. This should be more representative than the Group of Seven or the Bretton Woods institutions, and more effective than the present UN system. We propose the establishment of an Economic Security Council (ESC) that would meet at high political level. It would have deliberative functions only; its influence will derive from the relevance and quality of its work and the significance of its membership.

The ESC's tasks would be to:

- continuously assess the overall state of the world economy and the interaction between major policy areas;
- provide a long-term strategic policy framework in order to promote stable, balanced, and sustainable development;
- secure consistency between the policy goals of the major international organizations, particularly the Bretton Woods bodies and the World Trade Organization (WTO); and
- give political leadership and promote consensus on international economic issues.

The ESC should be established as a distinct body within the UN family, structured like the Security Council, though not with identical membership and independent of it.

With some 37,000 transnational corporations worldwide, foreign investment is growing faster than trade. The challenge is to provide a framework of rules and order for global competition in the widest sense. The WTO should adopt a strong set of competition rules and a Global Competition Office should be set up to provide oversight of national enforcement efforts and resolve inconsistencies between them.

The decision-making structures of the Bretton Woods institutions must be reformed and made more reflective of economic reality; gross domestic product figures based on purchasing power parity should be used to establish voting strength.

The role of the IMF should be enhanced by:

- enlarging its capacity for balance-of-payments support through low conditionality compensatory finance;
- having oversight of the international monetary system and a capacity to ensure that domestic economic policies in major countries are not mutually inconsistent or damaging to the rest of the international community;
- releasing a new issue of Special Drawing Rights; and
- improving its capacity to support nominal exchange rates in the interest of exchange rate stability.

For some countries, aid is likely to be for many years one of the main ways to escape from a low-income, low-savings, low-investment trap. There is no substitute for a politically realistic strategy to mobilize aid flows and to demonstrate value for money, including cofinancing between official aid donors, the private sector, and NGOs with a view to widening the support base.

A false sense of complacency has enveloped the developing-country debt problem. Radical debt reduction is needed for heavily indebted low-income countries, involving at least implementation of 'full Trinidad terms', including the matter of multilateral debt.

In response to environmental concerns, governments should make maximum use of market instruments, including environmental taxes and tradable permits, and should adopt the 'polluter pays principle' of charging. We support the European Union's carbon tax proposal as a first step towards a system that taxes resource use rather than employment and savings, and urge its wide adoption.

A start must be made in establishing schemes of global financing of global purposes, including charges for the use of global resources such as flight lanes, sea-lanes, and ocean fishing areas and the collection of global revenues agreed globally and implemented by treaty. An international tax on foreign currency transactions should be explored as one option, as should the creation of an international corporate tax base among multinational companies. It is time for the evolution of a consensus on the concept of global taxation for servicing the needs of the global neighbourhood.

| REFORMING THE UNITED NATIONS | We do not subscribe to the notion that the UN should be dismantled to make way for a new architecture of global governance. Much of the necessary reform of the United Nations system can be effected without amending the Charter, provided governments are willing. But some Charter amendments are necessary for better global governance, and those we propose will help to create an environment propitious to a return to the spirit of the Charter. |

UN reform must reflect the realities of change, including the new capacity of global civil society to contribute to global governance.

Reform of the Security Council is central to reforming the UN system. Permanent membership limited to five countries that derive their primacy from events fifty years ago is unacceptable; so is the veto. To add more permanent members and give them the veto would be regressive. We propose a process of reform in two stages.

First, a new class of five 'standing' members who will retain membership to the second stage of the reform process should be established. They will be selected by the General Assembly and we envisage two from industrial countries and one each from Africa, Asia, and Latin America. The number of non-permanent members should be raised from ten to thirteen, and the number of votes required for a decision of the Council raised from nine to fourteen. To facilitate the phasing out of the veto, the permanent members should enter into a concordat agreeing to forgo its use save in circumstances they consider to be of an exceptional and overriding nature.

The second stage should be a full review of the membership of the Council, including these arrangements, around 2005, when the veto can be phased out; the position of the permanent members will then also be reviewed, and account taken of new circumstances—including the growing strength of regional bodies.

The Trusteeship Council should be given a new mandate over the global commons in the context of concern for the security of the planet.

The General Assembly should be revitalized as a universal forum of the world's states. Regular theme sessions, effective exercise of budgetary authority, and the streamlining of its agenda and procedures should be part of the process of revitalization.

We also propose an annual Forum of Civil Society consisting of representatives of organizations to be accredited to the General Assembly as 'Civil Society Organizations'. The forum should be convened in the General Assembly Hall sometime before the Annual Session of the Assembly. International civil society should itself be involved in determining the character and functions of the Forum.

The Right of Petition proposed in the context of promoting the security of people requires the formation of a Council of Petitions—a high-level panel of five to seven persons, independent of governments, to entertain petitions. Its recommendations will go as appropriate to the Secretary-General, the Security Council, or the General Assembly, and allow for action under the Charter.

In the light of experience and in the context of the proposed Economic Security Council and our other recommendations, we propose that the Economic and Social Council (ECOSOC) be wound up. The UN system must from time to time also shut down institutions that can no longer be justified in objective terms. We believe this to be true also of the United Nations Conference on Trade and Development (UNCTAD) and the United Nations Industrial Development Organization, and propose an in-depth review to this end. Our proposals on these UN bodies are part of the integrated set of proposals we make for improving global economic governance including, notably, the setting up of an Economic Security Council. Balance in governance arrangements will not be well served if decision-making is preserved in the hands of a small directorate of countries while institutions such as UNCTAD, set up to correct imbalances, are dismantled.

The world community can take pride in UN achievements in the economic and social sectors through the specialized agencies and the programmes and funds. But there is scope for improvement in responding to new needs and in efficiency. There is also need to improve co-ordination and for the specialized agencies to enhance their position as centres of authority. The various programmes and funds require more efficient governance structures and improved funding systems, with fairer burden-sharing among a wider range of donor countries.

To help put women at the centre of global governance, a post of Senior Adviser on Women's Issues should be created in the Office of the UN Secretary-General, and similar positions should be established in the specialized agencies.

The UN must gear itself for a time when regionalism becomes more ascendant world-wide and assist the process in advance of that time. Regional co-operation and integration should be seen as an important and integral part of a balanced system of global governance. However, the continuing utility of the UN Regional Economic Commissions now needs to be closely examined and their future determined in consultation with the respective regions.

The procedure for appointing the Secretary-General should be radically improved, and the term of office should be a single one of seven years. The procedure for selecting the heads of UN specialized agencies, funds, and programmes should similarly be improved.

Member-states should face up to the need to pay their UN dues in full and on time.

The global neighbourhood of the future must be characterized by law and the reality that all, including the weakest, are equal under the law and none, including the strongest, is above it. Our recommendations are directed to strengthening international law and the International Court of Justice in particular.

All member-states of the UN that have not already done so should accept the compulsory jurisdiction of the World Court. The Chamber Procedure of that court should be modified to enhance its appeal to states and to avoid damage to the Court's integrity.

Judges of the World Court should be appointed for one ten-year term only, and a system of screening potential members for jurisprudential skills and objectivity introduced. The UN Secretary-General should have the right to refer legal aspects of international issues to the World Court for advice, particularly in the early stages of emerging disputes.

The Security Council should appoint a distinguished legal person to provide advice at all relevant stages on the international legal aspects of issues

STRENGTHEN-
ING THE RULE
OF LAW
WORLD-WIDE

before it. It should also make greater use of the World Court as a source of advisory opinions, with a view to avoiding being itself the judge of international law in particular cases.

We do not emphasize formal enforcement measures but failing voluntary compliance, Security Council enforcement of World Court decisions and other international legal obligations should be pursued under Article 94 of the Charter.

An International Criminal Court should be quickly established with independent prosecutors of the highest calibre and experience.

The International Law Commission, or other appropriate body, should be authorized to explore how international law-making can be expedited.

THE NEXT STEPS

If reform is left to normal processes, only piecemeal and inadequate action will result.

We have made many recommendations, some of them far-reaching. We would like in this chapter to go one step further by suggesting a process through which the world community could consider these and similar recommendations.

At several points in this report we have recalled the establishment of the United Nations fifty years ago. The passage of a half-century provides an appropriate occasion to assess how the UN system has measured up and how well it is equipped to cope with present and emerging challenges. The world has not stood still these fifty years. We started this report by noting how the world had been transformed in the post-war period. Accelerating change has been a prominent feature, even of the recent past.

During the time this Commission has been at work, we have witnessed the currencies of Europe held hostage by forces of speculation themselves out of control. Powerful economies confronted each other on the threshold of trade wars, while marginal ones collapsed. There was ethnic cleansing in the Balkans, a 'failed state' in Somalia, and genocide in Rwanda. Nuclear weapons lay unsecured in the former Soviet Union, and neo-Fascism surfaced in the West.

The United Nations has faced much greater demands. Its existence is a continuing reminder that all nations form part of one world, though evidence is not lacking of the world's many divisions. Today's interdependencies are compelling people to recognize the unity of the world. People are forced not just to be neighbours but to be good neighbours. The practical needs of a shared habitat and the instinct of human solidarity are pointing in the same direction. More than ever before people need each other—for their welfare, their health, their safety, perhaps even for their survival. Global governance must acknowledge that need.

Our report is issued in the year the UN marks a jubilee. It is not tied to that one event or to the UN system alone. It speaks to a longer time and a larger stage, but the UN and its future are a central part of our concerns. It is important that the international community should use the UN's anniversary as an occasion for renewing commitment to the spirit of the Charter and the internationalism it embodied, and establish a process that can take the world to a higher stage of international cooperation. This process must be centred on the UN but not be confined to it.

Ours are not the only recommendations that will be considered in the anniversary year. Many new ideas have been put forward by the UN Secretary-General in his *An Agenda for Peace* and its updates and in 'An Agenda for Development'; by Gareth Evans, the

Foreign Minister of Australia, whose study *Cooperating for Peace* has offered well-developed proposals for strengthening global capacity for preventive diplomacy, peacekeeping, and peacebuilding; and by *Renewing the United Nations System,* the comprehensive study of the UN done by Erskine Childers and Brian Urquhart.

Other major studies are in progress, one under the aegis of the Ford Foundation on the United Nations in its Second Half-Century and one by the Carnegie Commission on the Prevention of Deadly Conflict. The General Assembly itself will be offering ideas for reform resulting from the discussions of its Working Group.

The variety of reports and studies presenting the case for change and proposing the form it should take reflects the wide recognition that change is needed. That itself does not guarantee that action will be taken to bring about change. The will to change does not exist everywhere. It would be easy for all the effort to promote reform to be stalled by a filibuster or simply by inertia. Or, paradoxically, it could be overwhelmed by the onset of the very dangers that some of the changes proposed are meant to guard against.

We are prompted to recall the vision that drove the process of founding the United Nations and the spirit of innovation that ushered in a new era of global governance. We need that spirit again today, together with a readiness to look beyond the United Nations and nation-states to the new forces that can now contribute to improved governance in the global neighbourhood.

We fear that if reform is left to normal processes, only piecemeal and inadequate action will result. We look, therefore, to a more deliberate process. Article 109 of the UN Charter envisaged Charter revision. Interestingly, a mandatory revision was one idea canvassed at San Francisco in the context of the objections to the provision for a veto by countries that were not great powers. The Charter has been amended on four occasions: in 1963 to enlarge the Security Council from eleven to fifteen members, in 1965 to enable a review conference to be held at any time, and in 1971 and 1975 to enlarge ECOSOC from eighteen to twenty-seven and then to fifty-four members. But revision of the Charter is the ultimate stage in a process of reform and is not required for many of the changes we propose.

The ultimate process has to be intergovernmental and at a high level, giving political imprimatur to a new world order whose contours are shaped to the designs developed for the anniversary year.

For such a process to have the best prospect of securing agreement on the nature and form of a new system of global governance, there will need to be careful preparation. Civil society must be involved in the preparatory process, which should reach out beyond governments to even wider sections of society than the preparatory processes leading to recent world conferences did. Many views must be examined, and many ideas allowed to contend.

Our recommendation is that the General Assembly should agree to hold a World Conference on Governance in 1998, with its decisions to be ratified and put into effect by 2000. That will allow more than two years for the preparatory process.

We do not envisage that action on all recommendations needs to await the final conference. Indeed, some changes cannot be delayed without giving rise to the possibility of movement along dangerous lines, particularly in the area of peace and security. We would be happy to see the General Assembly taking up some matters, such as reform of the Security Council, without waiting for their consideration as part of the preparatory process. It should also be possible for decisions to be taken during the course of that process on recommendations that warrant early consideration.

Many of the changes proposed do not need an amendment of the Charter. Some changes are already under way. We encourage action on reform at all levels—provided, of course, that ad hoc decisions do not become a substitute for systematic reform through a fully representative forum. We recall that the nuclear arms race began because the process of disarmament blessed by the very first resolution of the General Assembly was talked out until it was too late to stop the race beginning.

A special responsibility devolves on the non-governmental sector. If our recommendations and those from other sources are worthy of support, international civil society must prevail on governments to consider them seriously. By doing so they would ensure that 'WE THE PEOPLES' are the main instruments of change to a far greater extent than they were fifty years ago. We call on international civil society, NGOs, the business sector, academia, the professions, and especially young people to join in a drive for change in the international system.

Governments can be made to initiate change if people demand it. That has been the story of major change in our time; the liberation of women and the environmental movement provide examples. If people are to live in a global neighbourhood and live by neighbourhood values, they have to prepare the ground. We believe that they are ready to do so.

We urge governments to set in motion a process of change that can give hope to people everywhere, and particularly to the young. Despite today's many complexities and hazards, the world has a unique opportunity to take human civilization to higher levels and to make the global neighbourhood a more peaceful, just, and habitable place for all, now and in the future.

THE NEED FOR LEADERSHIP

The world needs leaders made strong by vision, sustained by ethics, and revealed by political courage that looks beyond the next election.

Whatever the dimensions of global governance, however renewed and enlarged its machinery, whatever values give it content, the quality of global governance depends ultimately on leadership. Throughout our work, we have been conscious of the degree to which the effectiveness of our proposals—indeed, their very realization—depends on leadership of a high order at all levels within societies and beyond them.

As the world faces the need for enlightened responses to the challenges that arise on the eve of the new century, we are concerned at the lack of leadership over a wide spectrum of human affairs. At national, regional, and international levels, within communities and in international organizations, in governments and in non-governmental bodies, the world needs credible and sustained leadership.

It needs leadership that is proactive, not simply reactive, that is inspired, not simply functional, that looks to the longer term and future generations for whom the present is held in trust. It needs leaders made strong by vision, sustained by ethics, and revealed by political courage that looks beyond the next election.

This cannot be leadership confined within domestic walls. It must reach beyond country, race, religion, culture, language, life-style. It must embrace a wider human constituency, be infused with a sense of caring for others, a sense of responsibility to the global neighbourhood. Václav Havel gave it expression when addressing the US Congress in 1990 he said:
Without a global revolution in the sphere of human consciousness, nothing will change for the better in our

being as humans, and the catastrophe toward which
our world is headed...will be unavoidable....We are
still incapable of understanding that the only genuine
backbone of all our actions—if they are to be moral—
is responsibility: responsibility to something higher
than my family, my country, my firm, my success,
responsibility to the order of being where all our
actions are indelibly recorded and where, and only
where, they will be properly judged.

Acknowledging responsibility to something higher than country does not come easily. The impulse to possess turf is a powerful one for all species; yet it is one that people must overcome. In the global neighbourhood, a sense of otherness cannot be allowed to nourish instincts of insularity, intolerance, greed, bigotry, and, above all, a desire for dominance. But barricades in the mind can be even more negative than frontiers on the ground. Globalization has made those frontiers increasingly irrelevant. Leadership must bring the world to that higher consciousness of which Václav Havel spoke.

To a very particular degree today, the need for leadership is widely felt, and the sense of being bereft of it is the cause of uncertainty and instability. It contributes to a sense of drift and powerlessness. It is at the heart of the tendency everywhere to turn inwards. That is why we have attached so much importance to values in this report, to the substance of leadership and the compulsions of an ethical basis for global governance. A neighbourhood without leadership is a neighbourhood endangered.

International leadership is a quality easy to identify by its presence or its absence, but extraordinarily difficult to define, and even more difficult to guarantee. Political differences and conflicts between states, sensitivity over the relationship between international responsibility and national sovereignty and interest, increasingly serious national domestic problems, and the somewhat disorderly nature of the international system of organizations and agencies—all these constitute considerable obstacles to leadership at the international level.

Such leadership can come from a number of possible sources and in many different forms. Governments, either singly or in groups, can pursue great objectives. The American-led post-war planning that produced the new international system based on the United Nations was a classic example of such leadership. Individuals can put their reputation on the line for international innovation, as Lester Pearson of Canada did for UN peacekeeping. Specific governments can create a constituency for an international initiative—Sweden on the environment, for example, or Malta on the Law of the Sea.

In the UN itself, international leaders may also emerge. Ralph Bunche pioneered trusteeship and decolonization and set up a new standard for international mediation and, indeed, for international civil service in general. Dag Hammarskjöld was the dominant, and the most innovative, international leader of his time. Maurice Pate and Henry Labouisse spearheaded the drive to make the world's children an international concern. Halfdan Mahler led the World Health Organization into a vital international role.

By leadership we do not mean only people at the highest national and international levels. We mean enlightenment at every level—in local and national groups, in parliaments and in the professions, among scientists and writers, in small community groups and large national NGOs, in international bodies of every description, in the religious community and among teachers, in political parties and citizens' movements, in the private sector and among the large transnational corporations, and particularly in the media. NGOs can be of crucial importance in developing support and new ideas for important international goals. Recent examples have included the environment, women's rights, and the whole broad area of human rights world-wide.

At the moment, political caution, national concerns, short-term problems, and a certain fatigue with international causes have combined to produce a dearth of leadership on major international issues. The very magnitude of global problems such as poverty, population, or consumerism seems to have daunted potential international leaders. And yet without courageous, long-term leadership at every level—international and national—it will be impossible to create and sustain constituencies powerful and reliable enough to make an impact on problems that will determine, one way or another, the future of the human race on this planet.

A great challenge of leadership today is to harmonize domestic demands for national action and the compulsions of international co-operation. It is not a new challenge, but it has a new intensity as globalization diminishes capacities to deliver at home and enlarges the need to combine efforts abroad. Enlightened leadership calls for a clear vision of solidarity in the true interest of national well-being—and for political courage in articulating the way the world has changed and why a new spirit of global neighbourhood must replace old notions of adversarial states in eternal confrontation.

The alternative is too frightening to contemplate. In a final struggle for primacy—in which each sees virtue in the advancement of national self-interest, with states and peoples pitted against each other—there can be no winners. Everyone will lose; selfishness will make genius the instrument of human self-destruction. But the leadership to avert this is not sufficiently evident. The hope must be people—people demanding enlightenment of their leaders, refusing to accept the alternative of humanity at war with itself. And that hope is balanced by the promise of the leadership that future generations will bring.

In a real sense the global neighbourhood is the home of future generations; global governance is the prospect of making it better than it is today. But that hope would be a pious one were there not signs that future generations come to the task better equipped to succeed than their parents were. They bring to the next century less of the baggage of old animosities and adversarial systems accumulated in the era of nation-states.

The new generation knows how close they stand to cataclysms unless they respect the limits of the natural order and care for the earth by sustaining its life-giving qualities. They have a deeper sense of solidarity as people of the planet than any generation before them. They are neighbours to a degree no other generation on earth has been. On that rests our hope for our global neighbourhood.

THE COMMISSION AND
ITS WORK

The Commission on Global Governance was established in 1992 in the belief that international developments had created a unique opportunity for strengthening global co-operation to meet the challenge of securing peace, achieving sustainable development, and universalizing democracy.

The first steps leading to its formation were taken by former West German Chancellor Willy Brandt, who a decade earlier had chaired the Independent Commission on International Development Issues. In January 1990, he invited to Königswinter, Germany, the members of that Commission and individuals who had served on the Independent Commission on Disarmament and Security Issues (the Palme Commission), the World Commission on Environment and Development (the Brundtland Commission), and the South Commission (chaired by Julius Nyerere).

Those attending the Königswinter meeting agreed that while the world situation had improved, the new decade would present major challenges that could be met only through co-ordinated multilateral action. They asked Ingvar Carlsson (then Prime Minister of Sweden), Shridath Ramphal (then Commonwealth Secretary-General), and Jan Pronk (Minister for Development Co-operation of the Netherlands) to prepare a report on the opportunities for global co-operation on issues requiring multilateral action.

Following this group's report, some three dozen public figures met in Stockholm in April 1991 to discuss the needs of the 1990s. In the 'Stockholm Initiative on Global Security and Governance', they proposed that an international commission be set up to explore the opportunities created by the end of the cold war to build a more effective system of world security and governance.

Willy Brandt, after consulting Gro Harlem Brundtland and Julius Nyerere, invited Ingvar Carlsson and Shridath Ramphal to co-chair the proposed Commission. In April 1992, the co-chairs met UN Secretary-General Boutros Boutros-Ghali to explain the purpose of the Commission. He commended the initiative and assured them of his support.

By September 1992, the Commission was established with twenty-eight members from around the world. All have served in their personal capacities, and not under instruction from any government or organization.

The following individuals participated in or formally endorsed the Stockholm Initiative on Global Security and Governance:

Ali Alatas, Indonesia

Patricio Aylwin Azocar, Chile

Benazir Bhutto, Pakistan

Willy Brandt, Federal Republic of Germany

Gro Harlem Brundtland, Norway

Boutros Boutros-Ghali, Egypt

Manuel Camacho Solis, Mexico

Fernando Henrique Cardoso, Brazil

Ingvar Carlsson, Sweden

Jimmy Carter, United States

Bernard Chidzero, Zimbabwe

Reinaldo Figueredo Planchart, Venezuela

Bronislaw Geremek, Poland

Abdlatif Al-Hamad, Kuwait

Mahbub ul Haq, Pakistan

Václav Havel, Czech and Slovak Federal Republic

Edward Heath, United Kingdom

Enrique Iglesias, Uruguay

Hongkoo Lee, Republic of Korea

Stephen Lewis, Canada

Michael Manley, Jamaica

Vladlen Martynov, Soviet Union

Thabo Mbeki, South Africa

Robert McNamara, United States

Bradford Morse, United States

Julius Nyerere, Tanzania

Babacar Ndiaye, Senegal

Saburo Okita, Japan

Jan Pronk, Netherlands

Shridath Ramphal, Guyana

Nafis Sadik, Pakistan

Salim Salim, Tanzania

Arjun Sengupta, India

Eduard Shevardnadze, Soviet Union

Kalevi Sorsa, Finland

Maurice Strong, Canada

Brian Urquhart, United Kingdom

THE COMMISSIONERS

Co-Chairmen

Ingvar Carlsson, Sweden   Prime Minister of Sweden 1986–91 and from October 1994, and Leader of the Social Democratic Party in Sweden. Deputy Prime Minister from 1982 to 1986. Member of Parliament since 1964. Served as Minister of Education (1969–73), Minister of Housing and Physical Planning (1973–76), and Minister of the Environment (1985–86). In April 1991, hosted the Stockholm Initiative that led to the creation of the Commission on Global Governance.

Shridath Ramphal, Guyana   Secretary-General of the Commonwealth from 1975 to 1990, and Minister of Foreign Affairs and Justice of Guyana from 1972 to 1975. Currently the Chairman of the International Steering Committee of LEAD International—the international Leadership in Environment and Development Program; Chairman, Advisory Committee, Future Generations Alliance Foundation; and the Chancellor of the University of the West Indies and of the University of Warwick in Britain. Member of each of the five independent international commissions of the 1980s, and chairman of the West Indian Commission, which issued its report in 1992. President of the World Conservation Union–IUCN from 1991 to 1993, and author of *Our Country, The Planet,* written for the Earth Summit.

Members

Ali Alatas, Indonesia   Minister for Foreign Affairs of the Republic of Indonesia since 1988. Indonesia's Ambassador and Permanent Representative to the United Nations in New York (1982–88) and in Geneva (1976–78). Has represented Indonesia in several international fora, including as Chairman of the First Committee at the 40th UN General Assembly Session in 1985. President of the Amendment Conference of the States Parties to the Treaty Banning Nuclear Weapon Tests and was Co-Chairman of the Paris International Conference on Cambodia. At present, Indonesia also holds the Chairmanship of the Non-Aligned Movement.

Abdlatif Al-Hamad, Kuwait   Director-General and Chairman of the Arab Fund for Economic and Social Development in Kuwait. Former Minister of Finance and Minister of Planning of Kuwait. Member of the Independent Commission on International Development Issues and the South Commission, and chairman of the UN Committee on Development Planning. Board Member of the Stockholm Environment Institute.

Oscar Arias, Costa Rica   President of Costa Rica from 1986 to 1990. In 1987, drafted a regional accord, known as the Arias Peace Plan, to end the ongoing wars in Central America. This initiative was signed by all the Central American Presidents on 7 August 1987, and culminated in the award of that year's Nobel Peace Prize to Dr. Arias. In 1988, he used the monetary award to establish the Arias Foundation for Peace and Human Progress.

Anna Balletbo i Puig, Spain   Member of the Spanish Parliament since 1979. Member of the Committees on Foreign Affairs and on Radio and Television, and of the Executive Committee of the Socialist Party in Catalonia. General Secretary of the Olof Palme International Foundation in Barcelona since 1988. Previously, President of Spain's United Nations Association, a Scholar at the Wilson Center in Washington, D.C., and a Professor of radio and television at the Universidad Autonoma de Barcelona. An activist on women's issues since 1975.

Kurt Biedenkopf, Germany   Minister-President of Saxony since 1990. Active in German national and regional politics. Member of the Federal Parliament in Bonn (1976–80 and 1987–90) and of the State Parliament of Northrhine-Westphalia (1980–88). Secretary General of the Christian Democratic Union of Germany from 1973 to 1977, and later Chairman of its regional organization. Prior to entering politics, served as Professor, Dean, and President of the Ruhr University in Bochum.

Allan Boesak, South Africa   Minister for Economic Affairs for the Western Cape Region. Also Director of the Foundation for Peace and Justice in Cape Town. A leading figure in his country's struggle against apartheid, Chairman of the African National Congress (ANC) for the Western Cape Region and a member of the ANC's National Executive Committee. Previously, President of the World Alliance of Reformed Churches and a Patron of the United Democratic Front.

Manuel Camacho Solis, Mexico   Former Minister of Foreign Affairs and former Mayor of Mexico City. Served as Mexico's Secretary of Urban Development and Ecology (1986–88), where he was responsible for the reconstruction programme after the 1985 earthquake. As Peace Commissioner in Chiapas, played a key role in establishing the cease-fire in 1994 and face-to-face negotiations with the EZLN. Recently published 'Change Without Breakdown', a blueprint for democratic reforms in Mexico.

Bernard Chidzero, Zimbabwe   Senior Minister of Finance. Politically active in the international and domestic arenas since the 1960s. Has served in different capacities with the United Nations for twenty years, including Deputy Secretary-General of UNCTAD (1977–80) and President of the Seventh Session of UNCTAD (1987–91). Chairman of the Development Committee of the World Bank and the IMF (1987–90), and a member of the World Commission on Environment and Development.

Barber Conable, United States   President of the World Bank from 1986 to 1991. Currently Chairman of the Committee on US-China Relations, and a member of the Senior Advisory Committee of the Global Environment Facility. Member of the U.S. House of Representatives from 1965 to 1985, where he served on the Ways and Means Committee for eighteen years, the last eight as its ranking minority member, as well as on the Joint Economic Committee, the House Budget Committee, and the House Ethics Committee. Has served on the boards of multinational corporations and on the Board of the New York Stock Exchange. Currently Chairman of the Executive Committee of the Board of Regents of the Smithsonian Institution and a Trustee Fellow and Executive Committee member of Cornell University.

Jacques Delors, France   President of the European Commission since 1985. Served as Minister for Economics, Finance, and the Budget (1981 and 1983–84). Mayor of Clichy 1983–84. Adviser to the Prime Minister (1969–72), Member of the General Council of the Banque de France (1973–79), and Member of the European Parliament and President of its Committee on Economic and Monetary Affairs (1979–81). Previously, a Professor at the University Paris-Dauphine, Chairman of the research centre 'Travail et Societé', and founder of the association 'Echanges et Projets', of which he is Honorary President.

Jiri Dienstbier, Czech Republic   Chairman of the Free Democrats party in the Czech Republic and Chairman of the Czech Council on Foreign Relations. Deputy Prime Minister and Minister of Foreign Affairs of Czechoslovakia from 1989 to 1992. A signatory of and spokesman for Charter 77, and a key member of the group led by Václav Havel initiating political change in his country. As a result of his opposition activities, he was sentenced to three years in prison in 1979. First spokesman of the Civic Forum's Coordinating Centre on its establishment in 1989.

Enrique Iglesias, Uruguay   President of the Inter-American Development Bank since 1988. Served as Minister of External Relations of Uruguay (1985–88), as Executive Secretary of the UN Economic Commission for Latin America and the Caribbean (1972–85), and as President of the Central Bank of Uruguay (1966–68). Chairman of the Conference that launched the Uruguay Round of Trade Negotiations in 1986.

Frank Judd, United Kingdom   Member of the House of Lords, where he has been the Labour Opposition's principal spokesman on education and is now the principal spokesman on development co-operation. A specialist and consultant in international affairs working particularly on the UN, Third World issues, conflict resolution, and arms control. For thirteen years, a Member of Parliament, serving consecutively as Parliamentary Under-Secretary of State for Defence, Minister for Overseas Development, and Minister of State at the Foreign and Commonwealth

Office, where he was deputy to the Secretary of State. Director of Voluntary Service Overseas from 1980 to 1985, and Director of Oxfam from 1985 to 1991.

Hongkoo Lee, Republic of Korea   Deputy Prime Minister of Korea and the Minister of National Unification. Served as the Republic of Korea's Ambassador to the United Kingdom from 1991 to 1993, and as Minister for Unification between North and South Korea from 1988 to 1990. In 1985, founded the Seoul Forum for International Affairs and served as its Chairman until 1988. Professor of Political Science at Seoul National University from 1968 to 1988, and Director of the Institute of Social Sciences (1978–82). Currently also the Chairman of the Seoul 21st Century Committee and of the World Cup 2002 Bidding Committee.

Wangari Maathai, Kenya   Founder and co-ordinator of the Green Belt Movement in Kenya. An environmental conservationist and activist on women's issues and human rights. Formerly the Chairman of the National Council of Women of Kenya, and spokesman for non-governmental organizations at the 1992 Earth Summit in Rio de Janeiro. Previously, Associate Professor of Anatomy at the University of Nairobi.

Sadako Ogata, Japan   Currently United Nations High Commissioner for Refugees (since 1991) and previously Professor and Dean of the Faculty of Foreign Studies at Sophia University in Tokyo and Director of its International Relations Institute (1980–91). Japan's Representative on the UN Commission on Human Rights in 1982–85, and a member of the Independent Commission on International Humanitarian Issues. From 1978 to 1979, Japan's envoy to the United Nations as well as Chairman of the Executive Board of UNICEF.

Olara Otunnu, Uganda   President of the International Peace Academy in New York. As Uganda's Foreign Minister from 1985 to 1986, facilitated the peace talks culminating in the Nairobi Peace Agreement. During tenure as Uganda's Permanent Representative to the UN (1980–85), served as President of the Security Council (1981), Vice-President of the General Assembly (1982–83), and Chairman of the UN Commission on Human Rights. Has taught at The American University and at Albany Law School, and was a visiting fellow at the Institut Français des Relations Internationales in Paris.

I.G. Patel, India   Chairman of the Aga Khan Rural Support Programme in India. Has held key economic positions in India and internationally: Governor of the Reserve Bank of India, Chief Economic Adviser to the Indian Government, and Permanent Secretary of the Indian Finance Ministry. Previously, Director of the London School of Economics and Political Science. Has served as the Executive Director for India of the International Monetary Fund and as Deputy Administrator of the UN Development Programme.

Celina Vargas do Amaral Peixoto, Brazil   Director of the Getulio Vargas Foundation in Brazil. Director-General of the Brazilian National Archives from

1980 to 1990 and Director of the Center of Research and Documentation on Brazilian History from 1973 to 1990. Member of the Inter-American Dialogue and has been a member of several national commissions on cultural, historical, and technological issues.

Jan Pronk, Netherlands Minister for Development Co-operation of the Netherlands, a position he also held from 1973 to 1978. Vice-Chairman of the Labour Party (1987–89) and a Member of Parliament (1971–73; 1978–80; 1986–89). Served as Deputy Secretary-General of UNCTAD from 1980 to 1986. Previously, a Professor at the Institute of Social Studies in the Hague and at the University of Amsterdam. Member of the Independent Commission on International Development Issues.

Qian Jiadong, China Deputy Director-General of the China Centre for International Studies in Beijing. Previously, Ambassador and Permanent Representative in Geneva to the United Nations, Ambassador for Disarmament Affairs, and a representative to the Conference on Disarmament. Member of the South Commission.

Marie-Angélique Savané, Senegal A sociologist and currently Director of the Africa Division of the UN Population Fund in New York. Formerly Director of the UNFPA country support team in Dakar (1992–October 1994), Special Adviser to the UN High Commissioner for Refugees (1990–92), team leader at the UN Research Institute for Social Development (1979–88), and Editor-in-Chief of *Famille et Développement* (1974–78). Founder and former President of the Association of African Women for Research and Development. Member of the Boards of several international organizations and institutions, of the South Commission, and currently of the UNESCO Commission on Education for the 21st Century.

Adele Simmons, United States President of The John D. and Catherine T. MacArthur Foundation in Chicago. Member of the Boards of several organizations and corporations and an elected member of the American Academy of Arts and Sciences and the Council on Foreign Relations. In 1993, appointed by the Secretary-General of the UN to the High-Level Advisory Board on Sustainable Development. From 1977 to 1989, President of Hampshire College in Massachusetts, where she developed new programmes in population and health and in peace and international security. From 1978 to 1980, served on President Carter's Commission on World Hunger and from 1991 to 1992, on President Bush's Commission on Environmental Quality.

Maurice Strong, Canada Chairman and Chief Executive Officer of Ontario Hydro, and Chairman of the Earth Council. Has received the Order of Canada and is a member of the Queen's Privy Council of Canada. Secretary-General of the 1992 UN Conference on Environment and Development in Rio, and of the

1972 Stockholm Conference on the Human Environment. Member of the World Commission on Environment and Development.

Brian Urquhart, United Kingdom   Currently a Scholar-in-Residence at the Ford Foundation's International Affairs Program. Involved in the formation of the United Nations in 1945 and served as Under Secretary-General for Special Political Affairs from 1972 to 1986. Main fields of interest and operation at the UN were conflict resolution and peacekeeping. Publications include *A World in Need of Leadership: Tomorrow's United Nations* (with Erskine Childers, 1990); *Towards a More Effective United Nations* (with Erskine Childers, 1991); *Ralph Bunche: An American Life* (1993); and *Renewing the United Nations System* (with Erskine Childers, 1994). Member of the Independent Commission on Disarmament and Security Issues.

Yuli Vorontsov, Russia   Ambassador to the United States, following a five-year term as Ambassador to the United Nations, and an Adviser to President Boris Yeltsin on Foreign Affairs. Served as the USSR Ambassador to Afghanistan (1988–89), France (1983–86), and India (1977–83). Between foreign assignments, appointed First Deputy-Foreign Minister in 1986.

THE TERMS OF REFERENCE

The Commission's terms of reference, adopted at its third meeting in February 1993, are as follows:

> The Commission on Global Governance has been established at a time of profound, rapid and pervasive change in the international system—a time of uncertainty, challenge and opportunity.

> Freed from East-West tensions, the world's nations have more favourable conditions for working together to build a better world for all. The need for cooperation among them has also increased. They have become more interdependent in many respects. New problems have appeared that call for collective action. Global society faces the forces of both integration and division.

> These trends pose fresh challenges to the existing structures of international cooperation. It is therefore necessary to reassess their capacity and the values and concepts that underlie them. It is time to review the arrangements for the governance of our global society.

> Five decades after World War II and in the aftermath of the Cold War, a new world is taking shape. It could give new meaning to the common rights and responsibilities of nations, peoples and individuals. It could bring greater peace, freedom and prosperity. The Commission has been established to contribute to the emergence of such a global order.

The elements of change

Wide-ranging changes have taken place in international relations. The number of nation states has multiplied, and shifts have occurred in their relative importance. The East-West division has come to an end. Several countries have formed closer relationships, ceding some sovereign power to collective entities. Other nations have fragmented, as ethnic, religious or other groups assert their separate identities.

Authoritarian rule is giving way to more democratic government, but the transition is not complete and human rights are still widely violated. Apartheid has begun to be dismantled but progress is halting and there has been a surge of racism elsewhere.

The two superpowers have started to disarm but the level and proliferation of arms, including nuclear weapons, continues to endanger peace. New sources of instability and conflict—economic, ecological, social, humanitarian—call for rapid collective responses and new approaches to security.

Economically, the last half century has seen unparalleled growth and transformation. They have been spurred by expanding world trade and investment and accelerating technological change. Widespread trade liberalisation and financial deregulation have created an increasingly global market. But many protectionist barriers remain and weaker countries risk being marginalised. The gap between rich and poor, among nations and within them, has widened. Though economic progress has benefitted billions, a fifth of the world's people live in abject poverty. Even rich countries are troubled by a deprived underclass. World disparities could deepen as the capacity to use knowledge through new communication and information technologies becomes the key to economic success. Growing disparities, made more visible by the media's wider reach, accentuate discontent and, among other things, produce pressure for migration, not just from rural to urban areas in developing countries, but now also from poorer to richer countries.

Migration has been a safety valve, easing pressure on and from desperate people. Today, while frontiers are breached by economic forces, they are being closed against people, even as poverty, famine, conflict and environmental deterioration drive more people from their homes. This narrowing of access could produce tension and potential for conflict.

The concept of the international system is also changing. People have begun to see it not just as a scene for states and their representatives but more as a global society with legitimate roles for many more actors. This new worldview values cultural diversity and sees equity and justice as essential underpinnings of institutions of governance.

Cultural variety and indigenous values suffer as homogenisation is promoted by global exposure to Western communication and entertainment industries and other purveyors of Western lifestyle. This tends to create divisions between younger and older generations and to prompt countermovements that sometimes take extremist or obscurantist positions.

Despite greatly expanded international cooperation, global and regional institutions have not been able to keep pace with the challenges of increasing interdependence. At all levels, there is a gap between the demands of individuals, peoples and nations and the capacity of the system to meet their needs. In a world turning into a global village, the rights and responsibilities of its different actors must be redefined—and respected—as we move towards a new global democracy.

The task of the Commission

The Commission's basic aim is to contribute to the improvement of global governance. It will analyse the main forces of global change, examine the major issues facing the world community, assess the adequacy of global institutional arrangements and suggest how they should be reformed or strengthened.

The Commission will be able to draw on the work of the previous independent commissions chaired by Willy Brandt, Olof Palme, Sadruddin Aga Khan and Hassan bin Talal, Gro Harlem Brundtland, and Julius Nyerere. These contributed to a better understanding of policies and measures necessary to address key issues in important fields: North-South relations, security and disarmament, humanitarian questions, environment and development, and the progress of the developing countries.

The Commission does not have to go over the same ground, but will examine their proposals for continuing relevance and consider how their acceptability may be enhanced. It will explore what factors may have caused past efforts to improve global governance to fail—and what conditions helped them to succeed. The Commission will suggest how global, regional and national institutions should be developed to better support cooperation in today's world.

The principal challenge will be to mobilise political will for multilateral action. Attitudes must be fostered that enable enduring collaborative solutions to global problems to be put into effect. The political and economic arguments for action in the common good need to be well marshalled. It will be the Commission's task to articulate a vision of global cooperation that may inspire nations—leaders and people—to intensify their collective endeavours.

Some basic issues

The improvement of global security in its many aspects will be a prime concern of the Commission. The world has been spared a great war in recent decades, but conflict and violence have not diminished. In particular, there has been a rise in strife within states. Some conflicts have highlighted the vulnerability of minorities. Some have resulted in large-scale suffering, gross abuses of human rights and massive refugee problems; these have generated demands for external intervention. There is also cause for growing concern over the threats to stability that could arise from non-military factors. In considering security issues, the Commission will examine what approaches the world community should adopt to deal with threats to security in the broadest sense.

The Commission will study measures that could strengthen the system of collective security under the Charter of the United Nations to prevent or halt conflicts between states. An important linked issue is arms control and action by which the world community could prevent potentially destabilising situations arising from arms proliferation and the trade in arms which assists it. A system of collective security that inspires confidence could reduce the urge of individual states to build up large arsenals, freeing valuable resources for socially useful purposes. The Commission will also pay attention to disarmament by the major powers and the prospects for securing a part of the savings for action to accelerate development.

The Commission's concern with security will extend to the considerations that should govern international action, whether preventive diplomacy or coercive intervention, to deal with conflicts within states that may trigger wider involvement or that cause outrage on humanitarian grounds. With increasing internal conflicts prompting calls for intervention, clear guidelines are desirable so that such action is both effective and consistent. The Commission will need to examine what the world community may set down as the limits of permissible behaviour in a range of areas, and consider mechanisms—in the context of a future regime of international law—to encourage and, if necessary, enforce compliance with these norms.

The values upheld by the international community must be reinforced by the regulatory framework of the global rule of law. As sovereign states remain the primary units of the international system, the changing nature of state sovereignty and the relationship between national autonomy and international responsibility will be germane to the work of the Commission.

Together with the worldwide movement towards participatory democracy, there has been greater attention to the rights of individuals and of minorities, and to the role of civil society and its voluntary organisations in advancing the people's interest. The Commission will be concerned with the protection of these rights. It will consider how individuals, peoples and nations can be empowered to exercise greater control over their fate and how democratic accountability can be fostered at all levels, from local to global.

The economic turbulence of recent times calls for renewed efforts to improve coordination in policy in the interests of achieving more stable conditions for investment and growth worldwide. There is also a need for nations to ensure that progress towards multilateral free trade is maintained. These issues will receive the Commission's attention.

A central concern will be the need to accelerate development in less developed countries, so that absolute poverty may be brought to an end and the living standards of billions of people raised to acceptable levels. The Commission will consider ways to foster an international environment that is more supportive of developing countries, and actions to reduce external obstacles to these countries' own efforts to earn their way out of poverty. Fairer conditions for selling to developed countries through the removal of import barriers, better terms of trade for primary commodities, and improved access to capital and technology remain key issues. The proliferation of trade blocks may adversely affect non-member countries, especially those in the developing world. The debt problem, which continues to burden many countries, draining resources that could be invested to raise output and living standards, also calls for further action.

Another important concern will be the environment, with its close links to development and population growth. Both affluence and poverty contribute to environmental stress, and so does population pressure which often accompanies poverty. Grave environmental problems beyond national remedy, such as greenhouse warming, ozone depletion and, in some cases, natural disasters, have linked the fate of nations more closely together. They call for cooperative strategies based on the principle of equitably shared responsibility. Such strategies must be responsive to a common danger and be guided by concern for the interests of future generations, in order to promote sustainable development on a global basis.

The Commission will consider how the limited progress made at the Earth Summit of June 1992 can be consolidated and extended, and how recognition of the interdependence of the human family, signalled by ecological dangers, can be widened so as to evoke greater international support for sustainable development.

Focus on international institutions

An extensive system of international cooperation has been built up over the past fifty years. With the United Nations at its centre, the system has an array of important organisations.

However, these institutions of global governance—mainly created for a much less complex world with far fewer nations—fall short of today's demands. In many cases, current arrangements inhibit the development of an improved system of global security and the advancement of the human condition. A key objective of the Commission will be to propose how an adequate international institutional framework can be achieved.

The Commission will identify the tasks that need to be performed as clearly as possible. It will study the requirements for carrying them out effectively and the adequacy of the existing institutional arrangements. It will then develop proposals for improving these facilities.

The United Nations, as well as its specialised agencies, the Bretton Woods institutions and the GATT, will be an important focus for the Commission's recommendations. The composition of the Security Council and the use of the veto will be matters for review. The Commission will also study how a number of functions can be performed at the regional level, frequently outside the UN framework.

A crucial factor in the effectiveness of organisations is their perceived legitimacy. This is linked to participation and transparency in their decision-making processes and to the representative nature of bodies that exercise authority. In considering how global institutions can be reconciled with these requirements, the

Commission will examine how non-state actors—non-governmental organisations, business and labour, the academic community, cultural and religious movements, rights groups—can be usefully involved in the work of international institutions.

Effectiveness also depends on how well institutions are financed and staffed. A predictable and adequate resource base and a well-functioning international civil service are essential to the proper functioning of world organisations, which face rising demands. The Commission will suggest steps to improve the present position, which has manifest weaknesses.

In the spirit of San Francisco

The United Nations was founded and its Charter adopted at a conference in San Francisco in 1945.

As 1995, its fiftieth anniversary, approaches, the adequacy of our institutions of global governance and the need to strengthen them will increasingly claim the attention of world leaders and citizens alike.

Recent improvements in international relations have created an exciting opportunity to construct a world system that is more fully responsive to the interests of all nations and people. It should be possible to move the world to a higher level of cooperation than has ever been attempted, taking advantage of the growing recognition of global interdependence.

In making its own contribution to this endeavour, the Commission will aim to invoke the spirit of multilateralism that animated those who worked together in San Francisco to form the United Nations. It plans to issue its report in 1994, so that its conclusions and recommendations may be discussed before the General Assembly of the United Nations holds its 50th anniversary session.

WORKING FOR THE COMMISSION

In May 1992, the Commission established a secretariat in Geneva, first at Rue de Cendrier and later, with the assistance of the Canton of Geneva, at Avenue Joli-Mont. Members of the secretariat have been:

Secretary-General:
Hans Dahlgren
Executive Director (until March 1994):
Peter Hansen
Professional Staff:
Salma Hasan Ali, Information Officer
Edward Kwakwa, International Legal Adviser
Rama Mani, External Relations Officer
General Services:
Vibeke Underhill, Executive Assistant

In addition, the secretariat has had some temporary support staff, including *Jacqueline Ocholla* and *Ulla Tabatabay*. *Alberto Bin*, *Peter Due*, *Lorenzo Garbo*, and *Tomas Vargas* were summer interns at the secretariat.

The Commission's co-chairmen have also had staff support from persons working in their respective offices:

London office:
 Charles Gunawardena
 Janet Singh
Stockholm office:
 Mats Karlsson
 Christina Örvi

A number of persons contributed to various parts of the report. *Michael Clough* served as rapporteur for three of the four working groups, and drafted early versions of the text. *Susan Berfield* assisted in drafting early text for Chapters One and Two. *Vincent Cable* worked on Chapter Four throughout. Other contributors were *Christoph Bail, Barry Blechman, Lars Danielsson, Jan Eliasson, Jeremy Pope,* and *Marti Rabinowitch*. *Charles Jones* and *Benedict Kingsbury* reviewed the manuscript from an academic perspective. *Yves Fortier* served as a special adviser. *Jonathan Thomson* helped the London office with some research.

Linda Starke edited the report. *Gerald Quinn* was responsible for the design and illustrations, and desktopping was done by *Peggy Miller*.

COMMISSION MEETINGS

The first meeting of the Commission took place in Geneva in September 1992, and was spent discussing the Commission's mandate and its terms of reference.

The second meeting was held in Geneva in December 1992. Here, the terms of reference were discussed in detail, and a work programme was adopted.

The third meeting, also in Geneva, in February 1993, finalized the text of the terms of reference. The Commission members divided themselves into four working groups: on global values, global security, global development, and global governance. The meeting included a discussion with the chairmen of two previous independent commissions: Prime Minister Gro Harlem Brundtland of Norway, and former President Julius Nyerere of Tanzania.

The fourth meeting, in Geneva in May 1993, was spent almost entirely in parallel meetings of the four working groups. The entire Commission also had a discussion with Dr. Harlan Cleveland, former U.S. ambassador to NATO. After its own sessions, the Commission had a one-day meeting with a group of representatives of international non-governmental organizations.

The fifth meeting was held in New York in September 1993, and coincided with the opening of the General Assembly. The four working groups met, and reported on their work to the full Commission. The Minister for Foreign Affairs of Australia, Senator Gareth Evans, discussed his forthcoming study on coopera-tive security with the Commission. Presentations were also made by UNDP Spe-cial Adviser Mahbub ul Haq and by Ambassador Juan Somavia, Chairman of the Preparatory Committee for the World Summit on Social Development.

The sixth meeting was held in Geneva, in December 1993. At this time, the four working groups had completed their tasks, and reported their conclusions and recommendations to the Commission, for joint discussion.

The seventh meeting was held in January 1994 in Cuernavaca, Mexico, upon the invitation of Manuel Camacho Solis and the Government of Mexico City. Commissioners discussed the outline for the report, as well as first drafts of several chapters. They also had a discussion in Mexico City with President Carlos Salinas, and a group of members met with a cross-section of Mexican non-governmental organizations.

The eighth meeting was held in Tokyo, and was co-sponsored by the United Nations University (UNU). The programme included a one-day public seminar on global governance at UNU. During their own meeting in Tokyo, Commission members continued to discuss draft texts for the report. The City of Hiroshima and two Japanese citizens' groups then hosted a Commission visit to Hiroshima. This included a tour of the Peace Park and a visit to the Memorial Museum, as well as a public conference attended by more than a thousand people.

The ninth Commission meeting took place in Brussels, in June 1994, upon the invitation of Jacques Delors and the European Commission. At this time, drafts for all chapters of the report were discussed.

At the tenth meeting, in Visby, Sweden, in July 1994, the entire manuscript for the report was reviewed, and its recommendations were adopted in principle. The Commission also had a discussion on ways to launch and disseminate the report and to promote its ideas.

The eleventh meeting of the Commission, in Geneva in October 1994, ap-proved the final text of the report and set up a programme for its launch, dissemination, and promotion in 1995.

Papers Prepared for the Commission

An important basis for the discussions in the working groups was the expert papers prepared specially for the Commission. These papers are to be published in a separate volume in 1995 by Martinus Nijhoff (Dordrecht), and include the following:

Georges Abi-Saab: 'The Unused Charter Capacity for Global Governance'

Sverker Åström: 'Security Council Reform'

Pablo Bifani: 'Technology and Global Governance'

Lincoln Bloomfield: 'Enforcing Rules in the International Community: Governing the Ungovernable'

Jorge Casteñeda: 'Athens in Ipanema: Exclusion and Citizenship, Thinking About Equality and Living Without It'

Johan Galtung: 'Global Governance for and by Global Democracy'

Bimal Ghosh: 'Global Governance and Population Movements'

Peter Haas: 'Protecting the Global Environment'

Ernst and Peter Haas: 'Some Thoughts on Improving Global Governance'

Shafiq ul Islam: 'Global Economic Governance'

Ramatullah Khan: 'The Thickening Web of International Law'

Alister McIntyre: 'Reforming the Economic and Social Sectors of the United Nations'

Ruben Mendez: 'Proposal for the Establishment of a Global Foreign Currency Exchange'

Bhaskar Menon: 'The Image of the United Nations'

Jeremy Pope: 'Containing Corruption in International Transactions— The Challenge of the 1990s'

James Rosenau: 'Changing Capacities of Citizens'

James Rosenau: 'Changing States in a Changing World'

James Rosenau: 'Organizational Proliferation in a Changing World'

Emma Rothschild: 'The Changing Nature of Security'

Osvaldo Sunkel: 'Poverty and Development: From Economic Reform to Social Reform'

Herbert Wulf: 'Military Demobilization and Conversion'

THE COMMISSION AND ORGANIZATIONS OF CIVIL SOCIETY

The Commission has valued the input of non-governmental and peoples' organizations to its discussions and has actively sought out their collaboration in the course of its work.

In early 1993, the co-chairs personally contacted more than fifty leading global NGO networks, asking them to disseminate information about the Commission to their member organizations and to solicit direct feedback from them. In response, the secretariat received hundreds of replies—proposals, recommendations, and other relevant material—which have helped discussion within the Commission.

A variety of meetings enabled the Commission to get a wide cross-section of views and perspectives from NGOs and citizens' groups. At its December 1992 meeting, the co-chairs met Geneva representatives of international NGOs to discuss the work they had begun. In June 1993, also in Geneva, members of the Commission discussed issues of global governance with a diverse group of NGO representatives from around the world. In December 1993, the Commission invited the NGOs represented in Geneva to an informal briefing on the progress made. At its last meeting in Geneva, the Commission briefed NGOs on the principal recommendations of its report.

To ensure a diversity of perspectives, discussions with NGOs and citizens' movements were also organized in association with the Commission's meetings in New York, Mexico City, and Tokyo. A meeting with leading Indian NGOs was held in connection with the Commission's Asian consultation in Delhi. Additionally, members of the Commission have participated in many public and NGO events to discuss their work.

CONSULTATIONS

A number of organizations hosted or helped organize discussions and symposia for the Commission. The Common Security Forum hosted three such seminars: on 'NGOs and Governance' at Harvard University in May 1993, and on 'Nationalism and Religion' in June 1993 and 'Democratization of International Financial Institutions' in August 1993, both in Cambridge, United Kingdom. The Norwegian Ministry for Foreign Affairs hosted a symposium on 'Collective Responses to Common Threats' in June 1993 in Oslo, Norway. In September 1993, a conference on 'Rethinking Global Institutions' was organized by the

London School of Economics and Political Science's Centre for the Study of Global Governance. Some Commission members participated in the Palme Commission Review Conference in November 1993 in Ditchley Park, United Kingdom. In April 1994, the United Nations University co-hosted a public symposium on issues of global governance in Tokyo, and the Future Generations Alliance Foundation and the Kyoto Forum organized in Hiroshima a public conference on 'What Can We do for Future Generations?'

When the drafting of its report was well under way and the recommendations were being formulated, the Commission again sought outside advice, especially from scholars and experts from developing countries. For this purpose, three regional consultations were held, in Latin America, Africa, and Asia, bringing together leading experts to discuss the principal issues of the report.

The Latin American consultation was held in San Jose, Costa Rica, in March 1994 in collaboration with the Arias Foundation for Peace and Human Progress. The African consultation was held in Cairo in May 1994, in collaboration with the International Peace Academy, the Egyptian Foreign Ministry, and the Organisation of African States. The Asian consultation was held in Delhi in May 1994, in collaboration with the Rajiv Gandhi Institute for Contemporary Studies.

These meetings provided an opportunity to discuss the main issues and recommendations in such fields as security, institutional reform, global economic management, and development, and constituted another important input for the drafting of the report.

FINANCIAL AND OTHER CONTRIBUTIONS

Initial funding, which permitted the Commission to begin its work, came from the governments of the Netherlands, Norway, and Sweden. Further financial contributions were given by the governments of Canada, Denmark, India, Indonesia, and Switzerland. Through the support of the government of Japan, funds were made available from two United Nations trust funds. The Commission also received grants from the Arab Fund for Economic and Social Development (Kuwait) and the World Humanity Action Trust (United Kingdom), as well as from the MacArthur Foundation, the Carnegie Corporation, and the Ford Foundation (all based in the United States). The Government of Mexico City paid for travel to and local costs of the Commission meeting in Mexico, and the European Commission did the same for the meeting in Brussels. The Friedrich Ebert Stiftung (Germany) paid some of the travel costs for the New York meeting. The Canton of Geneva provided the Commission with the free use of a house in Geneva for its secretariat.

FOLLOW-UP

The Commission decided at an early stage that it would engage in active efforts to disseminate the report, and to promote its ideas and recommendations. This will be done mainly through speaking engagements, working with governments, international organizations, NGOs and other civil society organizations, and the media; organizing workshops and discussions; and distributing material.

The Commission's secretariat will also continue to operate in Geneva. As of November 1994, the Director of the secretariat is *Stefan Noreén*. The address and contact numbers are:

The Commission on Global Governance
Case Postale 184
CH–1211 GENEVA 28
Switzerland
tel +41 22 798–2713
fax +41 22 798–0147

ACKNOWLEDGEMENTS

The Commission has received help and advice from a large number of individuals, institutions, and organizations around the world. It expresses its special thanks to all of them.

Marie-Clare Acosta, Commission for the Defence and Promotion of Human Rights, Mexico

Sergio Aguayo, Academia Mexicana de Derechos Humanos, Mexico

Francisco Aguilar, Arias Foundation for Peace and Human Progress, Costa Rica

Gabriel Aguilera, FLACSO, Guatemala

Dominik Alder, Permanent Mission of Switzerland to the United Nations, Switzerland

Mohammed Amr, Deputy Foreign Minister, Egypt

Bahá'í International Community, United States

Brian van Arkadie, Institute of Social Studies, The Netherlands

Torsten Andersson, Governor of Gotland, Sweden

Peter Anyang' Nyong'o, African Association of Political Science, Kenya

Victoria Aranda, United Nations Conference on Trade and Development, Switzerland

Giorgi Arbatov, Institute of the USA and Canada, Russia

Oscar Arguelles, Mexico

Marcus Arruda, International Council of Voluntary Associations, Switzerland

John Ashworth, London School of Economics, United Kingdom

Göran Bäckstrand, International Federation of Red Cross and Red Crescent Societies, Switzerland

Lennart Båge, Ministry for Foreign Affairs, Sweden

Egon Bahr, University of Hamburg, Germany

Edith Ballantyne, Women's International League for Peace and Freedom, Switzerland

Mr. Bakshi, Rajiv Gandhi Institute for Contemporary Studies, India

Ashok Bapna, Society for International Development, India

Regina Barba, Union of Environmental Organizations, Mexico

Magne Barth, Norway

Tim Barton, Oxford University Press, United Kingdom

Miguel Basanez, ACUDE, Mexico

Jacques Baudot, United Nations, United States

Margarita Benitez, Universidad de Puerto Rico en Cayey, Puerto Rico

Douglas Bennet, Assistant Secretary of State for International Organization Affairs, United States

Mats Berdal, International Institute for Strategic Studies, United Kingdom

Sverre Bergh Johansen, Ministry of Foreign Affairs, Norway

Keith Best, World Federalist Movement, United Kingdom

Jagdish Bhagwati, Columbia University, United States

Austin Bide, World Humanity Action Trust, United Kingdom

Harold S. Bidmead, Norway

Jérôme Bindé, World Commission on Education and Culture, France

Alan Blackhurst, International Community Education Association, United Kingdom

Selma Brackman, War and Peace Foundation, United States

Ove Bring, Uppsala University, Sweden

Anthony and Gita Brooke, Operation Peace Through Unity, New Zealand

Andrew Brown, Foundation for International Environmental Law and Development, United Kingdom

Gro Harlem Brundtland, Prime Minister, Norway

Anne-Marie Burley, University of Chicago, United States

Richard Butler, Permanent Mission of Australia to the United Nations, United States

Campaign for Nuclear Disarmament, United Kingdom

The Carter Center of Emory University, United States

Jorge Castañeda, National University of Mexico, Mexico

Maria Cattaui, World Economic Forum, Switzerland

Lincoln Chen, Harvard University, United States

Martha Chen, Harvard University, United States

Erskine Childers, United States

Kamala Choudhri, Vikram Sarabhai Foundation, India

Patricio Civili, United Nations, United States

Harlan Cleveland, University of Minnesota, United States

Solita Collàs-Monsod, University of Philippines, Philippines

Common Security Forum, United Kingdom

Conference of Catholic Bishops, United Kingdom

Conference of Non-Governmental Organisations in Consultative Status with the United Nations, Switzerland

Conferences on a More Democratic United Nations, United Kingdom

George Cox, World Disarmament Campaign, United Kingdom

Julie Dahlitz, Australia

Christine Dawson, Aspen Institute, United States

Gurgulino de Souza, United Nations University, Japan

Tarcisio Della Senta, United Nations University, Japan

Francis Deng, Brookings Institute, United States

Meghnad Desai, Centre for the Study of Global Governance, United Kingdom

Ali Hillal Dessouki, University of Cairo, Egypt

Development Gap, United States

P.N. Dhar, India

Rut Diamant, Universidad de Buenos Aires, Argentina

Peter Dicken, University of Manchester, United Kingdom

Adama Dieng, International Commission of Jurists, Switzerland

Terje Disington, Norway

Julian Disney, Australian National University, Australia

David Doerge, Stanley Foundation, United States

James Dooge, International Council of Scientific Unions, France
Muchkund Dubey, Council for Social Development, India
Daniel Dufour, United Nations, Switzerland
Nicholas Dunlop, EarthAction Network, United Kingdom
John Dunning, University of Reading, United Kingdom
Juan Enriques, Mexico
Armando Entralgo, Cuban Center on Africa, Cuba
Dwain Epps, World Council of Churches, Switzerland
Gareth Evans, Foreign Minister, Australia
Richard Falk, Princeton University, United States
Arghyris Fatouros, United Nations Conference on Trade and Development,
    Switzerland
Eric Fawcett, University of Toronto, Canada
René Felberg, former President of the Swiss Confederation, Switzerland
Anders Ferm, *Arbetet*, Sweden
Dietrich Fischer, Pace University, United States
Inga Eriksson Fogh, Permanent Mission of Sweden to the United Nations,
    United States
Thomas Franck, New York University, United States
Friends of the Earth International, Netherlands
Enzo Friso, International Confederation of Free Trade Unions, Belgium
Maud Frölich, Swedish United Nations Association, Sweden
Gerard Fuchs, French Socialist Party, France
Moises Garcia, Mexico
Dharam Ghai, United Nations Research Institute for Social Development,
    Switzerland
Robert Gillespie, Population Communication, United States
Global Citizens Association, Canada
P. Gopinath, International Labour Organisation, Switzerland
Branislav Gosovic, South Centre, Switzerland
Ricardo Govela, Mexico
Kennedy Graham, Parliamentarians for Global Action, United States
Greenpeace, United Kingdom
GreenCross International, Switzerland
Martin Griffith, ActionAid, United Kingdom

Christian Grobet, former Conseiller d'Etat, Switzerland

S. Guhan, Madras Institute of Development Studies, India

Pranay Gupte, *Earth Times*, United States

Ahmed Haggag, Organization of African Unity, Ethiopia

Marek Hagmajer, World Federation of United Nations Associations, Switzerland

Roger Hällhag, International Union of Socialist Youth, Austria

Fred Halliday, London School of Economics, United Kingdom

Stuart Hampshire, Stanford University, United States

Sven Hamrell, Dag Hammarskjöld Foundation, Sweden

Robert Harris, Education International, Switzerland

John Harriss, London School of Economics, United Kingdom

Sohail Hashmi, Harvard University, United States

Luis Hernandes, Centro de Estudios para el Cambio en el Campo Mexicano, Mexico

Staffan Hildebrand, Sweden

Wolfgang Hirschwald, Berlin University, Germany

John Hobcraft, London School of Economics, United Kingdom

Michael Hoffman, Social Democratic Party, Germany

Stanley Hoffmann, Harvard University, United States

Kamal Hossain, Bangladesh Bar Council, Bangladesh

Richard Hudson, Center for War and Peace Studies, United States

Eric Hundewadt, Danish United Nations Association, Denmark

Mahbub ul Haq, United Nations Development Programme, United States

Johan Jörgen Holst, former Foreign Minister, Norway

Abid Hussain, Rajiv Gandhi Institute for Contemporary Studies, India

Sa'ad Eddin Ibrahim, Ibn Khaldoun Center for Development Studies, Egypt

Jean Ingram, Centre for the Study of Global Governance, United Kingdom

InterAction Council, United States

International Cooperative Alliance, Switzerland

International Peace Bureau, Switzerland

Shafiq ul Islam, Council on Foreign Relations, United States

Asma Jahangir, Supreme Court of Pakistan, Pakistan

Amir Habib Jamal, South Centre, Switzerland

Peter Jay, BBC, United Kingdom

Rani Jethmalani, Supreme Court of India, India

Richard Jolly, United Nations Children's Fund, United States

Anthony Judge, Union of International Associations, Belgium

Mary Kaldor, Sussex European Institute, United Kingdom

Hal Kane, Worldwatch Institute, United States

Michael Kane, Environmental Protection Agency, United States

Tatsuro Kanugi, International Christian University, Japan

Inge Kaul, United Nations Development Programme, United States

Vijay Kelkar, United Nations Conference on Trade and Development, Switzerland

Ashok Khosla, Development Alternatives, India

Dalchoong Kim, Yonsei University, Korea

Uner Kirdar, United Nations Development Programme, United States

Yuji Kumamaru, Ministry of Foreign Affairs of Japan, Japan

Radha Kumar, Helsinki Citizens' Assembly, Czech Republic

Ferdinand Lacina, Minister of Finance, Austria

Maurice Laing, World Humanity Action Trust, United Kingdom

Sarwar Lateef, World Bank, United States

Bernie Lee, United Kingdom

Georg Lennkh, Chancellor's Office, Austria

James Leonard, United States

Iain Levine, United Kingdom

Ioan Lewis, London School of Economics, United Kingdom

Carl Lidbom, Sweden

Warren Lindner, Centre for Our Common Future, Switzerland

Börge Ljunggren, Swedish Institute for Development Assistance, Sweden

John Logue, Common Heritage Institute, United States

Jan Lönn, International Youth and Student Movement for the United Nations, Switzerland

Jim MacNeill, Institute for Research on Public Policy, Canada

C. Mahendran, Sri Lanka

Manmohan Malhoutra, India

Mahmood Mamdani, Centre for Basic Research, Uganda

Ibbo Mandaza, South Africa Political Economy Series Trust, Zimbabwe

Elsa Mansell, United Kingdom

Mayor of Brussels, Belgium

Mayor of Hiroshima, Japan

Mayor of Mexico City, Mexico

Ali Mazrui, State University of New York at Binghamton, United States

Media Natura, United Kingdom

Medical Action for Global Security, United Kingdom

Brian Mulroney, former Prime Minister, Canada

K. G. Mohan Chandra, Development Alternatives, India

Rod Morris, Center for Global Citizens, United States

Robert Mueller, University for Peace, Costa Rica

Max Muth, Switzerland

C. B. Muthamma, India

K. Natwar-Singh, Jawarhalal Nehru Memorial Fund, India

Mazide Ndiaye, Forum for African Voluntary Development Organizations, Senegal

Thomas Netter, United Nations Information Service, Switzerland

The New Economics Foundation, United Kingdom

Hanna Newcombe, Peace Research Institute, Canada

NGO Network on Global Governance and Democracy, Switzerland

Lars Norberg, Ambassador of Sweden, Switzerland

Nuclear Age Peace Foundation, United States

Julius Nyerere, Former President, Tanzania

Olusegan Obasanjo, former Head of State, Nigeria

Waafas Ofosu-Amaah, WorldWide Network, United States

One World Action, United Kingdom

Oxfam, United Kingdom

Peter Osvald, Permanent Mission of Sweden to the United Nations, United States

John Otranto, Global Committee Against Radioactive Energy, Germany

David Owen, International Conference on the Former Yugoslavia, Switzerland

John Pace, World Conference on Human Rights, Switzerland

William Pace, Global Policy Institute, United States

Bernadette Palle, Burkina Faso

Lisbet Palme, Swedish UNICEF Committee, Sweden

Barbara Panvel, India

Asha Patel, Cambridge University, United Kingdom

Connie Peck, United Nations Institute for Training and Research,
Switzerland

Ellen Permato, Centre for Our Common Future, Switzerland

Vladimir Petrovsky, United Nations, Switzerland

Raymond Plant, Oxford University, United Kingdom

Stanley Platt, World Federalist Association, United States

Gerry Pocock, United Kingdom

Jonathan Power, United Kingdom

V. R. Punchamukhi, Research and Information Systems for Non-Aligned
and Other Developing Countries, India

Chakravarthy Raghavan, Third World Network, Switzerland

Indira Rajaraman, National Institute of Public Finance and Policy, India

V. Ramachandran, Rajiv Gandhi Institute for Contemporary Studies, India

Krishna Rao, Rajiv Gandhi Institute for Contemporary Studies, India

Paul Redfern, Centre for the Study of Global Governance,
United Kingdom

Michael Reisman, Yale Law School, United States

Paul Evan Ress, Switzerland

B.H.S. Roberts, Australia

Gabriela Rodrigues, Arias Foundation for Peace and Human Progress,
Costa Rica

Andrès Rozental, Ministry of Foreign Affairs, Mexico

John Ruggie, Columbia University, United States

Kumar Rupesinghe, International Alert, United Kingdom

Nafis Sadik, United Nations Population Fund, United States

SaferWorld, United Kingdom

Mohamed Sahnoun, International Development Research Centre, Canada

Karl Sauvant, United Nations Conference on Trade and Development,
Switzerland

Bengt Säve-Söderbergh, Ministry of Foreign Affairs, Sweden

Oscar Schachter, Columbia University, United States

Peter Schatzer, International Migration Organization, Switzerland

Stephan Schmidheiny, Business Council for Sustainable Development,
Switzerland

Pierre Schori, Minister for Development Co-operation, Sweden

Klaus Schwab, World Economic Forum, Switzerland

Gautam Sen, Poona University, India

Amartya Sen, Harvard University, United States

Monica Serrano, El Colegio de Mexico, Mexico

Kaushik Shridharani, United States

Sampooran Singh, India

Jasjit Singh, Institute for Defence Studies and Analysis, India

Karan Singh, People's Commission on Environment and Development, India

Manmohan Singh, Minister of Finance, India

Kusuma Snitwongse, Institute of Security and International Studies, Thailand

Karin Söder, former Foreign Minister, Sweden

Luis Guillermo Solis Rivera, Arias Foundation for Peace and Human Progress, Costa Rica

Juan Somavia, Permanent Mission of Chile to the United Nations, United States

Gillian Sorenson, United Nations 50th Anniversary Committee, United States

James Gustave Speth, United Nations Development Programme, United States

Rodolfo Stavenhagen, Colegio de Mexico, Mexico

Stockholm International Peace Research Institute, Sweden

Thorvald Stoltenberg, International Conference on the Former Yugoslavia, Switzerland

Paul Streeten, University of Sussex, United Kingdom

Nishkala Suntharalingam, International Peace Academy, United States

Sussex Alliance for Nuclear Disarmament, United Kingdom

John Sutter, World Federalist Association of Northern California, United States

Alberto Szekely, Mexico

Joaquin Tacsan, Arias Foundation for Peace and Human Progress, Costa Rica

Zenebeworke Tadesse, Ethiopia

Daniel Tarschys, Council of Europe

Paul Taylor, London School of Economics, United Kingdom

Carl Tham, Minister of Education, Sweden

Raj Thamotheram, United Kingdom
Bhekh Thapa, Institute of Integrated Development Studies, Nepal
Rita Thapa, United Nations Population Fund, Nepal
Marta Turok, AMACUP, Mexico
Takeo Uchida, United Nations University, Japan
Jakob von Uexkull, Right Livelihood Award Foundation, United Kingdom
United Nations Association—Merton Branch, United Kingdom
United Nations Association of Great Britain and Northern Ireland
United Nations Association of New Zealand
Cyrus Vance, former Secretary of State, United States
Margaret Vogt, Nigerian Institute of International Affairs, Nigeria
Béat Vuagniaux, Republique et Canton de Genève, Switzerland
Thomas Weiss, Academic Council on the United Nations System, United States
Marc Weller, Cambridge University, United Kingdom
Morten Wetland, Prime Minister's Office, Norway
Joan Wicken, Tanzania
Anders Wijkman, SAREC, Sweden
Guy Willms, European Union, Belgium
Woods Hole Research Center, United States
David Woollcombe, Peace Child International, United Kingdom
Women's Environment and Development Organization, United States
World Council of Churches, Switzerland
World Vision International, Switzerland
Tetsuji Yasumaru, Future Generations Alliance Foundation, Japan
Katsuhiko Yazaki, Chairman, Future Generations Alliance Foundation, Japan
Gisele Yitamben, Cameroon

(The Commission apologizes for any oversight or inaccuracy in this list.)

BIBLIOGRAPHY

CHAPTER ONE

Anspanger, Franz. 1989. *The Dissolution of the Colonial Empires*. London: Routledge.

Bairoch, P. 1993. *Economics and World History: Myths and Paradoxes*. Hertfordshire, U.K.: Harvester Wheatsheaf.

—. 1982. 'International Industrialization Levels from 1750 to 1980.' *Journal of European Economic History* (Fall): 268–333.

Brown, Lester R., Hal Kane, and David Malin Roodman. 1994. *Vital Signs 1994*. New York: W.W. Norton & Company.

Gilbert, M. 1989. *Second World War*. London: Weidenfeld and Nicholson.

IMF (International Monetary Fund). 1993. *World Economic Outlook* (October). Washington, D.C.: IMF.

International Commssion on Peace and Food. 1994. *Uncommon Opportunities: An Agenda for Peace and Development*. London: Zed Books.

Ishikawa, E. and D.L. Swain. 1981. *Hiroshima and Nagasaki—The Physical, Medical and Social Effects of the Atomic Bombings*. London: Hutchinson.

Michel, H. 1975. *The Second World War*. London: Andre Deutsch.

Senghaas, Dieter. 1993. 'Global Governance: How Could it be Conceived?' *Security Dialogue* 24 (3): 247–56.

UNEP (United Nations Environment Programme). 1993. *United Nations Environmental Programme: Environmental Data Report 1993–1994*. London: Blackwell Publishers.

UNIDO (United Nations Industrial Development Organization). 1992. *The Handbook of Industrial Statistics 1992*. Vienna: United Nations.

United Nations. 1993. *World Population Prospects: The 1992 Revision.* New York: United Nations.

United Nations Department of Public Information. 1992. *Basic Facts About the United Nations.* New York: United Nations.

World Bank. 1994. *World Development Report 1994.* New York: Oxford University Press.

CHAPTER TWO

Cleveland, Harlan. 1993. *Birth of a New World.* San Francisco: Jossey-Bass.

Deng, Francis. 1993. 'Reconciling Sovereignty with Responsibility.' Paper presented at the Oslo symposium on Collective Responses to Common Threats (Commission on Global Governance and the Norwegian Ministry of Foreign Affairs, June 22–23).

Eisner, Michael. 1992. 'A Procedural Model for the Resolution of Secessionist Disputes.' *Harvard International Law Journal* (Spring): 408–25.

Etzioni, Amitai. 1992–93. 'The Evils of Self-Determination.' *Foreign Policy* (Winter): 21–35.

Falk, Richard. 1975. *A Study of Future Worlds.* New York: The Free Press.

Franck, Thomas. 1992. 'The Emerging Right to Democratic Governance.' *American Journal of International Law* (January): 46–91.

Hoffman, Stanley. 1981. *Duties Beyond Borders: On the Limits and Possibilities of Ethical International Politics.* Syracuse: Syracuse University Press.

Kidder, Rushworth M. *Shared Values for a Troubled World.* San Francisco: Jossey-Bass.

Mazrui, Ali A. 1994. 'The Failed State and Political Collapse in Africa.' Paper presented at the Cairo Consultation on the OAU Mechanism on Conflict Prevention, Management and Resolution (Organization of African Unity, Government of Egypt, and International Peace Academy, May 7–11).

Miller, Lynn H. 1990. *Global Order: Values and Power in International Politics.* San Francisco: Westview Press.

Pope, Jeremy. 1993. 'Containing Corruption in International Transactions— The Challenge of the 1990s.' Background paper for the Commission on Global Governance.

South Commission. 1990. *The Challenge to the South.* New York: Oxford University Press.

United Nations. 1945. *Charter of the United Nations.* New York.

Chapter Three

Adeniji, Oluyemi. 1993. 'Regionalism in Africa.' *Security Dialogue* 24 (2): 211–20.

Anthony, Ian. 1993. 'Assessing the UN Register of Conventional Arms.' *Survival* 35 (4): 113–29.

Berdal, Mats. 1993. 'Whither UN Peacekeeping?' Adelphi Paper 281, International Institute of Strategic Studies, London.

Blechman, Barry. 1993. 'Current Status of the Palme Commission Proposals.' Background paper for the Palme Review Conference, Ditchley Park (November 13–14).

Boutros-Ghali, Boutros. 1992. *An Agenda for Peace: Peacemaking and Peace-Keeping.* Report of the Secretary-General Pursuant to the Statement Adopted by the Summit Meeting of the Security Council, January 31. New York: United Nations.

Cleveland, Harlan. 1993. *Birth of a New World.* San Francisco: Jossey-Bass.

Evans, Gareth. 1993. *Cooperating For Peace.* Australia: Allen & Unwin.

Grimmett, Richard F. 1994. 'Conventional Arms Transfers to the Third World, 1986–1993' (A Congressional Research Service Report for Congress). Washington, D.C.: The Library of Congress.

Helman, Gerald B. and Steven R. Ratner. 1992–93. 'Saving Failed States.' *Foreign Policy* (Winter): 3–20.

Homer-Dixon, Thomas F. 1991. 'On the Threshold: Environmental Changes as Causes of Acute Conflict.' *International Security* 16 (2): 76–116.

Independent Commission on Disarmament and Security Issues. 1989. *A World at Peace: Common Security in the Twenty-First Century.* Stockholm.

Independent Commission on Disarmament and Security Issues. 1982. *Common Security: A Programme for Disarmament.* London: Pan Books.

Independent Commission on International Humanitarian Issues. 1988. *Winning the Human Race?* London: Zed Books.

Keegan, John. 1993. *A History of Warfare*. New York: Alfred A. Knopf.

Nanda, Ved P. 1992. 'Tragedies in Northern Iraq, Liberia, Yugoslavia, and Haiti-Revisiting the Validity of Humanitarian Intervention Under International Law—Part I.' *Denver Journal of International Law and Policy* 20 (2): 305–34.

Ogata, Shijuro, Paul Volcker and others. 1993. 'Financing an Effective United Nations: A Report of the Independent Advisory Group on U.N. Financing.' A Project of the Ford Foundation. February.

Roberts, Adam. 1994. 'The Crisis in UN Peacekeeping.' *Survival* (Autumn): 93–120.

—. 1993. 'The United Nations and International Security.' *Survival* (Summer): 3–30.

Rothschild, Emma. 1993. 'The Changing Nature of Security.' Background paper for the Commission on Global Governance.

Scheffer, David. 1992. 'Toward a Modern Doctrine of Humanitarian Intervention.' *University of Toledo Law Review* (Winter): 253–93.

SIPRI (Stockholm International Peace Research Institute). 1994. *SIPRI Yearbook: World Armaments and Disarmament*. New York: Oxford University Press.

—. 1993. *SIPRI Yearbook: World Armaments and Disarmament*. New York: Oxford University Press.

Sivard, Ruth Leger. 1993. *World Military and Social Expenditures 1993*. Leesburg, Va.: World Priorities Inc.

UNDP (United Nations Development Programme). 1994. *Human Development Report 1994*. New York: Oxford University Press.

UNICEF (United Nations Children's Fund). 1994. *Anti-Personnel Land-Mines: A Scourge on Children*. New York: UNICEF.

United Nations Department of Public Information. 1994. 'Background Note: United Nations Peace-Keeping Operations March 1994.'

Urquhart, Brian. 1993. 'A UN Volunteer Force—The Prospects.' *New York Review of Books* (July 15): 52–56.

Wulf, Herbert. 1993. 'Military Demobilization and Conversion.' Background paper for the Commission on Global Governance.

Chapter Four

Bifani, Pablo. 1993. 'Technology and Global Governance.' Background paper for the Commission on Global Governance.

ECE (Economic Commission for Europe). 1992. *The Environment in Europe and North-America: Annotated Statistics*. New York: United Nations.

GATT (General Agreement on Tariffs and Trade). 1993. *International Trade Statistics 1993*. Geneva: GATT.

Ghosh, Bimal. 1993. 'Global Governance and Population Movements.' Background paper for the Commission on Global Governance.

Grubb, Michael. 1991. *The Greenhouse Effect: Negotiating Targets*. London: Royal Institute of International Affairs.

Haas, Peter. 1993. 'Protecting the Global Environment.' Background paper for the Commission on Global Governance.

IMF (International Monetary Fund). 1993. *World Economic Outlook May 1993*. Washington, D.C.: IMF.

—. 1993. *IMF Annual Report 1993*. Washington, D.C.: IMF.

—. 1992. *Measurement of International Capital Flows*. Washington, D.C.: IMF.

—. 1991. *Determinants and Systemic Consequences of International Capital Flows*. Washington, D.C.: IMF.

Islam, Shafiq ul. 1993. 'Global Economic Governance.' Background paper for the Commission on Global Governance.

Korten, David C. 1990. *Getting to the 21st Century*. West Hartford, Conn.: Kumarian Press.

Mendez, Ruben. 1993. 'Proposal for the Establishment of a Global Foreign Currency Exchange.' Background paper for the Commission on Global Governance.

—. 1993. 'The Provision and Financing of Universal Public Goods.' Background paper for the Working Group on Development, Commission on Global Governance.

OECD (Organisation for Economic Co-operation and Development). 1994. *Development Co-operation: Efforts and Policies of the Members of the Development Assistance Committee 1993.* Paris: OECD.

—. 1993. *Development Co-operation Report.* Paris: OECD.

—. 1991. *The State of the Environment.* Paris: OECD.

Streeten, Paul, Louis Emmerij, and Carlos Fortin. 1992. *International Governance* (Silver Jubilee papers, Institute of Development Studies, University of Sussex). Brighton: University of Sussex.

Sunkel, Osvaldo. 1993. 'Poverty and Development: From Economic Reform to Social Reform.' Background paper for the Commission on Global Governance.

UNDP (United Nations Development Programme). 1994. *Human Development Report 1994.* New York: Oxford University Press.

—. 1993. *Human Development Report 1993.* New York: Oxford University Press.

UNEP (United Nations Environmental Programme). 1993. *Environmental Data Report 1993–94.* Oxford: Blackwell.

UNESCO (United Nations Educational, Scientific and Cultural Organization). 1993. *World Science Report.* Paris: UNESCO.

United Nations. 1992. *World Investment Report 1992: Transnational Corporations as Engines of Growth.* Department of Economic and Social Development, Transnational Corporations and Management Division. New York: United Nations.

World Bank. 1994. *World Development Report 1994.* New York: Oxford University Press.

—. 1993. *World Development Report 1993.* New York: Oxford University Press.

—. 1993. *World Tables 1993.* Baltimore: Johns Hopkins University Press.

—. 1993. *The World Bank and the Environment 1993.* Washington, D.C.: The World Bank.

World Commission on Environment and Development. 1987. *Our Common Future.* Oxford: Oxford University Press.

CHAPTER FIVE

Abi-Saab, Georges. 1993. 'The Unused Charter Capacity for Global Governance.' Background paper for the Commission on Global Governance.

Åström, Sverker. 1993. 'Security Council Reform.' Background paper for the Commission on Global Governance.

Bloomfield, Lincoln. 1993. 'Enforcing Rules in the International Community: Governing the Ungovernable.' Background paper for the Commission on Global Governance.

Caron, David. 1993. 'The Legitimacy of the Collective Authority of the Security Council.' *American Journal of International Law* (October): 552–88.

Childers, Erskine with Brian Urquhart. 1994. *Renewing the United Nations System*. Uppsala: Dag Hammarskjöld Foundation, *Development Dialogue* 1994:1.

—. 1992. *Towards a More Effective United Nations*. Uppsala: Dag Hammarskjöld Foundation, *Development Dialogue* 1991:1–2.

Galtung, Johan. 1993. 'Global Governance for and by Global Democracy.' Background paper for the Commission on Global Governance.

Haas, Ernst and Peter Haas. 1993. 'Some Thoughts on Improving Global Governance.' Background paper for the Commission on Global Governance.

Hansen, Peter. 1992. 'Some Notes on Global Governance.' Background paper for the Commission on Global Governance.

Khan, Ramatullah. 1993. 'The Thickening Web of International Law.' Background paper for the Commission on Global Governance.

Kwakwa, Edward. 1993. 'Changing Notions of Sovereignty.' Background paper for the Commission on Global Governance.

Mani, Rama, 1993. 'The Role of Non-Governmental Organisations in Global Governance—Some Notes' Background paper for the Commission on Global Governance.

McIntyre, Alister. 1994. 'Reforming the Economic and Social Sectors of the United Nations.' Background paper for the Commission on Global Governance.

Menon, Bhaskar. 1993. 'The Image of the United Nations.' Background paper for the Commission on Global Governance.

Pace, William R. 1993. 'The United Nations at a Crossroads' (unedited version of guest editorial for *The Go-Between*, newsletter for the Non-Governmental Liaison Service of the United Nations). February.

Rosenau, James. 1993. 'Changing Capacities of Citizens.' Background paper for the Commission on Global Governance.

—. 1993. 'Changing States in a Changing World.'Background paper for the Commission on Global Governance.

—. 1993. 'Organizational Proliferation in a Changing World.' Background paper for the Commission on Global Governance.

—. 1992. *The United Nations in a Turbulent World* (Occasional Paper Series, International Peace Academy). Boulder, Colo.: Lynne Rienner.

Salamon, Lester M. 1994. 'The Rise of the Nonprofit Sector.' *Foreign Affairs*. July/August: 109.

United Nations. 1945. *Charter of the United Nations*. New York.

CHAPTER SIX

Burley, Anne-Marie Slaughter. 1993. 'International Law and International Relations Theory: A Dual Agenda.' *American Journal of International Law* (April): 205–39.

Charney, Jonathan. 1994. 'Progress in International Maritime Boundary Delimitation Law.' *American Journal of International Law* (April): 227–56.

Chayes, Abram and Antonia Handler Chayes. 1993. 'On Compliance.' *International Organization* (Spring): 175–205.

Damrosch, Lori Fisler, ed. 1987. *The International Court of Justice at a Crossroads*. New York: Transnational Publishers, Inc.

Reisman, Michael. 1993. 'The Constitutional Crisis in the United Nations.' *American Journal of International Law* (January): 83–100.

—. 1990. 'International Law after the Cold War.' *American Journal of International Law* (October): 859–66.

Schachter, Oscar. 1991. *International Law in Theory and Practice*. Dordrecht: Martinus Nijhoff.

Sources for Figures

Page 8:	UNDPI (United Nations Department of Public Information). 1993. *Basic Facts About the United Nations*. New York: United Nations.
	United Nations. 1994. *World Population Prospects: Annex Tables 1994*. New York: United Nations.
	Hunter, Brian (ed.). 1994. *Statesman's Yearbook 1994–95*. New York: Macmillan Press.
	New Zealand Ministry of Foreign Affairs and Trade. 1994. *United Nations Handbook 1994*. Auckland: Ministry of Foreign Affairs and Trade.
Page 13:	UNDP (United Nations Development Programme). 1993. *Human Development Report 1993*. New York: Oxford University Press.
Page 19:	UNDP. 1994. *Human Development Report 1994*. New York: Oxford University Press.
	World Bank. 1982. *World Development Report 1982*. New York: Oxford University Press.
Page 20:	UNDP. 1994. *Human Development Report 1994*. New York: Oxford University Press.
Page 25:	United Nations. 1994. *World Investment Report 1994*. New York: United Nations.
	World Bank. 1993. *World Development Report 1993*. New York: Oxford University Press.
	UNDP. 1993. *Human Development Report 1993*. New York: Oxford University Press.
	UNDP. 1994. *Human Development Report 1994*. New York: Oxford University Press.
Pages 32 and 33:	Union of International Organizations. 1993. *Yearbook of International Organizations 1993–1994*. Munich: K.G. Saur Verlag.
Page 103:	UNDPI. 1994. *United Nations Peace-Keeping, Update: May 1994*. New York: United Nations.
	UNDPI. 1994. *Background Note: Peace-Keeping Operations*. New York: United Nations.
Page 113:	Data on peacekeeping budgets compiled from UN sources.

| Page 125: | UNDP. 1994. *Human Development Report 1994*. New York: Oxford University Press. |

Page 125: UNDP. 1994. *Human Development Report 1994*. New York: Oxford University Press.

Page 137: World Bank. 1993. *World Debt Tables 1993–94.* Washington D.C.: World Bank.

OECD (Organisation for Economic Co-operation and Development). Press Division. June 20, 1994. 'Sharp Changes in the Structure of Financial Flows to Developing Countries and Countries in Transition.' Paris: OECD.

Page 143: UNDP. 1994. *Human Development Report 1994*. New York: Oxford University Press.

Page 144: Earth Council. 1994. 'Consumption: The Other Side of Population for Development.' Paper prepared for the International Conference on Population and Development.

UNDP. 1992. *Human Development Report 1992*. New York: Oxford University Press.

Page 148: UNDP. 1993. *Human Development Report 1993*. New York: Oxford University Press.

Page 165: UNCTAD (United Nations Conference on Trade and Development). 1994. *A Preliminary Analysis of the Results of the Uruguay Round and Their Effects on the Trading Prospects of Developing Countries*. Geneva: United Nations.

Pages 174 and 175: ITU (International Telecommunications Union). 1994. *Multimedia Markets: Driving the Information Superhighway*. Geneva: ITU.

Page 206: ILO (International Labour Organisation), IOM (International Organization for Migration), and UNHCR (United Nations High Commissioner for Refugees). 1994. *Migrants, Refugees and International Cooperation*. Geneva: ILO, IOM, and UNHCR.

Page 207: Data compiled from UNHCR sources.

Page 236: Data compiled from UN sources.

Page 297: Data compiled from UN sources.

INDEX

United States (*cont.*):
    and international law, 308, 312, 314
    population/consumption within,
        145
    and trade policy, 166–67
    and UN, 234, 243, 299, 300
    and weapons, 14, 114, 116, 117
Uniting for Peace Resolution (1950),
    244, 249
Universal Declaration of Human Rights
    (1948), 55, 244
Universal Postal Union, 266
urbanization, 9, 28
Urquhart, Brian, 246, 292, 298, 350
Uruguay Round, 165–67, 171, 222
US National Academy of Sciences, 116

values, *see* global ehics
Versailles Peace Conference, 68, 73
Vietnam, 165
violence
    culture of, 16–17
    and demilitarization, 131
    and extremist movements, 52
    and global security, 48–49, 97–98
Volcker, Paul, 297
voting, *see* democracy; elections

war, *see* armed conflict
Ward, Barbara, 47
Warsaw Pact, 104
weapons, *see* arms
Western European Union, 105
West Guinea, 249
West Irian, 249
women
    and citizen empowerment, 36
    and global economy, 143
    and poverty, 22
    and reform of UN, 284–85, 346
    and UN conference on, 34, 143, 284
    and violence, 17
World Bank, 108, 147, 168, 290
    and Demilitarization Fund, 126
    and Global Environment Facility,
        272

and International Center for the
    Settlement of Investment
    Disputes, 326
and International Development
    Association, 187, 192–96, 223
and International Finance
    Corporation, 195
and UN economic operations, 156,
    161, 222, 268, 273, 296
World Commission on Environment and
    Development, 11, 146, 215
World Conference on Governance
    (proposed for 1998), 351
World Conservation Union–IUCN, 209
World Court, 100, 333
    Article 38(1) of, 306
    and chamber procedure/arbitration,
        313–14
    compulsory jurisdiction of, 303, 308–
        13, 316–18, 347
    and selection of judges, 315–16
    and UN Secretary-General, 318–19
    and UN Security Council, 319–23
    see also rule of Law
World Health Organization, 266, 267, 269
World Meteorological Organization, 209,
    266
World Resources Institute, 209
World Summit on Social Development,
    34, 143
World Trade Organization, 138, 223,
    317, 342
    and global competition, 164–76
    and UN economic operations, 157,
        158, 161, 268
World Wide Fund for Nature, 209

Yemen, 15, 202
Yugoslavia, 73, 105, 324
    armed conflict in, 15, 128
    and economic sanctions, 107
    and UN action, 72, 86, 237
    see also Bosnia-Herzegovina

Zaire, 87
Zambia, 202